SMALL GROUPS AND FOREIGN POLICY DECISION-MAKING

Dean A. Minix

UNIVERSITY
PRESS OF
AMERICA

Copyright © 1982 by
University Press of America, Inc."
P.O. Box 19101, Washington, D.C. 20036

All rights reserved

Printed in the United States of America

ISBN (Perfect): 0-8191-2373-0
ISBN (Cloth): 0-8191-2372-2

Library of Congress Number: 80-8128

To Debbi

Mr. Wiggins:

Thank you for your unflagging support since I've been at Campbell. It has not gone unnoticed nor unappreciated.

Dean

ACKNOWLEDGEMENTS

This volume is a culmination of many years of research with a legion of individuals who lent considerable behind-the-scenes support. To name them all would be difficult at least, impossible at most. However, an effort must be made.

Collegial support came from Dr. Willian Klocke and Mr. Roger Stuebing of the Behavioral Sciences Lab of the University of Cincinnati. Since this volume sprang from my dissertation research, much credit is due to: Dr. Andrew K. Semmel (director); Dr. Stephen E. Bennett; and Dr. Norris L. Johnson. A finer doctoral committee will never exist. Dr. Semmel, in particular, deserves much credit for this book. I learned much from this scholar and co-author; perhaps the best that I can do is to pass some of his wisdom on to my students. If so, they will truly benefit.

I also must acknowledge my friend, colleague, and chairman, Dr. Elmer L. Puryear, whose professionalism in all areas of life is so contagious. His encouragement, not only with this project, but with everything I attempt, is greatly appreciated.

Professor Dorothea Stewart deserves much credit for editing this work. Her expertise is reflected throughout this volume.

My family as well, Mom and Dad, Reg and Jeanne, deserves credit for being so patient and understanding. I could *not* have done this without your help--especially you, Mom and Dad.

But most of all, I would not be who or where I am today without the support of my wife Debbi. She really deserves the credit for this book.

Thank you to all those mentioned and unmentioned. You have been so kind; you should all be co-authors. I alone, though, committed the errors in this volume.

DAM
Campbell University
January, 1982

TABLE OF CONTENTS

I	Introduction	1
II	Crisis Decision-Making and Stress	19
III	Group Dynamics and Decisional Quality	37
IV	The Choice-Shift Phenomena	57
V	Methodology	83
VI	Decisional Polarization in Small Foreign Policy-Making Groups	103
VII	An Explanation of the Group Polarization Phenomena	123
VIII	Conclusion	159
	Appendix A	180
	Appendix B	188
	Bibliography	200
	Index	242

LIST OF TABLES

III-1	Frequency of Involvement of High-Level Officers in Crises	40
VI-1	Average Pre-Test, Post-Test, and Shift Values Per Sample and Sub-Sample	106
VI-2	Percentage Choice-Shifts for All Scenarios and for All Groups Across Scenarios	108
VI-3A	ANOVA for Pre-Test Responses	110
VI-3B	ANOVA for Post-Test Responses	110
VI-3C	ANOVA for Shift Scores	110
VI-4	Average Pre-Test, Post-Test, and Shift Decision Responses for Each Experimental Sub-Sample	113
VI-6	Cross-Tabulation of Pre-Test Means by Post-Test Scores Per Group Per Scenario	119
VII-1	Pearson Correlation Coefficients Between "Group" and "Pre," "Post," and "Shift" Variables	147
VII-2	A Listing of Group "Process" and "Attribute" Hypotheses on a Confirmed-Disconfirmed Continuum	151-152
VI-5	Pre-Test, Post-Test, and Shift Scores Per Group Per Sub-Sample Per Scenario	195-199

LIST OF FIGURES

Figure A	Comparative Pre-Test Responses of Sub-Samples Across Dilemmas	189
Figure B	Comparative Post-Test Responses of Sub-Samples Across Dilemmas	190
Figure C	Comparative Decision "Shift" Scores for Sub-Samples Across Dilemmas	191
Figure D	Mean Pre-Test and Post-Test Responses Per Sub-Sample	117
Figure E	Average Pre-Test - Post-Test Scores-- Officers	192
Figure F	Average Pre-Test - Post-Test Scores-- Cadets	193
Figure G	Average Pre-Test - Post-Test Scores-- Students	194

PREFACE

This investigation is designed to measure, compare, and evaluate differences between individual and small group decisional units within the foreign policy process. Specifically, this research stems from the work in psychology, sociology, and social-psychology in group dynamics known as extremization or polarization. Recent small group dynamics research on this subject has led analysts to conclude that small decisional units are more extreme (either to risk or caution) in their choice-making behavior than individuals acting alone. Building upon these social-psychological findings, a series of experiments were conducted to measure and evaluate the relative impact of different decisional units (individual and small group) on the degree of risk each unit would select in relation to protecting US interests in several international crises.

These experimental subjects were drawn from three diverse populations: 1) United States Army Officers stationed at the United States Army Armor Advanced School at Fort Knox, Kentucky (N=28); 2) Army and Airforce ROTC personnel enrolled at the University of Cincinnati (N=39); and 3) graduate and undergraduate students enrolled at the University of Cincinnati (N=56). The experiments utilized a classical pre-test, post-test design. The pre-test instructed the subjects to select privately a course of action designed to protect US national interests in a series of six hypothetical international crises. Under each scenario, a scaled list of options, obtained by the technique of paired-comparisons, was provided. The options ranged from low risk, bilateral negotiations, to high risk, nuclear war. In the post-test, subjects within each of the samples were aggregated into small groups of approximately five to six persons where the group affixed its response to each of the crises. The difference between the group decision and the average of the individual decisions for each dilemma (i. e., the "shift") represents the degree of risk or caution the group was willing to exercise over private, isolated decision-makers. In cases where the group response was greater than the average of the individual's responses, there was a choice-shift to risk; in cases where the group response was less, there was a shift to caution.

The data analysis reveals that: 1) there is a substantive as well as a statistical significance across the three sample populations with respect to the pre-test, post-test, and shift responses; 2) the Officers were heavily inclined to opt for the more coercive elements of foreign policy, that is, those options located on the risky end of the scale, while the students were disposed to choose the more cautious or diplomatic alternatives. The ROTC Cadets elected a more moderate set of responses, but pointing toward the direction set by the Officers; and 3) the variable "group membership" was the prime explanatory variable accounting for the pre-test, post-test, and shift scores of the groups.

These findings support the group polarization thesis found in group dynamics literature which states that groups will be more risky or more conservative depending upon the "cultural" values imported into the group. The fact that the three homogenous sample groups generally continued in the same direction they had initially selected as individuals leads this analyst to conclude that the dominant values of the group were a consequential factor in the group's choice-shift. The milieu of the small group provided an ambiance for the reinforcement of existing group and individual norms which translated into the group-induced shifts or decisional polarization. Group or committee decisions, in short, are more extreme than those decisions made by isolated decision-makers and this extremization is largely dependent upon the composition of the group. Who decides-- the group or individual-- is in no small way unrelated to the type of decision rendered by a nation's foreign policy machinery.

CHAPTER I

INTRODUCTION

The complexity of world politics has grown geometrically since the advent of the nation-state system in the seventeenth century.[1] The interdependence of nations brought about by the actions of transnational and non-state actors, inter-governmental organizations, and key individuals all reflect the "cobweb-like" structure known as international relations.[2] But the concept "international relations" is woefully inadequate and incomplete in today's world. To analyze only "international relations" is to focus narrowly on actions pertinent only to nation-states while ignoring the bulk of events conducted by other non-state actors. Henry Kissinger, a recent manager of United States foreign policy, noted that:

> the traditional agenda of international affairs - the balance among major powers, the security of nations - no longer defines our perils or our possibilities...Now we are entering a new era. Old international patterns are crumbling; old slogans are uninstructive; old solutions are unavailing. The world has become interdependent in economics, in communications, in human aspirations.[3]

Given the changing, tangled structure and complex dynamics of world politics, and the need to reflect it in analytical thinking, we raise the question: "How should we go about acquiring knowledge of the political dynamics of the world?"

Approaches to the study of world politics are almost as numerous as scholars in the discipline. Approaches range from Marxist-Leninist analyses to psychological perspectives. Through the unifying concept of the levels-of-analysis, however, there are several standard "lenses" one can adopt to impose some order on the broad scope and range of the subject matter.

At the most inclusive level-of-analysis, the __global level__, the analytical focus is not necessarily upon any particular actor, but instead it is on a range of world and global issues. Global analysts, for example, concentrate upon the interplay between such non-governmental organizations as guerrilla organizations (e.g., the Palestine Liberation Organization - PLO), transnational actors (e.g., multinational oil corporations like Gulf Oil), inter-governmental organizations (e.g., the Organization of Petroleum Exporting Countries - OPEC), and global institutions (e.g., the United Nations). Not only is the scope of this analytical level exceptionally broad, but the type of issues dealt with is typically unique. Instead of concentrating on military-strategic issues which have dominated international politics in the postwar years, the global perspective deals mainly with the politics of the quality of life on the planet Earth. Issues such as food and energy scarcity, desertification, technological superiority, the quantity and quality of global foreign assistance, or the need for new global institutions and cooperation set the new complex issue-agenda of the global level-of-analysis.[5]

By contrast, <u>international systems</u> level theorists contend, among other things, that there are similarities between structural characteristics of biological organisms and social structures.[6] In drawing this analogy, they attempt to provide a world view of the dynamic interplay between and among nation-states. As J. David Singer contends,

> by focusing on the system, we are able to study the patterns of interaction which the system reveals, and to generalize about such phenomena as the creation and dissolution of coalitions, the frequency and duration of specific power configurations, modifications in its stability, its responsiveness to changes in formal political institutions, and the norms and folklore which it manifests as a societal system.[7]

In short, international systems level theorists assume that, in the words of Charles McClelland, "organized complexity prevails" in international relations. Moreover, there are "repetitive patterning and deterministic processes in the world (that) are mixed with accidental, idiosyncratic, and random elements."[8] Because of the crisis-oriented focus of the news media, most international events will appear disjointed or out of context to the lay-observer. However, says McClelland, "any specific phenomena, entity, trait, relationship, or process should be considered in its context or milieu rather than in isolation."[9]

Some of the issues addressed from this analytical perspective include: the study of international conflict and conflict resolution,[10] coalition formation between nations in the international system,[11] international behavior patterns in world and regional organizations,[12] and so forth. By adopting this focus, however, systems theorists - like the globalists - pay less attention to the trees in order to study the forest. This approach "requires that we postulate a high degree of uniformity in the foreign policy operational codes of our national actors."[13] Internal and domestic variations as possible sources or causes of behavior are minimized and a "black box" or "billiard ball" conceptualization is promulgated as the most lucrative method of studying international politics.[14] The relatively homogeneous nature of the elements of the international system, posited by system-level theorists, may contribute to correlative statements about the political world, but it does not always yield, as Singer suggests, a base from which to espouse causal relationships.[15]

The principal deficiency of the systems-level approach lies in its narrow focus on inter-state relationships which reflect analytical thinking from the power politics paradigm; that is, it is an image of the world which looks to the relative power of states in the international system. From the systems-level then, "external" events are the prime explanatory variables in determining a nation's behavior. Ignored are a plethora of "internal" attributes such as cognitive processes, belief systems, and the images of national leaders. Though the systems-level approach would be more parsimonious in terms of theory-building, the conceptual blinders imposed by this perspective produces what may be a false (or perhaps, only as partially true) image of world society. On the other hand, the "basement level," to employ John Burton's terminology, "is concerned with world society as a whole, making no arbitrary boundaries between that which is national and that which is international, and consequently, no arbitrary boundaries among the general body of knowledge about man and his environment - psychological, sociological, economic, or political."[16]

The <u>nation-state</u>, or national attribute, level-of-analyses on the other hand, "avoids inaccurate homogenization which often flows from the global and systemic focus, but it also may lead to the opposite type of distortion - a marked exaggeration of the differences among our sub-systematic actors."[17] While the nation-state should not and can not be viewed as a unitary actor, this level-of-analysis leads analysts into a labyrinth of sub-national entities such as individuals, interest groups, and bureaucracies which compete for influence in the formation of public policy. "The nation-as-actor approach demands that we investigate the processes by which national goals are selected, the internal and external factors that impinge on those processes, and the institutional framework from which they emerge."[18]

Essentially this perspective asks several questions: What national attributes (economic institutions, social structures, educational systems, etc.) correlate with the basic behavior patterns of certain states? Are there particular determinants in certain types of states, for example, micro-states versus great powers? Instead of positing simply one system as systems-level theorists do, this focus provides analysts with over 150 "systems" for the study of world politics. While the nation-as actor approach is not a particularly innovative way to analyze world politics, recently many scholars have employed systematic and quantitative techniques in what is frequently referred to as the "comparative study of foreign policy."[19]

Research examples stemming from this focus are plentiful, but only a few examples are necessary for illustrative purposes. Henry Kissinger's study of national attributes, for instance, looks not at the governmental or economic structure of a system, but rather at its "leadership types."[20] Kissinger's assumption is that different leadership types will tend to produce various foreign policy acts.

James Rosenau, a principal theoretician within this perspective, isolates two salient variables at the national attribute level in his pre-theory of foreign policy.[21] The "government variable refers to those aspects of a government's structure that limit or enhance the foreign policy choices made by decision-makers."[22] The societal variable refers to "those non-governmental aspects of a society which influence its external behavior."[23]

Other analysts, such as Maurice East and Charles Hermann,[24] assume that nations can be ranked according to their power and that powerful nations somehow behave differently from less powerful nations. Factors such as size and development are used in hypothesis construction concerning their basic assumption.

While these research sketches are typical of this level-of-analysis, they are by no means exhaustive of the various types of research conducted from this perspective. However, more often than not, analytical thinking from this perspective appears oriented to non-human determinants which affect a nation's foreign policy behavior: for instance, size, geographical location, economic and political development, and military preparedness. There are analysts though who subscribe to the basic assumptions of this level concerning the impact of sub-national entities on foreign policy behavior, but who emphasize instead the dynamic interplay of individuals and groups upon the formation of such policy. Put differently, these latter analysts believe that the process by which policy is determined is a highly significant factor in analyzing a nation's behavior. For them a social-psychological focus yields a better pay-off in seeking the causes and correlates of a nation's political behavior.

The Social-Psychological Level-of-Analysis in International Relations

Herbert Kelman, in his seminal work International Behavior: A Social-Psychological Analysis, defines social-psychology as "the intersection between individual behavior and societal-institutional processes." And as such, he contends, "social interaction is thus the level-of-analysis that is most purely and most distinctively social-psychological."[25]

Instead of ignoring internal variables and seeking

causes solely external to the nation, this approach to the study of international relations works from the "inside-out," so to speak, for an explanation of a nation's foreign behavior. For many, decision-making analysis represents the core around which the inside view of foreign policy takes form. James Robinson and Richard Snyder state that "the main purpose of inquiries about decision-making processes is to determine whether and how decision processes affect the content of the decision outcome."[26] Thus, the social-psychological level-of-analysis in general, and the decision-making approach in particular, conveniently combine to determine whether different decision-making styles, procedures, structures, norms, and units have an impact upon the quality of the decision being rendered. "Different combinations of situations, individuals, and organizations," say Robinson and Snyder, "produce different policies."[27] Rosenau elaborates by stating:

> today it is commonplace to presume that what a state does is in no small way a function of how it decides what to do.... In other words, foreign policy action is a product of decisions, and the way decisions are made may substantially affect their content.[28]

In maintaining the line of reasoning established by Rosenau and similar advocates of social-psychological analysis of political behavior, Glenn Paige suggests that "decisions tend to vary with the composition of the decision unit."[29] Paige's own research into the causes of the U.S. entry into the Korean war conveys that "the initial decision to follow a diplomatic path in the crisis-- with an emphasis on international law and organization-- was a function of the presence of individuals in the decision-making unit who had been involved with the United Nations and were then with the State Department."[30]

Paige, in his research on the Korean decision, reaffirms the social-psychological belief that the most fundamental level-of-analysis in political life is the individual decision-maker. However, in most behavioral (and traditional) analyses, it is taken as a given, not as a hypothesis, that little variance in the behavior of nations can be explained by keying on national elites. Instead, the bulk of empirical studies in international politics/foreign policy take the systems-level focus-- articulated above-- with only occasional forays into governmental, societal, and bureaucratic explanations.[31] The psychological or cognitive level, in effect, remains inadequately researched and relatively unexplored when compared to the more traditional or mainline analyses of world politics.

Many factors can be cited as reasons for not viewing actors psychologically or foreign policy social-psychologically. Ole Holsti, in a cogently argued essay supporting cognitive approaches to the study of decision-making, cites three conventional wisdoms why such explanations centering on elite perceptions and cognitions are unlikely to expand our knowledge of foreign policy significantly.[32]

The first conventional wisdom deals with the confining or limiting aspect of bureaucratic politics upon individual decision-makers. Such large organizations, it is believed, severely constrain the individual by organization memory, prior policy commitments, standard operating procedures (SOPs), normal bureaucratic inertia, and conflict resolution by bargaining. These, in addition to other bureaucratic attributes, limit the impact of a particular decision-maker upon the foreign policy process. In other words, it is believed that so much variance can be explained by organizational and bureaucratic factors that one's personality plays only a tangential role (if any) in explaining foreign policy behavior.

The second conventional wisdom for discounting a cognitive approach rests on the belief that foreign policy is the "external manifestation of domestic institutions, ideologies, and other attributes of the polity."[33] Whereas the names and faces of the foreign policy elite may change, the interest and overall policy of the nation do not radically vary over time. This, of course, assumes that the structural features of a nation's foreign policy machinery are permanent and transcend the more transient nature of the personalities occupying the machinery's various offices.

Point three takes a wholistic or systemic approach to studying international behavior. Many analysts argue that structural and other attributes of the international system shape and constrain policy choices to such a degree that this is the logical starting point of analysis.[34] As Holsti states, those who feel this way would be in favor of extending their analysis to cover the national and domestic levels-of-analysis, but they would be reticent to dig deeper in analyzing the cognitive process of even the highest leaders.[35]

Therefore, conventional wisdom has it that after one has studied international politics/foreign policy at the systemic level, most of the variance in foreign policy behavior has been accounted for. The residual of unexplained variance is then frequently attributed to the cognitions and perceptions of the national leadership.[36]

It should be noted (as Holsti does) in the case of the first criticism which centers on the dynamics of bureaucratic organizations, that such a focus does not necessarily exclude a concern for belief systems. In other words, belief systems may be the basis for prescriptive or normative evaluations in periods of bureaucratic conflict. Holsti adds that a bureaucratic perspective may describe slippage between policy proposals and actual policy outputs, but such a focus is rarely valuable in explaining how the decision was made in the first place. Moreover, the homogeneity of a nation's foreign policy elite, which is assumed in traditional analysis, is, at best, a questionable assumption.[37] Bernard Mennis, in his study of United States military officers and Foreign Service Officers, for example, concludes that the "political viewpoints of the members of the two organizations actually are dissimilar."[38] Many others point to the same conclusion. The plurality of viewpoints among foreign policy participants invites the question: Why? Answering the question leads one invariably to adopt some variant of the social-psychological approach to foreign policy and international relations.

Many of those analysts who focus on system-level variables of national behavior and who argue that policy options and individual behavior are constrained because of the structural attributes of the system would nonetheless support (to a degree) the above positions argued by Rosenau, Robinson and Snyder, Kelman, and others. Some would even extend their analysis to include intra-nation dynamics and a few would go even further to promote the cognitive analysis of key national elites.[39]

This analyst, therefore, finds the theoretical premise advanced (often by systems-level theorists)-- that the individual level-of-analysis is relatively unimportant in analyzing world politics-- difficult to support. Such theoretical blindness consumes valuable time in discerning the causes and correlates of a nation's political behavior.[40]

Unlike much of foreign policy research, then, this research argues for the importance of psychological and social-psychological factors and variables in explaining the behavior of nations. However, "social interaction" as used here focuses on those relevant social relationships among members of small experimental decision-making groups. Ignored here is the larger milieu of social intersections such as those between the individual and his government; non-governmental organizations; inter-governmental organizations; and/or the international system. While these other relationships are highly relevant and certainly within the scope of the social-psychology of international politics, this study will focus primarily upon the dynamic interactions within small groups who make decisions during periods of international crisis. To repeat, it is this social-psychological orientation to political research that departs from the normal study of international politics and foreign policy.

Specifically, this research is interested in the effects of decision-making organization on the "quality" of the decisions produced in international crisis situations.[41] The "quality" of decision here refers to the degree of decisional extremization undertaken by the decision unit. Research findings from psychology, social-psychology, and sociology point to the fact that small decision-making groups are more inclined to take more extreme stands on an issue than are isolated individuals.[42] These findings have flown in the face of conventional wisdom regarding outcomes of group versus individual decision-making. Traditionally, groups were regarded as cautious, conservative entities which produced "happy-medium" or consensus decisions with extreme positions moderated by group deliberations. Extremely conservative or risky individuals were thought to be muted by the collective wisdom of the larger group membership. Subsequent research-- including this analysis-- has modified this view and has elaborated a more detailed explanation of group behavior.

Contributions of the Study of World Politics
Viewed Social-Psychologically

International politics viewed social-psychologically provides the analyst with several alternatives for contributing to the scientific study of world society.[43] By adopting such a perspective, perhaps this study will aid "in counteracting and correcting the tendency of analysts (principally systems-level theorists) who reify the state and treat it as a human agent."[44] When foreign policy behavior is viewed social-psychologically, it is possible to scrutinize in detail the processes which contribute to such behavior. Moreover, the analysis of the social dynamics between individuals and groups provides an alternative perspective for the analysis of international politics and foreign policy.

Now that the general direction of this research is clear, it is necessary to elaborate upon its predetermined route. <u>Chapter II</u> discusses two very fundamental variables in small group crisis decision-making: the impact of the restricted size of the decisional unit on the decision-making process; and the effects of stress on decision-making behavior under crisis conditions.

<u>Chapter III</u> examines the social and psychological effects of small group dynamics upon decisional extremization. Factors such as group composition, role structure, membership-- as well as cohesion and conformity-- are discussed in relation to the dependent variable, decisional extremization. Concomitantly, the group dynamic pathology of "groupthink" as developed by Professor Irving L. Janis is reviewed as a potential contributing factor in the decisional extremization phenomenon.

<u>Chapter IV</u> reviews the group decisional extremization/polarization literature from the earliest risky-shift research to the more current beliefs on decisional extremization and polarization. The early research focus on the dependent variable risk is compared to present thinking on the "new" dependent variable "commitment."

Collectively, Chapters II, III, and IV are designed to provide a conceptual framework for the investigation of small group decisional extremization/polarization in times of international crisis. In short, these chapters describe those salient variables the researcher should look to in describing and explaining this dynamic effect in small crisis-deliberating groups.

<u>Chapter V</u> explicates the methodology employed in the small group experiments. It performs the necessary duty of describing: 1) the sample of Fort Knox officers, Air Force and Army ROTC cadets, and college students; 2) the Choice Dilemma Questionnaire testing instrument; 3) salient independent variables; and 4) the procedures initiated in the individual/small group "runs." In sum, it describes the procedures utilized in the small group experiments.

<u>Chapters VI</u> and <u>VII</u> report the principal findings produced from the experiments. In particular, Chapter VI seeks to discern if there was a decisional extremization effect present within and across the sample groups of officers, cadets, and students. Chapter VII, on the other hand, amplifies upon the confirmation of the extremization phenomena and postulates several hypotheses for its occurrence. The tentative explanation proffered in this chapter is related to the conceptual framework produced in Chapters II-IV in order to test the validity of the construct.

Finally, <u>Chapter VIII</u> concludes by summarizing the study's major findings. It also suggests additional avenues for research in the field of small group dynamics and foreign policy decision-making.

NOTES

1. The state-centric model of international relations is generally dated from the historic period in which the state became a dominant form of political organization-- the Peace of Westphalia signed in 1648. See Parry (1968:14).

2. See Burton, <u>et al</u>. (1974:8). The author appreciates the conceptual distinctions between "international relations," "international politics," "world politics," and "foreign policy." In the strictest sense, this research deals with elite behavior in the sphere of public policy formation towards various external actors; that is, foreign policy. Except when specified, however, the above concepts may be used interchangeably

to facilitate style without intending to distort the conceptual character and uniqueness of each. See Dougherty and Pfaltzgraff (1971:23).

3. "A New National Partnership," speech by Secretary of State Henry A. Kissinger at Los Angeles, January 24, 1975. News release, Department of State, Bureau of Public Affairs, Office of Media Services, p.1.

4. As Kurt Lewin (1951:157) observed, "the first prerequisite of a successful observation in any science is a definite understanding about what size of unit one is going to observe at a given time." As a cautionary note, the concept level-of-analysis is used interchangeably with analytical perspective, foci, or approach. These terms are habitually used in several different ways. Richard Snyder, for example, has suggested at least three meanings: a) the level at which the phenomenon occurs; b) the level at which an explanation is formulated; and c) the level at which the data are collected. Indeed Kelman (1965: 20, fn 4) is correct in saying that "the term (level-of-analysis) is ambiguous, but it seems rather difficult to do without."

5. <u>Cf</u>. Keohane and Nye (1977); Sewell (1977); and Blake and Walters (1976).

6. Stephens (1972:322). <u>Cf</u>. McClelland (1966;1968) and Kaplan (1957).

7. Singer (1961:22).

8. McClelland (1968:6).

9. McClelland (1968:6).

10. See Singer and Small (1968).

11. See Russett (1967).

12. See Inglehart (1963).

13. Singer (1961:23).

14. Wolfers (1959). <u>Cf</u>. Burton, <u>et al</u>., (1974:3-30).

15. Singer (1961:23).

16. Burton (1974:5).

17. Singer (1961:24).

18. Singer (1961:25).

19. See Rosenau (1976) as an illustration.

20. Kissinger as in Rosenau (1967:267 ff.).

21. Rosenau (1976:43).

22. Rosenau (1976:43).

23. Rosenau (1976:43).

24. East and Hermann (1974).

25. Kelman (1965:22).

26. Robinson and Snyder (1965:456).

27. Robinson and Snyder (1965:456).

28. Rosenau (1969:169, original emphasis).

29. Paige (1968:284).

30. Paige (1968:285).

31. This is not intended to slight those analysts who, comparatively speaking, only recently delved deeper into cognitive and intra-group behavior. For example, Holsti (1962: 1965a; 1965b; 1971; 1972a; 1972b); M. Hermann (1966; 1975); George (1967); de Rivera (1968); Hermann and Brady (1972); Bonham and Shapiro (1976); Axelrod (1976); and Etheredge (1978).

32. Holsti (1976:16-17).

33. Holsti (1976:17). See also Lowi (1967:300). Lowi, a major analyst of the pluralist persuasion, sides with the elitists' interpretation in the sphere of foreign policy-- especially international crises.

34. Cf. Singer (1961).

35. Holsti (1976:17). See Greenstein (1967) for a refutation of this line of analysis. Additionally, there are several methodological stigmas attached to

cognitive analyses which Holsti does not address within this trilogy. There are obvious problems of access to elite decision-makers, reliability of testing instruments, as well as the validity of the findings over periods of time. Such points are discussed further in Chapter V.

36. There appears to be an over-abundance of these "residual" categories in foreign policy analysis. For example, the impact of public opinion-- while being the key element in voting behavior studies-- is seldom investigated in relation to the area of foreign policy. As Bernard Cohen (1973:24) relates, "public opinion is treated as a residual category/variable in foreign policy theories." This is due to the inability to operationalize the concept, the strength of the prevailing political and ideological orthodoxies (which flourish because of the dearth of empirical theories), and the belief that public opinion is considered to be external to the decision-making process which envelops large sections of the national political process. Much of what Cohen and others have said about public opinion and its impact upon the foreign policy process can be repeated verbatim about cognitive and social-psychological variables which affect foreign policy behavior. Moreover, this residual of unexplained variance is frequently rather large and *if* we attribute it to psychological or social-psychological variables, then it would appear that this is an area of politics that merits considerable attention.

37. See Holsti (1974).

38. Mennis (1971:180). Andrew Semmel (1972) too, discovered that there are wide differences in a given issue-area among Foreign Service officers within a given foreign policy agency, the Department of State.

39. However, some systems-level theorists maintain a "hard-line" approach and argue like J. David Singer (1971:19-20) who says that:

> I urge here a clear and sharp distinction between behavior and the intrapsychic processes that precede and accompany behavior of the individual; let us simply equate behavior with actions. By doing so, we are free to speak of the behavior

of acts of any social entity,
from the single person on up, and
need never be guilty of anthropo-
morphizing our social system. To
use the metaphor of the S-R (stimulus-
response) psychologists, we can
treat all the psychological and
physiological processes that occur
within an individual as if they
unfolded in a "black box" which
cannot be penetrated, and try to
understand external behavior (or
output) strictly in terms of its
empirical association with external
stimuli (or input).

40. Fred Greenstein (1967:97 ff), a major analyst in the area of personality and politics, lists five traditional objections to personality studies in political analysis. Briefly they are:

1) Personality characteristics are randomly distributed throughout the foreign policy elite and bureaucracies. Personality cancels out.

2) Personality characteristics are less important than one's social characteristics.

3) Because individuals have little impact on foreign policy and world events, personality is a blind avenue of research.

4) Personality is not important; it is the role or position that one occupies within the foreign policy machinery that counts. "The clothes make the man" imagery.

5) There is a <u>class</u> of objections deprecating the relevance of personality in which personality is equated with particular aspects of psychological functioning. The alleged "deep psychological needs" (ego-defensive) do not have an

> important impact on behavior
> and consequently "personality"
> so defined need not be studied
> in relation to political life.

Greenstein in this article, and others, e. g., M. Hermann (1972; 1974); Holsti (1974); Axelrod (1976); and Etheredge (1978); (see note 23 for a more complete listing), refute these aforementioned points and maintain that such a research investment into the cognitive processes of elite national leaders is indeed as rewarding as any other research approached from other perspectives or levels-of-analyses.

41. This nominal definition of crisis-- high threat, short decision time, and surprise to the decisional unit-- is one that was first advanced by Charles F. Hermann (1965) and has since become widely accepted in international crisis research.

42. A small group is generally considered to consist of 20 or fewer members (though not fewer than three persons) who: 1) communicate over time; 2) interact frequently on a face-to-face basis; and 3) can form some type of impression of other group members. See Bales (1950:3) and Homans (1950:1). See Myers and Lamm (1976) for a discussion of the group extremization phenomena.

43. Kelman (1965:580) suggests that such a focus can:

> 1) contribute to the study of the one substantive problem that is well within the scope of the social-psychologists-- the role of public opinion in the foreign policy process;
>
> 2) provide analytical tools for investigating the individual decision-maker as the unit-of-analysis;
>
> 3) provide concepts and methods for a detailed study of the <u>processes</u> that are critically involved in international relations-- especially foreign policy decision-making and negotiation; and

    4) address itself to some of the
        assumptions that are made in the
        formulation of theory and policy
        in international relations.

44. Kelman (1965:586).

CHAPTER II

CRISIS DECISION-MAKING AND STRESS

Introduction

The study of the crisis behavior of nations, groups, and individual decision-makers has been of considerable interest to social scientists, particularly political scientists. Until recently, however, there have been few empirical or quantitative attempts which examine the behavior of such political entities during periods of crisis.[1] Though we need not elaborate upon the policy relevance or theoretical importance of the concept of crisis, the difficulty in conducting crisis-related research is stymied by the plethora of definitions that the concept has acquired. The examples of this over-usage or misusage of the concept of crisis are abundant. Pick up a copy of virtually any piece of mass print media or scholarly literature and soon every problem is of "crisis" proportions. As James Robinson laments, "'crisis' is a lay term in search of a scholarly meaning."[2] The many and varied definitions of crisis stem, in large measure, from the concept's transdisciplinary and multi-level conceptual character. A brief conceptual survey will illustrate this point.

Contemporary usage defines crisis as a situation in which the potential for violence or conflict is high. This, though, is hardly comparable to the traditional Greek meaning of crisis which meant a "turning point"-- a definition currently employed in medical terminology. Usage of the concept in political science may be broadly classified into <u>substantive</u> and <u>procedural</u> definitions. Robinson states that:

> <u>Substantive</u> conceptions of crisis are those that are specific to the content of a particular policy, problem, or situation. <u>Procedural</u> definitions are those that emphasize generic characteristics of crisis situations without regard to whether it is an international crisis, or an individual crisis.[3]

Several examples of the substantive definition of crisis are evident in the literature; for example, Herman Kahn's forty-four step, ladder-like approach

of military escalation. Kahn's definition, while
providing a scale on the level of violence, does not
yield any sort of behavioral predictions during periods
of crisis. System-level scholars, such as Charles
McClelland, define crisis as "conflict situations
between two or more parties in which the likelihood
of war, or the level of violent interaction, abruptly
increases."[4]

The other rather general classification of crisis
is subsumed under the rubric of procedural definitions
which are likely to inhere in any situation labeled
"crisis" be it personal, national, or international.
Weiner and Kahn enumerated twelve generic dimensions
of crisis which range from "an unfolding sequence
of events and actions" to a situation that "accentuates
tensions among the actors, expecially in political
crises involving nations."[5] Miller and Iscoe take
a different approach. They profile crisis found in
psychological and sociological investigations which
are concerned with such individual and group level
attributes as changes in behavior that can become
pathological; efficiency, frustration, and scapegoating
within the group; the degree and intensity of crisis
for the individual within the group; and related tension, frustrations, and anxieties in the organism.[6]

Other scholars, such as Charles Hermann, prefer
to place the concept in a decision-making framework
and analyze crisis as a situational variable which
increases the likelihood of a certain kind of decision
by the policy-makers. Here, the crisis situation
is viewed as a variable of stimulation-- one likely
to produce definite responses by, and consequences
for, the decision-making unit. Specifically, Hermann
posits that a crisis is a situation that: 1) threatens
high-priority goals; 2) restricts the amount of decision
time available for response; and 3) surprises the
members of the decision-making unit.[7] Until recently,
most crisis researchers have accepted the definition
offered by Hermann. Some scholars, however, have begun
to re-analyze the concept with respect to the element
of "surprise."[8] Michael Brecher reports that a consensus was reached in a Jerusalem "crisis seminar"
in 1975-1976 that frames the concept more precisely
and elaborately for systematic empirical research.
It was agreed that, in conceptual terms:

> a foreign policy crisis is a situational change in the external or

> internal environment which creates
> in the minds of the incumbent decision-
> makers of an international actor
> a perceived threat from the external
> environment to [the] basic values
> to which a responsive decision is
> deemed necessary.9

In operational terms:

> a foreign policy crisis is a break-
> point along the peace-war continuum
> of a state's relations with any
> other international actor(s). A
> crisis is a situation with four
> necessary and sufficient conditions,
> as these are <u>perceived</u> by the highest
> level decision-makers of the actor
> concerned:
>
> 1. a change in its external or internal environment, which generates
>
> 2. a threat to basic values, with a simultaneous or subsequent
>
> 3. high probability of involvement in military hostilities, and the awareness of
>
> 4. a finite time for their response to the external value threat.10

With these many and disparate definitions of the concept of crisis, the scholarly community is abundantly supplied with examples of the crisis behavior of individuals, groups, bureaucracies, nation-states, and international systems. Yet, three separate images seem to emerge in the literature of crisis behavior.11

The first image involves studies conducted from a decision-making framework which focus on the crisis behavior of individuals and small groups. Research on such factors as the stress associated with crises,12 the size of the decision set,13 the individual and collective patterns of decision-making,14 or the overall social-psychology of crisis decision-making15 illustrates this viewpoint. "The major focus within this perspective has been to emphasize the extraordinary nature of crisis decision-making, such as the change from routine to _ad hoc_ decision-making groups."[16]

The second image is provided by viewing crises as "changes in the patterns of interaction among participating countries."[17] Measurement of the concept from this image involves observation of national transactions at special periods. In other words, nations undergoing a crisis will alter drastically their behavior toward other nations. In the post-crisis period, relations between nations will again approach normalcy. A systems framework is employed here to analyze changes in international interaction patterns.

The final image focuses on crisis as a major change in the international system. Many analysts assume that crises impart new patterns and relationships in the international system.[18] For example, the Cuban missile crisis is often viewed as the watershed event in cold war tensions that initiated the process of detente between the two superpowers. Though major criticisms have been leveled at this conceptualization, "the notion of a _major_ crisis as an impetus to new directions and orientations in parts of the international system is clearly adhered to by some scholars and practitioners."[19]

Thus, the dilemma of conducting crisis-related research should be obvious. The scope of definitions and the range of usage of the concept is exceptionally broad and diverse. But given the social-psychological thrust of this research, Michael Brecher's reformulated definition of crisis appears most satisfactory because of its attempt to encompass micro-oriented definitions as well as the more explicit macro conceptualizations. This reformulated definition departs from the conventional view (for example, Hermann's) on four points: 1) the omission of "surprise" as a necessary condition; 2) the addition of perceived "high probability of involvement in military hostilities;" 3) the replacement of "short" time by "finite" time for response; and 4) the recognition that the situational change which induces a crisis may originate in the _internal_ as well as the external environment of the crisis actor.[20]

Crisis Decision-Making Models

The definitional dilemmas of the concept of crisis presage an even more difficult problem in that not only do we lack a theory of crisis itself, but also we rarely (if ever) incorporate the concept into already existing theories of decision-making. The closest we have come to a theory of crisis decision-making is what Robinson refers to as <u>ad hoc</u> predictions [21] (where he refers to the early work of Charles Hermann).[22]

Traditional theories of decision-making such as economic decision-making theory, psychological decision theory, choice theory, game theory, Bayesian choice models, and others, can be subsumed under the classification of "rational choice models" of human behavior. These models "are strong theoretically (deductive) and relatively precise, formal, and mathematical."[23] However, the conceptual framework employed by these rational choice models assumes a pure situation; that is, all alternatives are known, all consequences of these alternatives perceived, and a ranking of the alternatives and consequences is possible. This is highly unrealistic because true decision-making is a continuous selection among alternatives that are frequently associated with unknown results.[24] This is especially true in crisis situations where stress increases dramatically over normal or routine decision-making; in such cases, decision-makers will tend to perceive the range of alternatives open to themselves as narrowing while the range of alternatives open to their adversaries as expanding.[25] Therefore, such traditional or pure models of decision-making in the context of crisis (<u>e</u>. <u>g</u>., Allison's Model I) are not always accurate or satisfying since national options simply do not just develop for the decision-making unit or group.[26]

For the most part, these types of traditional or rational choice models of political decision-making have conspicuously overlooked the role of interpersonal group dynamic or social-psychological variables such as decision-making styles, leadership, conformity to group norms, risk-taking, and so on. In effect, these models have "black-boxed" the small group decision-making process and have even avoided the concept of crisis itself in any theorizing about political decision-making. Thus, the deductive and mathematical elegance of such rational choice models has stirred a reaction among those analysts who find the many questionable assumptions about human behavior to be unrelated to actual decision behavior.[27] To many, other forces militate against a complete acceptance of the assumptions of the rational model view

of individual and collective behavior. This reaction
has spawned attempts by some political scientists
to cross-over into sister disciplines and borrow new
concepts and findings applicable to the dynamics of
inter-personal relations in, for example, small group
settings.[28]

Small Group Dynamics and Crisis Decision-Making

The relevance of small groups in political decision-
making, particularly in crisis decision-making, was
underscored by Sidney Verba when he wrote,

> If we are to understand the political
> process, greater consideration must
> be given to the role of face-to-
> face contacts. Primary groups of
> all sorts mediate political relation-
> ships at strategic points in the
> political process. They are the
> locus of most decision-making, they
> are important transmission points
> in political communications, and
> they exercise a major influence
> on the political beliefs and attitudes
> of their members.[29]

Most real-world political (and non-political) decision-
making groups tend to be small in size-- usually between
two and seven members, and frequently up to twenty
members. It is almost axiomatic that during crises
the locus of decision will be found in a group whose
size tends to diminish. This was true in such prominent
US foreign policy crisis situations as Korea (1950);
Indo-China (1954); Cuba (1962); Vietnam (1965); and
the Arab-Israeli dispute of October 1973.

Whatever the organizational location and function,
groups will have an overwhelming impact upon the policy-
making process and hence, upon the substance of the
policy itself. Groups provide the essential services
of information search, processing, evaluation, and
frequently, execution. As Janis notes, the small
decision group is often the principal and final decision body itself.[30]

In addition to these functional factors, groups
also provide several social-psychological benefits.
They provide psychological reference points to the

membership; they are potential sources of both cohesion and conflicts which, in moderate doses, allegedly improve the decisional product; and groups provide a means of bolstering (magnifying the chosen alternative and down-playing the attractiveness of those not chosen) and shielding the anonymity of individual groups members should the decision be a fiasco. Obviously, many of these traits are undesirable in terms of the quality of the decision being rendered-- particularly if these traits are overplayed or allowed to become dominant. Nonetheless, the importance and centrality of such groups should be classified as a given in the process of political decision-making.

If small decisional groups are indeed central to the study of political decision-making as Verba suggests, it is surprising that there have not been more systematic attempts to incorporate these potentially valuable social-psychological findings about small groups into the study of foreign policy decision-making.

One example of crisis modeling on the small group level is the research of Charles Hermann and Linda Brady. Given the prominence of such small decisional units in crisis deliberations, they have formulated an alternative model of crisis decision-making which gives greater consideration and emphasis to the role and behavior of such groups compared to rational choice models. In brief, Hermann and Brady's model of Organizational Response posits that:

> crisis decisions are concentrated in the hands of a small number of the government's foreign policy leaders. Thus, crisis decision-making can be contrasted with "normal" decision-making in which a much larger number of individuals at various levels throughout the foreign policy bureaucracies become involved. Notice (the statements) do not assert that all of the highest level foreign policy-makers will be involved. The head of state will most likely select persons who enjoy his personal trust, whose judgment he respects, and who he feels have special knowledge of the substance of the issue. He may also include one or more individuals

> strictly on the basis of his appreciation of their advice even though they presently hold no high position in any foreign policy bureaucracies. This personal selection of participants often makes the decision units <u>ad hoc</u> rather than a permanent and formally constituted organ of government. The occasional inclusion of trusted persons from outside the foreign policy bureaucracies explains the qualification that the decision unit consists primarily of high-level foreign policy office holders...31

Thus, it is apparent that research in the area of decision-making-- particularly crisis decision-making-- has moved beyond the initial formulations of the rational-choice school to include both intra-psychic and inter-personal dynamics as well. To illustrate this trend, several scholars have begun to give closer analytical attention to the phenomena of stress, which are believed inherent to crisis deliberations and critical decision outcomes.

The Effects of Crisis-Induced Stress Upon Crisis Decision-Makers

To the layman, stress is a pejorative term-- something to be avoided at all costs. It is felt that the many demands placed upon an individual by family, friends, co-workers, and even society itself, produce anxiety and tension which, if not released, lead to dysfunctional behavior and perhaps ultimately to the physical and/or emotional collapse of the individual. While an oversimplification, this description is quite accurate. In certain instances, however, stress can be a stimulant to higher or improved performance. How an administrator, such as the President, copes with the intense stress accompanying a crisis situation is a partial indicator of how well he will function in his role as chief executive. Richard Nixon, for example, asserted that crises brought out the best in him.32 Conversely, others have indicated that the severe pressures placed upon them in critical situations lead to a breakdown in mental and physical functioning.

During the Cuban missile crisis, for example, it

was reported that one Assistant Secretary was so exhausted that he drove his automobile into a tree at four a.m.33 Robert Kennedy recalled that: "the strain and hours without sleep were beginning to take their toll....That kind of pressure does strange things to a human being, even to brilliant, self-confident, mature, experienced men."34 Moreover, James David Barber, in his profiling of Presidential character, relates that President Warren Harding "found most of the decision process almost unbearably stressful."35

Alexander George and Ole Holsti, in their synthesis of the effects of stress on political decision-makers, state that:

> it is customary to regard "stress" as the anxiety or fear an individual experiences in a situation which he perceives as posing a severe threat to one or more values. In this connection, a useful distinction has been made between "psychological" and "physiological" stress (Lazarus 1964). Psychological stress requires an interpretation by the subject of the significance of the stimulus situation. Psychological stress occurs either when the subject experiences damage to his values or anticipates that the stimulus situation may lead to it. "Threat," therefore, is not simply an attribute of the stimulus; it depends on the subject's appraisal of the implications of the situation. Thus, the perception of threat is regarded as the central intervening variable in psychological stress.36

Generally speaking, experimental evidence shows that intense stress-- like that produced in international crises-- may improve psychomotor output, but it impairs cognitive performance.37 The best summary statement regarding cognitive performance and stress is that the relationship is curvilinear. As such, this relationship has frequently been referred to as the "inverse U" curve. Otherwise stated, low to moderate stress facilitates cognitive performance; high stress, on the other hand, tends to destroy such performance.38

Holsti and George cite several typical conclusions drawn from the experimental literature on stress as it affects individuals:[39]

 a) Perceptual behavior becomes distorted or disrupted. Major dimensions of perceptual function are affected; for example, selection of percepts from a complex field becomes less adequate and sense is less well differentiated from nonsense. There is a maladaptive accentuation in the direction of aggression and escape. Untested hypotheses are fixated recklessly.[40]

 b) ...shift to more rigid, primitive, less adequate and less realistic efforts at mastery... ineffective, rigid, and primary forms of coping, such as reality-distorting defenses.[41]

 c) ...more recent and usually more complex behavior disappear and simpler and more basic forms of behavior reappear.[42]

 d) When political leaders are faced with the necessity of making decisions the outcomes of which they can not forsee, in crises which they do not wholly understand, they fall back on their own instinctive reactions, traditions, and models of behavior. Each of them has certain beliefs, rules, or objectives which are taken for granted.[43]

With these findings even further distilled, three salient characteristics seem to summarize the effects of stress on the actions of political decision-makers. It can be said that they suffer from a reduced attention span, exhibit an increase in cognitive rigidity, as well as suffer from an attenuated time perspective.

Because crises create a reduced attention span for the individual, this reduction may be a catalyst for still other related effects. For example, because of the reduced attention span, task and information overload and task and role conflicts are common.[44] Baddeley contends that decision-makers attempt to cope with stress by reducing their attention.[45] Broadbent, too, states that as stress increases, filtering is likely to be less discriminating.[46] As a corollary, the search procedures for decisional alternatives tend to be dominated by historical antecedents, that is, reasoning or decision-making by analogy.[47] However, the diminished attention span of the individual is not a singularly unattractive phenomenon if the reduction of attention eliminates trivia or irrelevant information and develops an agenda of priorities.[48]

Cognitive rigidity, a second stress-related phenomenon, leads to an erosion of cognitive abilities including creativity and the ability to cope with complexity. Accordingly, decision-makers tend to establish a dominant percept through which to interpret information in the light of information that might seem to call for a reappraisal.[49] In other words, because of the reduced attention span which contributes to an increase in cognitive rigidity, political decision-makers will resort to stereotyping which itself contributes to a diminished capacity for ambiguity. Also, crises produce what Thomas Milburn calls "caricatures of day-to-day motivational structures." He says that "energetic, active people tend to behave even more energetically and actively under pressure. Anxious people are more anxious; repressors repress more-- especially if they consider it important to operate that way."[50]

Other analysts contend that high-level decision-makers possess what they term a "high discount rate." In other words, "they assign a high value to immediate achievements and to discount heavily the value of those realized in the more distant future."[51] Because increased stress aids in caricature regression, it can also lead to an attenuated time perspective and ultimately to the premature closure of decision options.

Because stress is associated with international crisis situations, policy-makers may often exhibit characteristics or behaviors that they otherwise might not display during periods of international tranquility.

It can almost be said that a decision-maker's senses can become so sharp, so heightened, that they actually become dulled due to the intense pressure. Moderate stress often facilitates performance, while intense stress can lead to a complete disintegration of performance. Under severe stress, executives can regress to a point of perceiving adversarial motives in a standard, stereotyped fashion; or they may attempt to relate the specific crisis event to a panorama of events unfolding in the international system in which the culprit is perceived to be the same adversary as in the immediate crisis.[52] There is also the tendency to simplify the spatial and temporal focus and a diminished ability to make fine discriminations when such intense stress occurs.

Analysis and evaluation are likewise impaired by stress. There exists a serious temptation to overestimate the benefits of certain preferred alternatives and to overestimate the costs of others.[53] Bolstering is the concept used to describe such behavior. Choice also suffers in the midst of high stress. There is the tendency either to "learn from the lessons of history," or "sit down and keep still" as Calvin Coolidge did when faced with tough decisions.[54] There is undoubtedly a yearning on the executive's part to resolve the immediate dilemma in his favor as much as possible. The probable pressures of short decision time, high threat to the decision-maker's value systems, and the general element of surprise lead a decision-maker to simplify his decision calculus by adopting a learning model drawn from history to guide him out of his present dilemma. Decision-making by analogy may be a crude and simplistic scheme. Whatever likenesses exist may be superficial and generally inapplicable to the present situation.

Holsti and George state that "rarely does a situation permit the decision-maker to maximize all values with a single option; whatever exceptions exist are trivial and of limited interest."[55] Because of the high stress associated with crises, its "streamlining" effects upon one's decision rules may not allow the decision-maker to see that the selection of one option will not satisfy all values. But if he does indeed recognize this value-complexity dilemma, then this recognition may contribute further to the stress that the elite faces. Thus, stress is not only an externally produced variable, but also one which results from "the tasks associated with formulating a response to it."[56]

Stress is also associated with pressures for premature closure. In this case, action-- some action-- is perceived to be better than inaction. As a result, emphasis is placed on short-run goals and values instead of long-range ones. This may be a functional strategy; indeed, it may be a coping device designed to relieve the immediate stressful situation. However, this strategy may engender heavy long-run costs such as ignoring long-range adversarial goals which, as a result, could intensify or exacerbate international tensions at a later date.[57]

Thomas Milburn agrees that "learning under stress conditions appears to depend on the complexity of the task. Simple learning, such as classical defense conditioning, is usually facilitated by stress; more complex types of learning appear to be disrupted by stress."[58] Holsti and George relate that "the more difficult and distasteful the decision and the process leading up to it, the greater the tendency to see evidence confirming the choice, and the lower the probability that the decision will be subject to reexamination in light of subsequent feedback." This is, as they state, one of the non-obvious consequences of cognitive dissonance theory.[59]

Foreign policy analysts seem to agree that "efforts at rational calculation and choice of policy tend to take place in three interrelated contexts or subsystems: the individual context, the small group, and the organizational context."[60] Likewise, the crisis-produced phenomena of stress takes place on the same three levels. Stress, however, not only arises from the "external" events initiated by others, but also from a phenomenon which is closely attendant to internal pressures for policy formation. Such internal pressures might include concern over ideological consistency in formulating a national response, doubts about your nation's ability to execute the decision, and perhaps even strong doubts about the consequences and likely responses to your decision by the adversary. Whatever the origin-- internal or external-- of such crisis-related stress, decision-makers tend to exhibit several common behavioral symptoms: a reduced cue awareness and attention span; an increase in cognitive rigidity; and an attenuated time perspective.

Allied with these observations of stress primarily at the individual level, there are additional characteristics which may exhibit themselves at the group and organizational level. The concepts of bolstering (playing up the chosen alternative while denigrating those not chosen) and value complexity (the recognition that one's choice will rarely satisfy all values) are elements which, if recognized by the decision-makers, are stress-inducing agents also. Moreover, when combined with the right amounts of group cohesion and solidarity, these elements (and others) can promote a collective decision-making malaise referred to as groupthink. It is conceivable that such a decision-making pathology can compel a group to adopt alternatives which are more extreme (that is, either more risky or more cautious) than the pooled sum of individual preferences. A discussion concerning the effects of such small group dynamics on crisis deliberations is presented in the following chapter.

NOTES

1. Hermann (1965;1972); Holsti (1965;1972); Zinnes (1968); *inter alia*.

2. Robinson (1968:510).

3. Robinson (1970:112).

4. Hermann (1972:7).

5. Weiner and Kahn (1962).

6. Miller and Iscoe (1963).

7. Hermann (1972:13).

8. See Brecher (1977:42). Brecher's lengthy footnote 7 bears repeating here.

> Hermann's (1969a:69, 202, 203) early simulation analysis led to a finding of "no significant relationship between either the time and awareness [surprise] dimension or the threat and awareness dimensions; however, a significant correlation

did occur between decision time and threat." Further, among all the tests that approach the (.10) level of significance, "high threat-short time yields the largest number of relationships-- one more than is generated by crisis....the simulation data do not prove the proposition that crisis, as defined, results in distinctive patterns of foreign policy decision-making. Nor do the data lead to the rejection of the macro hypothesis." This was reaffirmed by Hermann (1972:207-208) in a later paper: "Crisis and threat-time both enter into four of the possible five relationships, whereas no other trait or combination of traits produces more than two.... Consistent with this...is a review of the crisis literature...that found the property of surprise mentioned less frequently than the other two traits." The lesser significance of "surprise" and the inadequacy of the overall definition are also evident in the findings of Brady (1974:3, 258): "Threat-opportunity explains the largest proportion of the variance in each behavior dimension. No interaction effects explain more than one percent of the variance in the behavior dimensions... In sum,...the absence of second-order interaction effects leads us to qualify our judgment concerning the typology's utility... The eight-fold situational typology [of Hermann] is not as successful as we would have predicted." McCormick (1975:16) went much further, questioning whether "surprise" could be operationalized at all: "Surprise...normally occurs only once when there is an unexpected outbreak of violence...we concluded that surprise is not measurable from content analysis."

9. Brecher (1977:42-43).

10. Brecher (1977:43-44).

11. See Hazelwood, et al. (1977:77).

12. Lazarus (1966); Holsti and George (1976).

13. Paige (1968); Semmel and Minix (1977).

14. Hermann (1972).

15. Janis (1972); George, et al. (1976).

16. Hazelwood, et al. (1977:77).

17. Hazelwood, et al. (1977:78). See also McClelland (1961; 1968).

18. Young (1968); Schlesinger (1965).

19. Hazelwood, et al. (1977:78).

20. Brecher (1977:44).

21. Robinson (1970:129).

22. Hermann (1965).

23. Kirkpatrick (1975:11).

24. Simon (1958); Snyder (1962); March and Simon (1965); Allison (1971;1972).

25. Holsti (1965); Wiegele (1973).

26. Steinbruner (1974); Snyder (1978).

27. Simon (1958); Snyder, et al. (1962); Allison (1971;1972).

28. Allison (1969); De Rivera (1969); Janis (1972); George (1975); Semmel (1976).

29. Verba (1961:2).

30. Janis (1972).

31. Hermann (1972:287-88). See also the pioneering work in the area of "non-rational" modeling by Janis (1972); Holsti (1962; 1965; 1971; 1972b); M. Hermann (1966; 1975).

32. Nixon (1962).

33. Nathan (1975:259).

34. Kennedy (1969:22; fn. 9); Sorenson (1969:705).

35. Barber (1972:193-94).

36. Holsti and George (1975:257).

37. Vogle, et al. (1959); Reynolds (1960); as in Holsti and George (1975:278). Holsti and George (1975:278, fn. 17) state that "if there is no task involvement-- personal involvement in the task or stake in the outcome-- stress may improve performance (Baker, et al. 1966). However, task involvement is presumably always present in foreign policy situations."

38. Rogow (1963), L'Etang (1970), and Weigele (1973) examine the psychological, medical, and biological aspects of stressful situations such as those accompanying crises. It is important to remember that individual stress thresholds may vary, but generally the "inverted U" pattern holds true.

39. Holsti and George (1975:278).

40. Postman and Bruner (1948:322).

41. Lazarus, Averill and Opton (1974).

42. Milburn (1972:265).

43. Joll (1968:6).

44. Holsti (1972:104-08).

45. Baddeley (1972).

46. Broadbent (1971:16).

47. Paige (1972); Milburn (1972:165).

48. Baddeley (1972).

49. Nalven (1961) as in Holsti and George (1975:279).

50. Milburn (1972:265).

51. Allison and Halperin (1972:50) as in Holsti and George (1975:280).

52. See Milburn (1972:275) for a question, hypothesis, decision-rule structure in relation to this problem. See also Holsti and George (1975:280)-- particularly their footnote 23 in which they state:

> In October 1962, when news of China's invasion of India reached those who were grappling with the problem of Soviet missiles in Cuba, some of them initially assumed that the two events were linked as part of a worldwide assault on the non-communist world, even though by this time there was no shortage of evidence indicating a deep split between Moscow and Peking.

53. Milburn (1972:273).

54. Fenno (1959).

55. Holsti and George (1975:281-82).

56. Holsti and George (1975:282).

57. Holsti and George (1975:282). As Nixon (1962:113) wrote after his 1962 California election defeat, "decisive action relieves the tension which builds up in a crisis. When the situation requires that an individual restrain himself from acting decisively over a long period, this can be the most wearing of all crises."

58. Milburn (1972:265).

59. Festinger (1957).

60. Holsti and George (1975:256).

CHAPTER III

GROUP DYNAMICS AND DECISIONAL QUALITY

This chapter is primarily concerned with the quality of decisions produced during international crises. In particular, it discusses some of the salient variables which impel small groups to reach more extreme choices than those reached by isolated, individual decision-makers. Since it is impossible to verify objectively quality from decision output, the term is generally reserved for the *processes* contributing to the final decisional outcome. It is generally assumed that certain procedures lead to increased decisional success, that is, meeting the decision-maker's objectives and having them adhered to in the future. High quality decisions, according to Irving Janis and Leon Mann, are conceptually characterized by "vigilant information processing" which stem from following a seven point checklist of "ideal procedures." These procedures include: 1) thoroughly canvassing a wide range of alternatives; 2) surveying all objectives to be fulfilled and the values implicated by choice; 3) weighing the costs and benefits of each alternative; 4) intensively searching for new, relevant information; 5) correctly assimilating this new information-- even if it opposes initially preferred choices; 6) re-examining the positive and negative consequences of all known alternatives; and 7) making detailed provisions for implementation of the chosen course of action with contingency plans available should known risks materialize.[1] Accordingly, these procedures-- if followed-- will tend to decrease "post-decisional regret" which frequently accompanies important or stressful decisions. If these criteria are side-stepped, it is possible that defective information processing could arise in such forms as "defensive avoidance" (avoidance in making the decision), "bolstering" (magnifying the attractiveness of the chosen alternative), or "hypervigilance" (panic).[2] Though it is possible to produce successful outcomes from low quality decision-making procedures, maladaptive coping mechanisms (like those cited above) are likely to surface.

Decisional extremization, on the other hand, is used to describe the phenomenon whereby small groups adopt more risky or more cautious choices compared to the pooled sum of individual preferences contained within the group.[3] In focusing on decisional quality, the analyst is forced to look closely at both intra-psychic and inter-psychic, or social factors, that may impinge on the policy-making process. Since a crisis is usually a stressful condition, it is likely that reactive social processes and coping reactions will not be unrelated to either the process or form of the final outcome. Just how much and what kind of effect crisis situations have on individual decision-making processes and group deliberations is the core focus of this research.

The social interaction and the intellectual interchange between individuals aggregated in a nation's foreign policy apparatus is highly significant because these individuals-- arranged in small groups-- frequently thrash out, argue, and "politick" matters of the highest concern during a foreign policy crisis. And, it is quite likely that the final group decision-- regardless of its degree of risk-- will be quite different from what "a simple aggregation of individual preferences and abilities might otherwise suggest."[4] It is such a proposition that compels this study of small group versus individual foreign policy decision-making behavior.

The purpose of this chapter is to aid in the development of a conceptual framework for studying the decisional extremization phenomenon as it relates to small group decision-making. This is no small task and not all pertinent ground can be covered. Nonetheless, the belief is that the factors and variables discussed here contribute to the amount of risk or caution a small group is willing to adopt during a crisis.

The studies, findings, and hypotheses set forth in this chapter have been discussed and evaluated by others. However, it is anticipated that the synthesis of findings from psychology, sociology, social-psychology, and political science which follows will illuminate potential sources of small group decisional extremization in political decision-making.

In addition to the reduced size of the decisional set, the membership composition and role structure of the group are likely to influence the extremity, and, in general, the "quality" of the decision made in periods of crisis-induced stress. To such a discussion this chapter now turns.

Size, Membership Composition, and Role Structure

Size. Even during normal or routine periods of foreign policy decision-making, the size of the decisional unit is generally restricted to a small coterie of individuals in the foreign policy apparatus. For example, the "routine" decision by the Carter administration to cancel funding for the full-scale production of the B-1 bomber included no more than a handful of top government officials at any given time: the President, the Vice-President, the Secretary of State, the Secretary of Defense, National Security Advisor Brzezinski, plus the President's top-eschelon subordinates.[5] During crises, however, the number of involved personnel frequently becomes even more restrictive. Research indicates that the size of the decision unit is generally between two and seven members.[6]

Charles Hermann, in his edited volume, International Crises: Insights from Behavioral Research, outlines reasons why crises generally involve only the elite of a nation's foreign policy machinery.[7] As one contributor to this volume, James Robinson, contends:

> a crisis tends to bring a problem or an issue to the top of an organization's hierarchy, it permits bypassing much of the bureaucratic lethargy that often characterizes foreign offices. A crisis decision will be taken by officials near the top and, given the demands of time, they can afford to bypass many customary procedures in making decisions.[8]

Glenn Paige reinforces Robinson's remarks by investigating two substantive examples: the Korean War and the Cuban Missile Crisis.[9] In the former case, the officials involved in the decision numbered fourteen; in the latter case, they numbered about sixteen. Moreover, Paige, among others, notes that these crisis groups are generally ad hoc in nature. Conventional national security machinery devised to handle crisis situations (for example, the National Security Council or the Cabinet) was bypassed in favor

of a coterie of individuals both within and outside
the government who were respected for their expertise
on a particular subject or for their general abilities
in dealing with foreign policy matters. Second, these
participants were generally held in close regard by the
chief executive. Former Secretary of State Dean
Acheson quickly comes to mind in the case of the Cuban
missile crisis. Acheson was, no doubt, chosen because
of his former positions in government, his link to
Democratic presidents, as well as his knowledge of
foreign affairs. Howard Lenter, in his perceptual
analysis of crisis by State Department officials,
buttresses the "consolidation of decision-making" thesis
in times of crisis.[10] His figures (reproduced below)
show that State Department officials feel overwhelm-
ingly that: a) crisis precipitates concern at a
higher level; and that b) crisis decision-making takes
place at a higher level than is customary.

Table III - 1

Frequency of Involvement of High-Level Officers in Crises

	No Response*	Always	Often	Sometimes	Never
a) A crisis precipitates concern at a higher level than normal	0	54 (68.4%)	22 (27.8%)	3 (3.8%)	0
b) A crisis precipitates decision-making at a higher level than normal	1	40 (51.3%)	37 (47.4%)	1 (1.3%)	0

*Excluded in calculating percentages.

Lenter's data reveal that State Department officials who believe that crises "always" precipitate concern at a higher level (68.4%) are more assured of this belief than those who replied that this was "often" the case (27.8%). If these two categories are combined and compared with the "sometimes" and "never" classifications (3.8% and 0%, respectively), then it can be concluded that an overwhelming majority (96%) of those State Department officials queried feel that crises do indeed created concern at higher levels than is the normal case with "routine" or customary decision-making in the Department of State.

The same data are supportive of the "reduced crisis decision-making set" thesis in regard to part B - "a crisis precipitates <u>decision-making</u> at a higher level than normal." Fifty-one percent replied that crises "always" generate decision-making at higher levels while 47% stated that this was "often" the case. Only one individual (1.3%) felt that this phenomenon occurs "sometimes." As in the case questioning "concern," no individuals felt that crises "never" rise in the bureaucratic decision-making hierarchy.

Charles Hermann, in his own simulation research, substantiates the claim that crisis decision-making is handled by a rather small group of participants. For example, he found that: 1) as time decreases, the number of participants in a decision tends to decrease; and 2) the larger the nation, the fewer decision-makers engaged in all situations.[11]

Therefore, during crises, it is taken as a given that the organization of the decision-making unit will be such that it will be considerably smaller in size when compared to "normal" or "routine" foreign policy decisions. By the unit's being small, however, there are potential factors which affect the internal group dynamics of the deliberation process. These factors, if present, affect the quality of the decision being rendered. Several factors, such as membership composition and role structure, are two of the salient variables most scholars agree will affect internal structure and interaction patterns in committees.[12]

<u>Membership Composition and Role Structure</u>. Robert Bales, a prominent scholar of small group interaction processes, states that committees tend to form informal power prestige offerings" from the outset.[13]

That is, members engage in a perceptual evaluation of the membership's early contributions and then form preliminary personal evaluations of everyone's relative "worth" to the committee. From this preliminary perceptual analysis conducted by each individual, expectations are made regarding one another's potential committee contribution; moreover, "opportunities to participate in the discussions are differentially allocated by the members to each other."[14] This evaluation process of committee members by one another leads to a status ranking with respect to a member's contributions to discussion. This perceptual ranking models the informal power and influence structure in a group, e. g., high contributors are more powerful and influential than low contributors. Moreover, "high participators interrupt others, but are not interrupted; they tend to get agreed with more than others; and they have more control over the interaction process than low participators."[15]

Bales' model, therefore, helps in understanding a small group or a committee's role structure and interaction. But, small group decision-making can have other consequences. For example, smaller groups tend to have simpler role structures which reflect less differentiation of tasks and less division of labor and specialization within the group, in addition to less formalized modes of procedure than larger, more complex organizations.[16] One of the consequences of this simplified role structure is conformity to group norms, practices, and procedures resulting in increased group cohesion.

Conformity: Group Pressures on the Individual

Cohesion among group members refers to "the members' positive valuation of the group and their motivation to continue to belong to it."[17] Cohesion, according to psychologist Irving Janis, "looms very large and exerts considerable influence on (an individual's) choice when he is participating in a group decision-- namely, the social approval or disapproval he anticipates receiving from the leader or from fellow members."[18]

There are two sides to this issue of group cohesion as Janis intimates. As an asset, cohesion reflects group solidarity, mutual good will, and a high feeling of task participation. Moreover, highly cohesive groups, according to Kurt Lewin and his followers, afford members "with a source of security, with solace and support against anxiety or distress, and help them to maintain self-esteem."[19]

But as a liability, "highly cohesive groups are not necessarily high performance groups."[20] This seems particularly true with respect to the phenomena under investigation: foreign policy crises. During a crisis then, the group may realize the fundamental threat to national values, goals, and lives and subsequently reduce in-group conflicts in favor of converging upon a particular course of action. In other words, in a crisis situation, it is believed better to have a quick consensus on a national policy than to have protracted debate, minority reports, and so on, which waste valuable time and energies. As George and his colleagues report:

> The policy consensus arrived at under these conditions may be more than simply the convergence of individual opinions on a particular issue; rather it may also express fundamental individual needs and group values that transcend normal cannons of objectivity, and it may reflect a tacit agreement within the group to agree unquestioningly upon whatever course of action causes least interpersonal strife.[21]

For example, Chester Cooper, in his volume _The Lost Crusade_, describes part of the Vietnam policymaking process in the Johnson administration:

> The NSC meetings I attended had a fairly standard format: the Secretary of State first presented a short summary of the issues, the Secretary of Defense added his comments, and there was some fairly bland and desultory discussion by the others present. Because many around the table had not participated in, nor indeed been told of the detailed advance discussions, "gut"

issues were seldom raised and searching questions were seldom asked.

The President, in due course, would announce his decision and then poll everyone in the room - Council members, their assistants, and members of the White House and NSC Staffs. "Mr Secretary, do you agree with the decision?" "Yes, Mr. President." "Mr. X, do you agree?" "I agree, Mr. President." During the process I would frequently fall into a Walter Mitty-like fantasy: When my turn came I would rise to my feet slowly, look around the room and then directly at the President, and say very quietly and emphatically, "Mr. President, gentlemen, I most definitely do not agree." But I was removed from my trance when I heard the President's voice saying, "Mr. Cooper, do you agree?" And out came a "Yes, Mr. President, I agree."[22]

By Cooper's own account, the pressures for conformity to the Administration's Vietnam policy were immense. In order to reduce cognitive dissonance, dissenters quietly conformed. When dissent did surface, other group members attempted to force the dissident to conform by making him the center of attention by invoking collegial "peer pressure." If these efforts failed, the dissident, as George and his colleagues state, "may be isolated by the group, being placed in the distressing position of having either to maintain his unpopular stand without support, or to withdraw into silence and inactivity. In extreme cases the deviant member may be rejected altogether by the group."[23]

This was apparently the case when George Ball began to question administration policy on Vietnam. President Johnson at first tolerated Ball's deviance by jocularly greeting him as "here come Mr. Stop-the-bombing." Ball was then useful to Johnson because he could be counted on to plot an alternate, though highly unfavorable course in Vietnam strategy, thereby allowing the Administration to deflect the criticism that all sides of the war issue were not being given just attention. But, as the war dragged on, Ball's usefulness had run its course. In-house dissent began to grow and with it the need to close ranks with like-minded advisors. This persuaded the President that Ball (and those like Robert McNamara who shared his views) should leave. As Halberstam relates, McNamara's departure to the World Bank is indicative of the group-induced pressures for conformity to the Administration's bombing policy in Vietnam.[24]

Conformity to group norms has been confirmed repeatedly both in scientifically controlled laboratory experiments and in everyday inter-personal relations.[25] Norms are rules of behavior, defined corridors for a group member's acceptable conduct. Such norms are generally derived from the group itself and the goal(s) that the group has selected. Hare states that:

> When the norms refer to the expectations for a single individual they constitute the individual's role. The norms are then, in effect, the expectations for the role of an "undifferentiated group member." Each person has within him a set of norms and goals which are a composite of his own idiosyncratic ideals, the expectations of other groups of which he is also a member.[26]

When either the individual or the group feel that a member has transcended the normal codes of behavioral conduct, there are but four options remaining for the person: 1) change the group norms; 2) remain a deviant; 3) leave the group; or 4) conform. Conformity is the likely behavior in such small, elite foreign policy-making bodies because of the cohesiveness of the group to begin with as well as the intra-psychic pressures for remaining on a powerful, prestigious policy-making organ.

Coincident to the pressures of group cohesion lies the danger that the chief executive will become isolated by myopic advice. Such pressures led Robert Kennedy to recall in his memoirs on the Cuban missile crisis that he "had frequently observed efforts being made to exclude certain individuals from participating in a meeting with the President because they held a different point of view..."[27] And, according to

Townsend Hoopes, Vice-President Humphrey's attempt to stop the bombing of North Vietnam in February 1965 was received by the White House "with particular coldness, and he was banished from the inner councils for some months thereafter, until he decided to 'get back on the team.'"[28] As Hoopes remarks in his book,

> it was my impression that the President's sense of incongruity reflected the extent to which he had become the victim of (1) Rostow's "selective briefing"-- the time-honored techniques of underlining, within a mass of material, those particular elements that one wishes to draw to the special attention of a busy chief-- and (2) the climate of cozy implicit agreement on fundamentals which had no longer characterized discussions within the inner circle on Vietnam, wherever was heard a disparaging word.[29]

Groupthink: Stress-induced Cohesion

Irving Janis, a social-psychologist, begins his seminal book, The Victims of Groupthink, by questioning Arthur Schlesinger's account of the Bay of Pigs incident. "How," Janis wonders, "could bright, shrewd men like John F. Kennedy and his advisors be taken in by the CIA's stupid, patchwork plan?"[30] Janis' research led him to note that this foreign policy "fiasco" (and others) were characterized by group decision-making processes which inhibited the Kennedy team from debating the issues. Specifically, Janis noted a high degree of concurrence-seeking behavior which resulted in a feeling of invincibility among group members. *Groupthink* is the concept employed by Janis to refer to a deterioration in the quality of group decision-making processes.

Janis finds support for the groupthink effect in many recent US foreign policy decisions.[31] His examples are drawn from the Bay of Pigs fiasco, the entry of the US into the Korean War, the attack on Pearl Harbor, and the escalation of US bombing attacks on North Vietnam. Other decisions can also be culled for potential pathologies regarding small group decision-making. The Bay of Pigs fiasco, which Janis labels "a perfect failure," is characteristic of the deficiency in reality-testing that accompanies high-level policy-making within such closed groups. The illusion of invulnerability was high to the "New Frontiersmen." As Robert Kennedy related to a colleague in the Justice Department on the day that the CIA launched its plan against Cuba:

> It seemed that, with John Kennedy leading us and with all the talent he had assembled, nothing could stop us. We believed that if we faced up to the nation's problems and applied bold, new ideas and hard work, we would overcome whatever challenged us.[32]

According to Arthur Schlesinger, Jr., "the dominant mood in the White House was 'buoyant optimism.' It was centered on the 'promise of hope' held out by the President. *Euphoria reigned; we thought for a moment that the world was plastic and the future unlimited.*"[33] However, the spirit of Camelot led the planners of the Kennedy administration to misperceive the strength and support of Castro as an adversary. They thought him weak and stupid-- an hysterical leader of a third-world nation who would do nothing to neutralize the Cuban underground.[34]

According to the groupthink hypothesis, a shared illusion of unanimity is also symptomatic of such stress-induced cohesion. Sorenson relates that:

> no strong voice of opposition was raised in any of the key meetings and no realistic alternatives were presented.[35]

And Schlesinger adds that:

> the massed and capricious authority of his senior officials in the realm of foreign policy and defense was unanimous for going ahead...Had one senior advisor opposed the venture, I believe that Kennedy would have cancelled it. No one

spoke against it.[36]

In addition to the illusion of invulnerability and the presence of unanimity, groupthink can also prohibit dissenters of policy from making their feelings known. Whether this censorship is self-imposed or accomplished with outside aid, matters of policy may not be given a just hearing if only one perspective is shown.[37]

According to Janis, Schlesinger was not hesitant about showing his discontent over policy, but he did so only via memoranda. In top-level White House meetings, however, Schlesinger was mute. As Schlesinger himself recalls:

> in the months after the Bay of Pigs I bitterly reproached myself for having kept so silent during those crucial decisions in the Cabinet Room though my feelings of guilt were tempered by the knowledge that a course of objection would have accomplished little save to gain me a name as a nuisance. I can only explain my failure to do more than raise a few timid questions by reporting that one's impulse to blow the whistle on this nonsense was simply undone by the circumstances of the discussion.[38]

This concurrence-seeking behavior among group members-- in this case, foreign policy decision-making groups-- is fostered by group-induced cohesion. Political decision-making is often stressful, but it is particularly so in foreign policy areas where the concommitant pressures for a quick and often forceful national option bring undue pressures upon the executive and his lieutenants. Such extremely stressful conditions like international crises pull the leadership together in order to permit a quick resolution to the crisis and to return operations to a less stressful, "normal," or "routine ' state. But to Janis, this stress-induced cohesion can be pathological. That is, members can become involved in the phenomena of "groupthink." Groupthink, according to Janis, is a

> quick and easy way to refer to a

> mode of thinking that people engage
> in when they are deeply involved
> in a cohesive in-group when the
> members' strivings for unanimity
> override their motivation to
> realistically appraise alternative
> courses of action...Groupthink
> refers to a deterioration of mental
> efficiency, reality testing, and
> moral judgment that results from
> in-group pressures.39

The so-called pathology of the groupthink phenomena stems neither from within the individual nor the organizational setting. Rather, the pathology arises from the cohesiveness often found in small foriegn policy decision-making groups. As Janis states, "the cohesion of small in-groups engenders a 'concurrence-seeking' tendency, which fosters excessive optimism, lack of vigilance, and sloganistic thinking about the weaknesses and immorality of out-groups."40 These symptoms are conducive to different forms of behavior, e. g., risk-taking, being aggressive, stereotyping adversaries, poor information processing, and so forth.

As George and his colleagues point out, the groupthink literature developed by Irving Janis is reminiscent of Leon Festinger's theory of informal social communication which Stanley Schachter later developed in his studies of conformity pressures.41 Schachter stressed that when there is no empirical referent for an issue, the sought-after referent then becomes the opinions of those around you. Thus, when individuals are confused or perplexed, they look to other group members in order to establish the validity of their own opinions.

But, as Janis admits, just because a foreign policy decision turns out to be a fiasco, it does not automatically mean that it was the result of groupthink or defective decision-making. Conversely, not every defective decision arising from groupthink will produce a fiasco. It is indeed possible to produce successful decisions contrived under poor decision-making conditions. But generally, how such decisions are rendered can, and will, affect the tone and the implementation of the nation's policy. Decisions produced without regard to excessive group cohesiveness, the channeling of information toward or away from a chief executive, and the membership composition and role structure of the group, among other decisional qualities, generally do not permit the proper conditions for a rational consideration of the crisis at hand. While complete rationality in political decision-making is unobtainable, improving the decision-making process can enhance the probabilities for successful implementation and decrease post-decisional regret.

Nonetheless, the presence of the stress-induced phenomenon of groupthink can lead to a host of defective decision-making procedures which, in turn, increase the likelihood of foreign policy failures, i. e., poor quality decisions. The link between groupthink and such fiascos is, of course, imperfect. But, defects in the decisional dynamics of small groups can be prevented. Through detection, it is anticipated the incidence of group-induced foreign policy fiascos will decrease.[42]

Individual versus Group: The "Quality" of Decision

The question of which unit-of-analysis-- individual or small group-- performs better during crisis situations depends upon many factors in addition to those previously outlined. Social-psychological research indicates that each unit has particular assets and liabilities with respect to task accomplishment, data recall, and the quantity of options discussed. Evidence indicates that some individuals are positively stimulated in the presence of others; some are negatively influenced; while others remain unaffected. The group appears to be superior to the individual on manual as compared to intellectual tasks.[43] Groups will also have a tendency to report fewer, but more accurate, facts than individuals because of the group's willingness to merge with perceived group norms. Moreover, groups will generally recall more information than individuals presumably, says Hare, "because of their greater capacity to store information."[44]

It is clear, though, that group processes do affect the decisional outcomes of the group. Janis reinforces this point by saying that:

> a group whose members have properly
> defined roles, with traditional
> and standard operating procedures

> that facilitate critical inquiry,
> is probably capable of making
> better decisions than any indi-
> vidual in the group who works on
> the problem alone. And yet, the
> advantages of having decisions made
> by groups are often lost because
> of psychological pressures that
> arise when the members work closely
> together, share the same values,
> and above all face a crisis
> situation in which everybody is
> subjected to stresses that
> generate a strong need for
> affiliation.45

Alexander George and his colleagues stress that group interaction processes "include efforts to deal with the emotional needs and stress that can be aroused by the value complexity and uncertainty which...are often associated with foreign policy decision-making.46

To the previous discussion on the dynamics of group decision-making that included such factors as group size, composition, role structure, and cohesion, the variable of group norms must be added. Norms establish behavioral parameters for both the individual acting alone as well as in the context of the social group. Particularly in the latter case, norms conceivably influence such potential pathological symptoms as cohesion, conformity, membership composition, and task accomplishment. Therefore, if the potential advantages of small group decision-making are to be secured and decision-making pathologies avoided, then it is necessary that (1) a differentiated role structure develop within the group so as to permit cogent contributions from all members; and (2) the processes of reaction, questioning, and suggestion-making within the group not be inhibited.47

Summary

Thus, the quality of the decision depends, as was stated, on several organizationally related factors, as well as the function of the decision unit itself. If a small group is charged with responding to a crisis event, then norm-promoted factors such as size and cohesion play a crucial role in shaping the decision outcome. If, on the other hand, an individual in isolation is to respond to the same crisis, factors such as belief-systems, psychological tensions, or stress can play a large role in mapping a response.[48] Of course, such factors are not restricted to only one particular unit-of-analysis. Norms, for instance, permeate all behavioral responses-- individually defined or within the dynamic context of the small group. Stress, too, appears within groups just as it does within individuals. But, by treating the attributes of the decisional unit as independent variables along with these other social-psychological factors, it is then possible to discover how the quality of the decisions reached may differ. The concepts of decisional extremization and polarization are employed to measure and analyze such differences.

NOTES

1. Janis and Mann (1977:11).

2. Janis and Mann (1977:6;82).

3. Polarization is a more narrowly defined concept than extremization. While the latter simply refers to movement by the group to either a more risky or more cautious position, polarization refers to the movement by the group to an already preferred pole. If, for example, the average of the individual preferences tended toward risk, then in all likelihood the final group decision would surpass this average of individual opinions and result in a group decision even more risky.

4. George, et al. (1975:40).

5. *Newsweek*, July 11, XC, 2, pp. 14-17.

6. Snyder and Paige (1958:362) and James (1951:474-77).

7. Hermann (1972).

8. Robinson (1972) as in Hermann (1972:34).

9. Paige (1972) as in Hermann (1972:45-56).

10. Lenter (1972) as in Hermann (1972:130-31). For additional reference to this centralization process, see Berelson and Steiner (1964), Weiner and Kahn (1962) and Buchan (1966).

11. Hermann (1972:197). Thomas Milburn (1972) as in Hermann (1972:266) also supports this contention by saying that "as crises last longer or become more intense, centralization of authority tends to occur in the decision-making process."

12. George, et al. (1972:41).

13. Bales (1950).

14. George, et al. (1972:41).

15. George, et al. (1972:41).

16. George, et al. (1972:42).

17. George, et al. (1972:44).

18. Janis (1977:133).

19. George, et al. (1972:44).

20. George, et al. (1972:44).

21. George, et al. (1972:44).

22. Cooper (1972:273-74).

23. George, et al. (1972:45).

24. Halberstam (1972:604-05; 783-84); Cooper (1972:343-44).

25. Sherif (1936); Asch (1952).

26. Hare (1976:19).

27. Kennedy (1969:117).

28. Hoopes (1969:31).

29. Hoopes (1969:218).

30. Janis (1972:iii).

31. Since groupthink is an elusive phenomenon to observe and measure, Janis does not offer his studies as "proof"-- only as hypotheses and plausibilities.

32. Guthman (1971:88).

33. Schlesinger (1965:259). In fact, Schlesinger was reputed to have said that the motto of the Kennedy phalanxe was: "we happy few."

34. Schlesinger (1965:293).

35. Sorenson (1966:314) as in Janis (1972:39).

36. Schlesinger (1965:258-59) as in Janis (1972:39).

37. Janis refers to those individuals who "protect" their superiors from information and material that is uncomplimentary or contrary to the consensus as fulfilling the role of "mind-guards." See Janis (1972: 41-43).

38. Schlesinger (1965:255).

39. Janis (1972:9).

40. Janis (1972:13). See pages 184-224 for Janis' suggestions as to who succumbs to groupthink; when; and why. Within these pages he offers several suggestions or prescriptions for the prevention of this effect.

41. See George, et al. (1975:47).

42. This presentation is just the tip-of-the-iceberg of the group decision-making pathology called groupthink. For a detailed discussion, see Janis (1972) and Janis and Mann (1977).

43. As Hare (1976:329) says: "the group will lose its superiority in accuracy and efficiency if (1) no division of labor is required; (2) problems of control are too great; or (3) the group develops a standard of productivity which is lower than that of a separate individual. In terms of man-hours the individual is usually more productive."

44. Hare (1976:329). With respect to decision-making "quality"-- the individual and collective processes involved-- see Holsti and George (1975); Axelrod (1976);

and Janis and Mann (1977).
45. Janis, as in George, et al. (1975:40).
46. George, et al. (1975:40).
47. George, et al. (1975:49).
48. Holsti (1962); Bennett (1972).

CHAPTER IV

THE CHOICE-SHIFT PHENOMENA

Conventional wisdom in such places as corporate board rooms, university departments, and, of course, all levels of government, is that the correct solution to problem-solving or decision-making lies with the operation of a committee. It is thought that such small groups-- generally consisting of the organization's top management personnel-- will reach a more judicious decision than a private, isolated individual. Small groups, the belief goes, will produce a more moderate and wiser decision because extremely risky or cautious members will be muted by the more cautious collective wisdom of the group's majority.

However, in 1961, James Stoner, a graduate student in business at the Massachusetts Institute of Technology, empirically tested this conventional wisdom. His findings indicated that groups were generally _more risky_ in their decisions than individuals acting alone. This phenomenon was quickly dubbed "shift-to-risk" or the "risky-shift." The traditional beliefs pertaining to the inherent conservatism of group decision-making were gradually disbanded by a flood of generally supportive research. However, not all findings followed with a "riskier-than-thou" conclusion. Some studies showed groups to be more conservative, while others showed absolutely no shift at all between individual preferences and group decisions. Generally, though, research during the 1960's produced little evidence contradicting the basic _risky_-shift. As a result, the conventional wisdom of cautious group decision-making was beginning to be eroded by a new belief in the inherent riskiness of small groups. Risk-taking perhaps inadvertently, became the prime dependent variable for analysts of small group behavior.[1] The principal testing device used in these so-called "risky-shift" studies has been the Choice Dilemma Questionnaire.

First developed by Kogan and Wallach in 1959 to measure individual risk-taking, the Choice Dilemma Questionnaire (CDQ) is further evidence regarding the volume of investigation applied to group risk-taking.[2]

Cartwright notes that "the average number of items added to it (the CDQ) each year rose from 4 to 8, to 23, for the successive three-year periods beginning with 1961 and reached 40 for the period 1970-71."[3] A decade after the initial Stoner discovery, the <u>Journal of Personality and Social Psychology</u> devoted an entire issue to the "risky-shift" phenomena.[4] As the journal subtitle implies, there was still, in 1971, a research bias favoring risk as a dependent variable over the more general phenomenon of group extremization.

Recent research on small group decision-making, however, focuses on developing a theory that is broad enough to handle "risky-shifts," "cautious-shifts," as well as "no-shifts," that is, "choice-shifts." As Vinoker states, "if we are to develop an adequate theory of individual and group decisions involving uncertainty, it should include an explanation of the decision-making process and should account for both risky and conservative shifts."[5]

"Choice-Shift Findings"

The "risky-shift," or the more general "choice-shift" effect, has been identified among a host of different nationalities and subjects. However, the vast majority of studies have been conducted on students from Western cultures. For example, the choice-shift effect has been found to be operative among individuals from: the United States,[6] Canada,[7] England,[8] France,[9] Germany,[10] Italy and Switzerland,[11] Israel,[12] New Zealand,[13] British Columbia,[14] as well as two African cultures, Uganda and Nigeria.[15]

In addition, the choice-shift phenomenon has also been explored across various subjects. Middle managers,[16] professionals and managers,[17] workers,[18] industrial workers and head nurses,[19] students, teachers, and principals,[20] college students, ROTC Cadets and Army Officers,[21] as well as housewives, clerks, technicians, and foremen[22] have all been subjects of this research genre.

Also, various cultural and typological variances among the subjects have been studied. For example, subjects' age, sex, and group size (N) have been included as independent variables.[23] Age of the participants has ranged from 18 to 60 and group size has spanned dyadic relationships to groups up to eighteen members.[24] Most studies, though, are conducted with a group "N" of four to six persons. The spate of "risky-shift" studies has also shown that the sex of the individuals within the group makes little difference in determining shifts. Sexually heterogeneous and homogeneous groups have persuaded analysts to agree with R. D. Clark, who says that "the data unequivocally reveal a strong and pervasive tendency by persons of both sexes to view themselves as being at least as risky as their peers."[25]

The prevalence of the CDQ instrument in the choice-shift research has provoked some analysts into questioning whether immediate or proximate contact or communication with other group members is essential for shifts to occur. Researchers have modified the simple pretest - post-test, face-to-face discussion CDQ procedures to incorporate situations whereby participants only would listen to, not discuss, the decision dilemma;[26] the participant would observe discussion through a one-way glass.[27] In some cases, scientists have asked subjects to compare notes without discussing the CDQ items.[28] However, these variations on a theme seem to indicate, as Pruitt and Teger state, that "some sort of communication among group members is essential for a shift to occur."[29] Although Haley and Rule, who applied Robert Bales' Interaction Process Analysis (IPA) to small group interactions, "found no difference in the frequency of initiating conversation in low risk, moderate risk, or high risk conditions...," they did, however, find that there is evidence that group discussion produces greater choice-shifts.[30]

Thus, the choice-shift effect has had little difficulty in receiving world-wide confirmation, but it is precisely this easily replicated phenomenon that has eluded analytical explanation. The volume of research surely indicates that there is no dearth of interest in the choice-shift effect.

Choice-Shift Hypotheses

As was stated, since the initial discovery of the

"risky-shift" effect, well over 300 research pieces have appeared on the subject. At first, most studies tended to confirm the "risky" aspect of group deliberations. Later studies, however, were relating findings of cautious shifts as well as no shifts. What has not been absent is a series of hypotheses (frequently called theories and models) attempting to explain this group dynamic phenomenon. Not unlike the analyses of international political behavior conducted by political scientists, these findings and explanations appear less than cumulative. To weave through the mass of group dynamics literature on decision-making is, at best, a difficult and tedious task. What follows is an attempt to sort out some of these competing, frequently contradictory, "explanations" regarding the risky-shift.

The Diffusion of Responsibility Hypothesis. This thesis holds that individuals in the group will elect riskier positions because alone they are not responsible for the group decision. The decision is the responsibility of the group as a whole and no one person will be held accountable. In other words, the context of the group acts in such a way to reduce individual anxiety about the negative consequences of potential decisional outcomes. This thesis was later amended to include the argument that emotional bonds must exist or develop in the group discussion.[31] Since the subject can hide behind the cloak of group anonymity, recklessness is a more likely behavior. As is generally the case with most of the rival explanations, the findings are mixed with respect to the diffusion-of-responsibility thesis. Some analysts find support for the hypothesis,[32] while others do not.[33]

Familiarization Hypothesis. The Familiarization Hypothesis was proposed by Bateson in 1966.[34] It argues that as individuals become more familiar with a problem, they will engage in greater risks. Like the diffusion-of-responsibility thesis, the familiarization thesis accounts only for shifts-to-risk. And, like the diffusion-of-responsibility thesis, it has received mixed reviews regarding its explanatory powers.[35] Proponents of this hypothesis assert that the so-called "risky-shift" effect is a "pseudo group effect." That is, it occurs within a group but does not arise from any group process.[36]

Persuasion or Leadership Hypothesis. As some

suggest, the "risky-shift" can be described by a leadership or persuasion hypothesis.[37] Such an approach asserts that dominant, forceful, persuasive personalities within the group who tend to be high risk-takers exert their influence over other, more maleable personalities within the group. Although such assertive personalities are believed to elect greater risks than others in the group, the leadership hypothesis does allow for the opposite effect to occur. That is, such personalities could be overly conservative or cautious and, by the same process, persuade other group members to elect a similar position.[38] The leader of the group is seen to have more confidence in his adopted decision and can unduly influence those members who are no so convinced with respect to their choices, or he can persuade those who have not then made up their mind as to which option should be selected.

Subsequent research has cast doubt on the leadership/persuasion thesis. The thesis with repsect to the risky-shift has been dispelled.[39] Evidence supporting the leadership theory with respect to the choice-shift is mixed. Some studies show evidence for the persuasion hypothesis;[40] others, though, do not.[41]

The rhetoric one employs to convince others in the group to adopt the leader's preferred choice should not be undersold. However, the "rhetoric-of-risk" (or caution) is more than likely to account for only part of the group decisional estremization phenomenon.[42] Vinokur points out that "leadership is assumed to be a stable personality characteristic throughout the conditions, rather than allowing for a change in influence with a change in situation."[43] A person, notes Vinokur, may take an extremely risky stance on one particular dilemma; a moderate stance on another; and a conservative position on yet another. Moreover, one's conviction may not be as strong across all situations. A moderate position may indeed allow the formerly persuasive "leader" himself to be influenced by a more extreme individual. Therefore, individual influence is analogous to the concept of "power" in international politics. That is, influence is situation-specific and, as such, not necessarily transferable from time 1 to time 2. As Vinokur says, "the amount and direction of change would be based on the intensity and strength of preference of a particular issue rather than all issues.[44]

The Emergent Norm Hypothesis. This hypothesis asserts that during the group's interchange of ideas, members cue on others for help in deciding on a course of action. As the discussion continues, one alternative will somehow gain more support than the other alternatives. Once that occurs, group members will focus upon it.[45]

Norris Johnson and Dorwin Cartwright both contend that the emergent norm hypothesis has been neglected in research on group decision-making involving risk. According to Johnson, "this is due to the mistaken belief that emergent norm implied a convergence toward the mean of initial choices."[46] Furthermore, "this would occur only when all the individual members had the same influence and in choice-shift, one must look to unequal influence."[47]

Rabow and his associates tested for the emergent norm thesis in their 1966 research by utilizing risky, neutral, and conservative CDQ's. They concluded that:

> Group decisions are not necessarily "riskier" than individual decisions. Group decisions on problems involving risk can be riskier, more conservative, or may not differ at all when compared to the means of decisions prior to discussion...the nature of the decision to be made can significantly affect the relationship between group decisions and individual decisions...norms play an important role in group decisions....There is, in a word, social support for the person who exercises caution or takes risks. The support, however, is related to the circumstances involved or specifically to the problem under discussion.[48]

Value Hypotheses

The value hypotheses, of which there are five, hold in common the belief that groups shift in the direction that the majority of the group's membership is predisposed as individuals. Value hypotheses include several variants: social-comparison hypothesis, pluralistic-ignorance hypotheses, release hypotheses, relevant arguments hypothesis, and commitment hypothesis. As Pruitt says, "their names describe the assumed process, whereby individual attraction toward one end of the scale is translated into group shift. These theories are called 'value theories' because they identify the cause of this attraction, and hence the energy behind the shift, in widely held human values."[49]

Roger Brown describes the value hypothesis as accounting for the socially desirable trait of risk in our culture.[50] In such a milieu, most group members perceive themselves at least as risky as others. However, in the group discussions, some members realize they are more cautious than others and will shift to a riskier position to minimize loss of face. These hypotheses are, of course, predicated on the concept of risk as a preferred value. In support of this view, Madaras and Bem report that risk-takers are viewed more favorably than risk rejectors.[51]

Additionally, the value hypothesis can account for a cautious shift on certain items on a Choice Dilemma Questionnaire. The same psychology as previously outlined for the concept of risk as value is now applicable to the concept of caution as value. Stoner discovered that the group decision was more cautious when members positively viewed the cautious alternative and for which individuals tended to view themselves as relatively cautious.[52]

Value theory, therefore, asserts that the group decision, risky or cautious, is a product of the pre-established values of the group membership. As Fraser and his colleagues have found, "the basic shift phenomenon may be an intensification of attitude for or against the attractive alternative, rather than a shift on some substantive dimension such as subjective risk." The conception of the shift as a change in attitude seems compatible with all existing theories of this phenomenon.[53]

Social-Comparison Hypothesis. Roger Brown best explicates the social-comparison hypothesis variant of the general category of value theory.[54] This hypothesis asserts that risky behavior or attitude is culturally valued or an "ego ideal" which prescribes that

Americans should be at least as risky as anyone else. This process entails surveying others' attitudes and preferences on a topic (i. e., social comparison) and then adopting a position or stance at least as risky as everyone else's. According to Solomon Asch, one will likely "move in the direction of the perceived majority."55 As Brown states:

> When individuals talk together and disclose their decisions the actual distribution is made known. Those who find themselves below the mean of the...members of the group discover that they are failing to realize the ideal of riskiness that they may have thought they were realizing. Consequently they feel impelled to move in a risky direction both in accepting the decision of the group and in changing their private opinions. Subjects at or above the group mean feel no such impulsion; they are relatively risky just as they meant to be. The result would be, of course, a shift in the group decision toward greater risk than the mean of the individual decisions.56

The utility of the social-comparison hypothesis is that it also can account for cautious shifts as well.

Pluralistic-Ignorance Hypothesis. A second variant of value hypotheses is the pluralistic-ignorance hypothesis. This hypothesis postulates that there is a discrepancy between an "ideal preference," that is, what one would like to see done, and an "assumed group standard" which he believes others would do. Obviously, this produces a conflict-compromise situation (in Graham Allison's words, "the pulling and hauling that is politics...") closely akin to the concept of incrementalism in decision theory.57 Such a conflict therefore leads to a compromise situation in which the result is a decision somewhere between the two points. Levinger and Schneider postulate that group discussion reveals each member's choice or position which could lead to a re-evaluation of the member's choice.58

Release or Contagion Hypothesis. The release, or contagion, hypothesis as described by Pruitt applies to both risky and cautious shifts.[59] Like the two previously described value hypotheses, the release hypothesis also assumes that people are in conflict when asked to reach a decision involving risk on a risk-oriented decision problem. As Pruitt describes:

> The forces that produce this attraction are internalized and ego syntonic. On the other hand (and here the theory departs somewhat from pluralistic-ignorance theory), a cautious approach is compelling because of widely held values attaching to moderation and being reasonable. These values are adhered to not so much out of conviction as out of conformity motive, a sense that other people predominantly support the so-called "golden mean," and that it is essential to avoid being seen by others as "too far out on a limb."[60]

Basically, the release hypothesis postulates that as one member of the group (the model) endorses a particular position, this "releases" cautious members from assumed social constraints that are holding them back from risk-taking. This idea of release from social constraints is somewhat similar to the findings of Asch in which individuals felt pressured into making false declarations (i.e., conforming) because of group pressures. In fact, one need not look far for possible examples of the effect and the explanatory theory behind it.[61] The release hypothesis is also referred to as the "Walter Mitty Effect" and as contagion.[62] Discussion simply "releases" the individual from binding social constraints when someone else adopts a riskier position than his own. When this occurs, the riskier person is imitated by the one (Walter Mitty) wishing to be as risky.

Release differs from the leadership hypothesis as described earlier, in that the leadership hypothesis views the process of influence as directly resulting from the behavior of the risk-taker. The release hypothesis, however, attributes risk to the person's mere presence within the group.

The evidence supporting social-comparison and leadership hypotheses supports the release hypothesis as well. In Dean Pruitt's words:

> In terms of existing evidence, release theory would seem to have an edge over the two value theories previously presented as an explanation for that part of the shift produced by exchange of information about initial risk level. Of course, this edge may be only temporary.[63]

<u>Relevant Arguments Hypothesis</u>. The fourth value hypothesis is the relevant arguments hypothesis. The hypothesis, first described by Roger Brown and later elaborated by St. Jean, suggests that as group discussions progress, members will be exposed to "relevant arguments" previously unpronounced in the group debate. These arguments, it is believed, account for the group shift. Support for this hypothesis is mixed.

<u>Commitment Hypothesis</u>. The commitment hypothesis, last of the five value hypotheses, suggests that group discussion is a vehicle for individuals to further commit themselves to their elected position instead of a forum for the exchange of ideas. This hypothesis, first advanced by Serge Moscovici and M. Zavalloni, states that:

> In the course of handling the information, as he interacts with real or imaginary interlocutors, he chooses alternatives, binds himself to the choice, and thus commits himself to the work he is doing.[64]

The commitment hypothesis is flexible because it assumes that the individual is using the group context only to further intensify his initial decision. That is, one could move towards the risk end of the scale in the case of risk-oriented items and to the cautious end of the scale for cautious-oriented items. "This theory is classified as a value theory, because Moscovici and Zavalloni seem to imply that the value pull of each item will determine the direction of the initial decision and thus of the further commitment that ensues during discussion."[65]

Even though the commitment hypothesis exhibits flexibility in terms of the direction of shift, it has trouble explaining the fact that "risky shifts are obtained when the subject observes a live group discussion, or listens to a recorded discussion."[66] Because the role of the subject is so passive in these latter experimental variations, it is difficult to see where "commitment" applies. In these cases, it would appear that an explanation of choice-shift behavior would be in the direction of familiarization or information obtained from either watching or listening to other group members.[67]

The value hypotheses, not unlike the other "theories" attempting to explain choice-shift behavior, are not universally supported. As one analyst has commented,

> ...the value hypotheses in some form (have) generally been better able to explain choice-shifts or lack of shift (than) have the previously mentioned hypotheses. This could be due to the fact that the value hypotheses have received more attention as well as having so many diverse variations.[68]

Though it is abundantly evident that there is a lack of support within the "choice-shift" research community for any one particular explanation, analysts do tend to agree that more than one theoretical paradigm may be at work in the choice-shift effect. As Dion and his colleagues state, "when we reach a complete understanding of group decision-making and risk-taking, it should not surprise us if propositions from several of the competing theoretical positions turn out to be true."[69]

The Group Extremization and Polarization Phenomena

The spate of research on small groups and risk-taking which followed the initial Stoner experiment in 1961 were re-examined in the early 1970's. Some researchers believed the tangled mass of "risky-shift" findings to have been a "fruitless fad."[70] The seemingly endless number of studies which produced confirmations, "confirmations-with-qualifications," and disconfirmations, has indeed been a "less than heuristic" sport.[71]

It is now widely recognized, says David Myers and Helmut Lamm, that "the designation 'risky-shift' was a misnomer that unfortunately induced many investigators to perceive the phenomena from the perspective of the dependent variable, risk-taking, rather than to think in broader theoretical terms about the effects of intra-group communication on attitudes and behavior."[72]

One of the interesting results in the torrent of investigations on group decisional dynamics was that some of the original CDQ's were prone to produce "risky-shifts;" some, "cautious-shifts;" and others, "no-shifts." Accordingly, Alan Teger and Dean Pruitt show that the initial or individual response is highly correlated with the shift (generally .70 to .90).[73] By implication then, a shift or a collective group decision is readily predictable from viewing the mean of the group's pre-test scores. In other words, "items which elicit relatively risky initial tendencies generally elicit further shifts toward the risky extreme after discussion. Items with relatively cautious initial means are more likely to elicit further shifts in the cautious direction."[74]

As a result of this finding, the "risky-shift/choice-shift" paradigm was recast into a broader theoretical framework known as the <u>group polarization</u> hypothesis. The polarization hypothesis is closely akin to the previously described commitment hypothesis (one of the five value theories): the average post-group response will tend to be more extreme in the same direction as the average of the pre-group responses.[75] The commitment hypothesis and its reformulated offspring, the group polarization hypothesis, evolves from the work undertaken by Serge Moscovici and his colleagues.[76]

The polarization effect of group decision-making though, appears to be the species, rather than the genus. The more general phenomenon is referred to as group <u>extremization</u>: A group will move away from neutrality, regardless of direction.[77] With extremization, one has to show only movement, not direction. Consequently, this latter effect should be easier to demonstrate.

The generality of the group polarization phenomenon has been repeatedly demonstrated in various experimental situations and actual or real-world settings. Myers and Lamm, for example, identify seven (arbitrary) categories in which this effect has been observed.[78] While it is unnecessary to explicate each category by citing the relevant research, it is noteworthy that the polarization effect is generally confirmed quite strongly across each of these classifications. The one exception is the category of <u>judgment</u> where the phenomenon "is not as reliably confirmed as in studies requiring a greater degree of social evaluation."[79] The polarization phenomenon, therefore, does not lack sufficient empirical verification. And like the previously cited choice-shift studies, this effect does not suffer from a dearth of explanations. Several contenders for explanation have been refuted. For example, the leadership dynamics explanation shows "no relationship between the extremity of a person and the extent to which he dominates the discussion,"[80] although, state Myers and Lamm, "it is still possible that relatively extreme <u>positions</u> will tend to be more persuasive than neutral positions."[81] Another likely candidate, familiarization with the information, has been discredited also. Apparently group discussion produces greater polarization than merely isolated or private study of the materials. Neither is the effect the result of a "majority-rule" decision scheme where minorities are "pressured" into adopting the position of the majority of the group's membership. However, there are two hypotheses which are often advanced as having the greatest explanatory potential: the interpersonal comparison hypothesis and the informational influence hypothesis.

The <u>interpersonal comparision hypothesis</u> stresses the social characteristics of the group and assumes that people tend to perceive and present themselves favorably in relation to others.[82] When the group discusses the issue, individual positions are revealed.

In order to maintain a desirable self-perception, a person may shift his position when it is learned that others have the same proclivities-- but only in a stronger sense. Essentially, group discussion and the revealing of individual predispositions "releases" the group member to intensify his position by shifting to what he perceives to be the emerging group norm. With its strong emphasis on group norms, this hypothesis is "consistent with conformity studies which indicate that the example of only one person freely deviating from an imposed norm can liberate other individuals to act out their own impulses."[83] This is consistent with the research conducted on ideological groups which shows that extreme views and extremist members are considered more influential.[84]

This hypothesis assumes that one enters the decision-making group underestimating the predispositions of his fellow members. But because of our desire to perceive ourselves in a socially preferred or "correct" position, we merge to fit the perceived expectations. Relevant arguments, therefore, have little, if any significance in pulling group opinion in the already preferred direction. In terms of the interpersonal comparison hypothesis, it is desirable to move with the direction of the perceived majority. As Brown notes, "to be virtuous, in any of an indefinite number of situations, is to be different from the mean-- in the right direction and to the right degree."[85]

Research on the interpersonal comparison hypothesis has been approached from several distinct fronts in an attempt to ascertain the veridicality of the hypothesis. These fronts encompass: 1) the difference between self, presumed other, and ideal scores; 2) predicting shift with self, presumed other, and ideal difference scores; and 3) choice-shift following exposure to others' responses.[86]

The first front, <u>differences between self, presumed other, and ideal scores</u>, assumes (with considerable substantiation) that if a subject is asked to go back over the items once again to determine where the <u>average peer</u> would respond and then once more to determine the position that the subject personally admires most, then the subject generally finds his initial response falling between the average group member and the socially valued or <u>ideal</u> response. Generally speaking, subjects perceive themselves as more extreme in the preferred direction than most of the other group members, but less extreme than their ideal.

McCauley, Kogan, and Teger as well as Myers report some unexplained order effects on the choice dilemma task cited above. This tendency to place oneself ahead of the average group members exists, they say, when the self response is made prior to estimating the group norm.[87] One apparently establishes his position first and then looks backward to locate the average group member's position.

Also, subjects tend to view others who have responded more extremely than they (in the socially desired direction) as more socially desirable than others who are less extreme.[88] Eisinger and Mills report that "an extreme communicator on one's side of an issue tends to be perceived as more sincere and competent than a moderate."[89]

The theoretical significance of these findings in relation to the interpersonal comparison hypothesis has been clouded by the finding that subjects who communicate extreme views are believed to possess cogent arguments and are admired for their ability.[90] Thus, there is some question concerning the significance of self-other-ideal differences in predicting choice-shifts as implied by the interpersonal comparison hypothesis.

Predicting the shift with self, presumed other, and ideal difference scores is the second front from which this hypothesis has been researched. The question here is: does the perceived difference between oneself and others correlate with an individual's shift on a specific item?[91] The findings related to this question of self versus perceived other are somewhat mixed. Clark and his colleagues observed increased risky-shift when their subjects strongly underestimated peer risk acceptance, but Lamm and his associates did not find the same effect with a similar manipulation.[92] Composing groups on the basis of self versus ideal position, however, yields a shift response in accordance with the interpersonal comparison hypothesis.[93] As Myers and Lamm state, "the self-ideal discrepancy may be the more crucial element of a viable interpersonal comparison approach."[94]

The final analytic assault on the interpersonal comparison hypothesis predicts a <u>choice-shift following exposure to others' responses</u>. Many studies show that there is movement on the part of the subjects to a manipulated norm. Is this conformity due to the interpersonal comparison of positions, or is it attributable to the influence of information? When discussion is absent, there is either a reduced shift or no shift at all. Burnstein and Vinokur report that if knowledge of others' choices was denied or if an opportunity to rethink the item was denied, no shift occurred.[95]

Myers, Bach and Schrieber constructed an experiment in which subjects responded to three choice dilemma questionnaires after being informed of the responses of forty other individuals.[96] This maximized the interpersonal comparison effect while holding constant other variables.

Increased risk-taking was noted when the post-treatment responses were compared to the control responses the subjects observed. Myers states that the results were "counterintuitive" because they were the opposite of conformity. "The subjects were fairly accurate in their guess of the average of the responses they had observed, and yet this exposure elicited a differentiation (polarization) from the observed norm."[97] While there is unsupportive evidence concerning this hypothesis, there is still significant support for several aspects of interpersonal comparison as principal factor in the group polarization effect.

The second hypothesis, informational exchange, has been even more consistently supported by research in this area. It "suggests that during discussion, arguments are generated which predominantly favor the initially preferred alternative. These arguments can induce some persuasive points the typical person has not previously considered."[98] Implicit in this hypothesis is the premise of the interpersonal comparison hypothesis: the group learns the direction and preference of the majority's opinion.

While arguments are believed to play a key role in the choice-shift phenomenon, it is not known whether such arguments convey information that was previously unknown (informational influence or relevant arguments), or whether these arguments reveal the general tenor of the group's feelings (interpersonal comparison). Or, do cogent arguments do both?

Experimental support for this hypothesis is generally of two types: 1) those studies which show that an exchange of arguments produces polarization even if no mention is made of the initial response,[99] and those studies which contend that increased information leads to a polarization of opinion;[100] and 2) that research which lifts the cover of the "black box" to examine the arguments actually expressed. In other words, the shift is hypothesized to be a function of the direction, the persuasiveness or cogency, and the novelty of each argument.

The amount of overlap between the interpersonal comparison and the informational influence hypotheses is not insignificant. The essential difference between these two rather complementary explanations rests with the fact that the interpersonal comparison hypothesis stresses the group's <u>social characteristics</u> and diminishes the importance of argumentative exchange as a vehicle for polarization. The informational influence hypothesis, on the other hand, stresses our <u>rational capacities</u> in hearing inconceived initial <u>arguments</u> which help establish a perceived group norm. Both emphasize strongly the primacy of group norms as being a strong catalyst for group polarization. In short, "our arguments may convey information about our position on an issue, and we may select arguments that are biased in the socially desired direction."[101]

Crisis Decision-Making/Group Polarization Framework

An attempt has been made to set forth those salient factors that may impinge on the small group decision-making process by influencing the effect known as group extremization/polarization during crisis deliberations. Here, an attempt will be made to summarize some of the individual and group-level variables that frequently lead groups to choose more extreme decisions than private decision-makers. Posed as a question: How do sets of individual beliefs and values become transformed in the milieu of the small group-- the pivotal locus of crisis decision-making-- and how does the final group decision differ with respect to each individual's beliefs and preferences? The concept of the small group and its related dynamics have been cast as a conversion process mechanism. What goes "in" in terms of individual values and beliefs may differ radically with the end product of final group decision. In fact, it may differ so radically that it is unrecognizable to any of the group's participants because of the transformation that occurred through group dynamics.

The key to unlocking this conversion process mechanism remains undiscovered. What emerges from the previous discussion will not be presented as a theory, but rather as a framework for future empirical forays into the relatively unexplored dynamics of group decisional extremization during crises.

One reminder is needed before this framework is elaborated. The entry into the field of small group decision-making was gained by linking the analysis of crisis decision-making and the "groupthink" phenomenon to the literature on the choice-shift and extremization effect. In much of the crisis decision-making and all of the groupthink literature, the focal point of investigation lies with the small group as the unit-of-analysis. However, the small group/choice-shift literature makes no a priori assumptions concerning the formation of the group. In other words, the concept is taken as a given in this literature and how or why the group developed is ignored. Again, what this research will attempt to demonstrate is the logical link between the decision-maker's perception of external threat to the nation and the response to that perceived threat. How would the crisis have been handled if it had been done individually or in the social atmosphere of a group? As previous research indicates, "who" decides foreign policy is in no small way unrelated to the outcome of the decision process. However, the perception of a crisis is neither a necessary nor a sufficient condition to trigger group polarization. Realistically, the pressures applied upon a select group of a nation's foreign policy-makers in times characterized by high stress, seem likely to trigger anything but a cool, calculated, rational response. Therefore, it is precisely this decisional variance between the individual and the small group in times of national emergency that this research seeks to uncover.

The Decision-Maker's Perception of a Crisis. For a crisis to occur and have an effect upon a nation, a decision-maker(s) must subjectively perceive the change in environment to be one where there is a high threat to basic national values, one where the probability of involvement in military hostilities is high and the situation is perceived to have a very finite time frame for formulating a national response.[102] In adopting the decision-making framework rather than a systems framework, decision-makers "behave according to their interpretation of the situation, not according to its objective character as viewed by some theoretical omnipotent observer."[103] Thus, the decision-maker's perception of a crisis is crucial. It is the key intervening variable between the actual event or occurrence (stimulus) and the nation's responses.[104] As Holsti and George state, "in choosing whether and how to respond, the individual's cognitive processes--broadly encompassing his value preferences, knowledge, information, and repertoire of coping strategies--are of central importance."[105]

Filters. In a pure sense, there is no independent variable. The actual event must be mediated through the decision-maker's finely honed filtering mechanism. Once a crisis is perceived, a host of psychological and environmental functions is triggered. For example, there is likely to be a striving for cognitive consistency on the part of the decision-makers, a reduced attention span, plus an attenuated time perspective for the individual. These, in turn, set off a chain of related psychological attributes ranging from reduced cue awareness to an increased emphasis on short-run values.[106]

Group Norms: Social Influence and "Groupthink" Pathologies. The psychological stress induced from the perception of a crisis could conceivably stimulate a host of potential "pathologies" on the part of the individual perceiver as well as the decisional unit itself. One form of coping with this intense stress is to seek the shelter of a small coterie of trusted advisors or confidants. Because of the nature of the event, the group will be restricted in size compared to routinized situations. This small group size permits only those on a "need-to-know" basis and those who share a certain bond with the chief executive to be admitted to the group. Because of the smallness of the group and the shared threat to common values, the group will seek to retain members who share the dominant group norm. Dissenters and obstructionists will likely be purged. Concomitantly, this "solidification" process of the group can lead to a host of potential group decision-making pathologies, e. g., a decrease in reality testing, mental efficiency, and moral judgment-- essentially Professor Janis' "groupthink" symptoms. If these groupthink pressures and resultant behavioral maladies occur, they can, in part, lead to a restricted information search on the part of the group, a reduced choice among policy options, an increase in primitive decision rules (e. g., historical analogizing), and a lack of alternative analysis.

Decisional Quality. This barrage of psychological and social-psychological factors feeds directly into the dependent variable, decision quality. In this research, the quality of the decision refers to the group decision-making procedures which can lead to the group polarization/extremization phenomenon. In short, are group decisions more committed to risk or caution than individual decisions? What transpires within the dynamics of the group atmosphere to cause it to reach more extreme decisions is not adequately explained by this framework. Because of the exploratory nature of this study, the many hypotheses and "theories" regarding this mysterious dynamic remain to be tested. It is anticipated, however, that the primacy of the group's norms would be a consequential if not a determining factor in moving the group along its committed path of either risk or caution. This factor of group norms, among others, will be singled out for special consideration as a catalytic agent for the group extremization/polarization effect.

NOTES

1. Cartwright (1973:229) says that "although the available evidence is not conclusive, it appears that the editorial practices of journals may have contributed inadvertently to the inflexibility of thinking in this field." As a testimony to this devotion to the dependent variable risk, there have been well over 300 studies since Stoner's original 1961 Master's Thesis (Myers and Lamm, 1975:297).

2. The conventional CDQ instrument described here is

discussed in greater detail in Chapter V. Stated briefly, the Choice Dilemma Questionnaire is a research instrument designed to test individual and group levels of risk-taking and caution-taking. Subjects are given a questionnaire posing some sort of "everyday" moral dilemma and are asked to advise the subject as to what to do. Each dilemma has an accompanying set of probabilities for success, $\underline{i}.\underline{e}.$, either 1, 3, 5, 7, 9, or 10 chances in 10. The lower the probabilities advised, the riskier the individual/group decision. Alternately, the higher the probability, the more cautious the individual/group decision.

3. Cartwright (1973:223).

4. Journal of Personality and Social Psychology, Vol. 20, No. 3, December 1971 (special "Risky-Shift" issue).

5. Vinokur (1971:232).

6. Brown (1965); Kogan and Wallach (1967); Pruitt and Teger (1969); Johnson and Stemler (1974); Johnson (1974); inter alia.

7. Vidmar (1970); Ferguson and Vidmar (1971); Haley and Rule (1971).

8. Bateson (1966).

9. Moscovici and Zavalloni (1969); Doise (1969; 1971); Zaleska and Kogan (1971); Kogan, Lamm, and Trommsdorff (1972).

10. Lamm and Kogan (1970); Lamm, Schaude and Trommsdorff (1971); Lamm and Trommsdorff (1974).

11. Belovica and Finch (1971).

12. Rim (1964a).

13. Bell and Jamieson (1970).

14. Middleton and Warren (1972).

15. Carlson and Davis (1971).

16. Belovica and Finch (1971).

17. Marquis (1962); Rim (1964b); Siegel and Zajonc (1967).

18. Jamieson (1968).

19. Rim (1965).

20. Rim (1966).

21. Semmel and Minix (1977); Semmel (1977); Minix (1977).

22. Rim (1964b).

23. Jamieson (1968); Rim (1964).

24. Atthowe (1961); Jamieson (1968); Baron, Baron and Roper (1974); Myers and Aronson (1972); Lamm, Schaude, and Trommsdorff (1971).

25. Clark (1971:261) as in Glover (1977:4-5).

26. Kogan and Wallach (1967c).

27. Lamm (1967).

28. Teger and Pruitt (1967).

29. Pruitt and Teger (1969:124) as in Glover (1977:5).

30. Haley and Rule (1971:160).

31. Glover (1977:7).

32. Wallach, Kogan and Bem (1962; 1964); Bem, Wallach and Kogan (1965); Kogan and Wallach (1967); Wallach, Kogan and Burt (1967).

33. Marquis (1962); Graham and Harris (1970); Dion, Miller, and Magnum (1971).

34. Bateson (1961). See also Flanders and Thistlewaite (1967).

35. Pruitt and Teger (1967); Bell and Jamieson (1970); Dion and Miller (1971); Stokes (1971); and Vinokur (1971) do not find support for this hypothesis.

36. Clark (1971:265); J. Campbell (1974).

37. Kogan and Bem (1962); Marquis (1962); Collins and Guetzkow (1964).

38. Brown (1965); Rabow, et al. (1966); Doise (1969).

39. Slovic (1962; 1964); Kogan and Wallach (1964); Wallach, Kogan and Burt (1968).

40. Marquis (1962); Wallach, Kogan and Bem (1962); Wallach, Kogan and Burt (1965); Rabow, et al. (1966); Doise (1969); Burnstein and Katz (1971).

41. Stoner (1961); Teger and Pruitt (1967); Lamm (1967); Hoyt and Stoner (1968); Haley and Rule (1971); Clark (1971).

42. Pruitt (1971a).

43. Vinokur (1971:239) as in Glover (1977:9).

44. Vinokur (1971:239) as in Glover (1977:9).

45. Rabow, et al. (1966); Kogan and Zalleska (1969); Roberts and Castore (1972); Baur and Turner (1974); Myers, Schreiber and Viel (1974); Blascovich and Ginsburg (1974).

46. Johnson (1974:107).

47. Johnson (1974:108).

48. Rabow, et al. (1966:24-25).

49. Pruitt (1971a).

50. Brown (1965).

51. Madaras and Bem (1968).

52. Stoner (1968).

53. Fraser, et al. (1970).

54. Brown (1965).

55. Asch (1951).

56. Brown (1965:701).

57. Pruitt (1969).

58. Levinger and Schneider (1969).

59. Pruitt (1969).

60. Pruitt (1971a).

61. For a modest example, see the foreign policy examples used in Irving L. Janis' <u>Victims of Groupthink</u>, (1972) and James Thomson (1968). See also Chapter III.

62. The "Walter Mitty" effect is simply that people often envision themselves riskier than they actually are.

63. Pruitt (1971a; 354).

64. Moscovici and Zavalloni (1969).

65. Pruitt (1971a:355).

66. Pruitt (1971a:355). See also Lamm (1967) and Kogan and Wallach (1967c).

67. See Pruitt (1971a:355-56).

68. Glover (1977:11).

69. Dion, <u>et al</u>. (1970).

70. Smith (1972).

71. There are perhaps several reasons for the "300+" reported "risky-shift" studies: the phenomenon, when using a CDQ design, is easily replicated; the "inherent" interest in a subject running counter to "common snese;" and the state-of-the-art soon after the phenomenon was discovered, suggest that "risky-shift" studies were <u>perhaps</u> easily published because of editorial biases. See Cartwright (1971).

72. Myers and Lamm (1976:603).

73. Teger and Pruitt (1967) as in Myers and Lamm (1976:603).

74. Myers and Lamm (1976:603).

75. Myers and Lamm (1976:603 - emphasis added.).

76. Moscovici and Zavalloni (1969). See the previous

section on the commitment hypothesis as subsumed under the general heading "Value Theories."

77. Myers and Lamm (1976:603).

78. The categories are: attitude studies, jury decisions, ethical decisions, judgments, person perceptions, negotiation behavior, and risk measures other than the choice dilemmas. See Myers and Lamm (1976:604).

79. Myers and Lamm (1976:607).

80. Myers and Murdoch (1970).

81. Myers and Lamm (1975:300).

82. Myers and Lamm (1975:300).

83. Myers and Lamm (1975:301).

84. Raack (1970).

85. Brown (1974).

86. See Myers and Lamm (1976:613-15).

87. McCauley, Kogan and Teger (1971) and Myers (1974) as cited in Myers and Lamm (1976:613).

88. Baron, Monson and Baron (1973); Jellison and Davis (1973); Jellison and Riskind (1973); Madaras and Bem (1968).

89. Eisinger and Mills (1968) as in Myers and Lamm (1976:614).

90. Burnstein, Vinokur, and Pichevin (1974) as in Myers and Lamm (1976:614).

91. See Myers and Lamm (1976:614).

92. Clark, et al. (1971); Lamm, et al. (1972).

93. Lamm, et al. (1971).

94. Myers and Lamm (1976:614).

95. Burnstein and Vinokur (1975) as in Myers and Lamm (1976:615).

96. Myers, Bach and Schrieber (1975) as in Myers and Lamm (1976:615).

97. Myers and Lamm (1976:615).

98. Myers and Lamm (1975:301).

99. Burnstein and Vinokur (1973).

100. Sears (1969).

101. Myers and Lamm (1975:302).

102. See Brecher (1977:44).

103. Hermann (1972:12-13).

104. Holsti and George (1975:275).

105. Holsti and George (1975:275).

106. The psychological explanation of the individual functioning under stress is intended only as an entree (although a highly significant one) into group pressures resulting from stress. The reader is urged to seek the excellent synthesis provided by Ole Holsti and Alexander George (1975) for a further, more detailed accounting of the psychological pathologies resulting from stress.

CHAPTER V

METHODOLOGY

The Research Strategy

Research on crisis decision-making has employed several wide-ranging research strategies spanning from the one-shot case study[1] to the methodologically sophisticated technique of computer simulation.[2] Other research strategies applied to the study of crisis decision-making include elite surveys,[3] propositional inventories,[4] and content analysis.[5] But, the most frequently used research design in the study of small groups and foreign policy decision-making seems to be the one-shot case study approach.

The dependence upon this method, however, diminishes the scholar's ability to generate empirical generalizations regarding crisis decision-making unless a comparative approach is taken.[6] Generally, journalists, politicians, and academicians approach the phenomenon of crisis decision-making in different fashions for various reasons. Political scientists direct their study to a much smaller and specialized population. Non-academics generally recreate the event(s) of the crisis by informal, unsystematic elite surveys or by personal recollection if they were present during the crisis decision-making process. These writings or memoirs are often directed toward mass appeal.

Frequently, insider's accounts are tainted with either absolution or a distorted (intentional or otherwise) recreation of the event. Even when this is not the case, different accounts of the same incident will vary simply because of the position of the various players within the decision-making structures and also because of the individual's selective perception. Therefore, because of the prevalence of the one-shot case study or the memoir in crisis research, the scholarly community is left with many uncertain notions concerning the phenomenon of crisis and the related behavioral aspects of the persons and groups involved.

Given the research question, there are a number of possible alternative data generation techniques, each possessing particular strengths and weaknesses. For example, elite survey or specialized elite interviewing could be conducted, but the problems of gaining access to relevant decision-makers complicates this as a viable research route.[7] Moreover, decision-makers, as members of the decisional collectivity, may not be able, or willing, to answer accurately questions pertaining to the group decision-making process simply because of their intimacy of association with other group members and their proximity to the crisis event. In other words, they may not be able to perceive the many group dynamic pressures brought to bear upon the group since their attention was riveted to the immediate resolution of the crisis at hand and not at discerning questions of group leadership, cohesion, risk-taking, and so on.

A second potential avenue of data generation is a content analysis of the relevant government documents of a crisis situation.[8] Such a method could yield an unobtrusive, systematic, and empirical look into the group dynamics of crisis decision-making. Like elite interviewing, content analysis requires the use of government personnel, documents, and transcripts--most, if not all, of which are inaccessible and/or classified. Furthermore, records of crisis-deliberating small groups may not even exist because of the secrecy of the options being discussed and the limited and intense time frame generally associated with international crises.

Third, one could conceivably cull the extant literature on a specific crisis or crises.[9] However, the liabilities that are associated with the one-shot case study are inherent in this type of research. The grinding of personal axes has a way of showing up in this type of literature, thereby limiting the researcher to the current conventional wisdoms and beliefs.

Fourth, another unobtrusive measure, events data, or a focus on the outcomes and policies of a nation, could be utilized. This technique assesses a nation's capabilities and stance in the international system by using such aggregate indicators as war involvement[10] and national attributes[11] to arrange nations categorically on certain international dimensions. Yet, such a perspective rarely, if ever, reveals the dynamics or processes that contribute to the particular policy or outcome; instead, it evades the many variables inside the nation and focuses solely upon the outcome of a particular nation-state.

An alternative research strategy, experimentation, seems most appropriate given the research question. Experimentation allows the researcher to "re-create-- through analogy or modeling-- the relevant variables pertaining to the question at hand."[12] With this technique, controls can be established to discern the effects of various treatment variables upon the phenomena to be explained.

While experimentation has a long and successful history in psychology, social-psychology, and sociology, it is not viewed by political scientists as a principal tool or technique of data generation. Experimentation in political science is viewed by some to be in its "relative infancy, including the decision-making field."[13] However, when experimentation has been used by foreign policy analysts, they usually focus on the process of foreign policy rather than on the outcome of such processes.[14]

One frequently cited rationale for not using experimental techniques in political science is the inaccessibility of relevant sample groups-- for example, National Security Council Members. But, the rationale behind sampling and experimentation alleviates the need for studying actual foreign policy participants. It allows us to look at various treatment effects on certain samples and to generalize our findings to a larger and perhaps unobtainable population. As Guy Swanson noted over a quarter-century ago,

> ...psychologists perform laboratory experiments on small collectivities with the belief that (1) they are producing valid replicas of the concepts under study and that (2) the use, when possible, of experimental replicas, gives them results that are clearer and more precise than those they could obtain in any other way. They also stress the well known advantages of being able to manipulate variables in order to produce conditions that are theoretically important but that

> are difficult to find or observe
> in field settings and of the
> ability to make endless repetitions
> in checking research findings.[15]

Much later, J. Raser's comments regarding the use of simulation in sociology pointed to the position that "experimental laboratory analogs should be treated with the same respect and judgment as any other research technique utilized in sociological study."[16] He declared:

> Familiarity with simulation is a
> prerequisite for understanding
> contemporary social and behavioral
> science research and teaching
> techniques. In addition, there
> is an important reason for examining
> the methodological aspects of
> gaming and simulation. Simulation
> is, in essence, the process of
> analogizing. So is all science.
> One examines a universe as an entity
> that is supposed to be <u>representative</u>
> of another universe or entity and
> argues that the laws that can be
> demonstrated as applying to the
> one under study also can be generalized over greater numbers, over
> time, or over some other gap-- to
> the referent universe. Thus, the
> problems of theory building,
> sampling, hypothesis testing, inference, and validity, which are
> the stuff of gaming and simulation
> efforts, are also the stuff of
> scientific endeavor.[17]

Raser's comments with respect to simulation can be easily transmitted into justifications for using experimentation in other branches of the social sciences. As Maraline Glover states,

> In the utilization of experimental
> laboratory analogs, experimentors
> view the analogies as a means by
> which they can go from the simple to
> the complex, from the concrete to the
> abstract and from the specific to

> the larger system. The experimentor, in effect, attempts to describe the elements of and relationships within the laboratory experiment as a "representation" of some aspect of reality in a larger referent system.[18]

Admittedly, there are serious problems concerning experimentation and the science of induction. Donald Campbell and James Stanley warn that:

> The problems (of induction) are painful because of a recurrent reluctance to accept Hume's truism that <u>induction or generalization is never fully justified logically</u>. Whereas the problems of internal validity are solvable within the limits of the logic of probability statistics, the problems of external validity are not logically solvable in any neat, conclusive way. Generalization always turns out to involve extrapolation into a realm not represented in one's sample. Such extrapolating is made by <u>assuming</u> one knows the relevant laws.[19]

These authors carry this reasoning to its ultimate conclusion by saying, "we cannot logically generalize beyond (the limits of the experimental design)." In other words, "we cannot generalize at all."[20]

However, generalization is at the very heart of science. By generalizing, we "make guesses as to the yet unproven laws, including some not even explored."[21] "The sources of external validity are thus guesses as to general laws in the science of a science: guesses as to what factors lawfully interact without treatment variables, and, by implication, guesses as to what can be disregarded."[22]

In this research, an attempt has been made to incorporate real-world or potential real-world decision-makers into the experimental design. By no stretch of the imagination do we sample some of the truly key participants of the foreign policy elite; but, it is to these types of players to which we wish to generalize. The more this, or any other design, approximates conditions and characteristics of the population to which you wish to generalize, the greater the reduction in what Campbell and Stanley refer to as "complex interactions and curvilinear relationships... (which) confuse attempts at generalization."[23] In effect, these authors seem to be advocating a greater degree of isomorphism between sample and real-world conditions or characteristics.

With these limitations delineated, these authors also remind us that:

> successful sciences such as physics and chemistry made their strides without any attention to representativeness (but with great concern for reproducibility by independent researchers). An ivory-tower artificial laboratory science is a valuable achievement even if unrepresentative, and artificiality may often be essential to the analytic separation of variables fundamental to the achievements of many sciences.[24]

Thus, even if this research fails to meet the suggested criteria of isomorphism in terms of selecting and sampling real-world decision-makers, it is still a potentially valuable piece of research insofar as it attempts to separate analytically those fundamental variables of group versus individual decision-making behavior.

Given these liabilities of conducting experimental research, "these problems need not be a deterrent to imaginative research and creative hypothesis-testing."[25] Short of this technique of experimentation, "hypothesis testing must wait upon when and what the natural world chooses to yield."[26] Science, in other words, can not allow research interests to be directed from the standpoint of easily accessible data. Frequently, portions of the real-world will have to be reconstructed to allow the researcher a greater insight into the intricate processes and dynamics at work.

The Research Design

The classical "risky-shift" experimental design in social-psychology has relied upon a test - re-test, or within-subjects, design that asks each participant to reach a decision on some real-life dilemma confronting a fictional character. This test and re-test instrument is commonly referred to as a Choice-Dilemma Questionnaire or CDQ.

In the "test" portion of the experiment, subjects (Ss) are requested to make one selection per scenario for as many scenarios as the researcher has constructed. Each dilemma has an accompanying set of probabilities for success, i.e., either 1, 3, 5, 7, 9, or 10 out of 10 chances of success. A classic example is:

> Mr. K is a successful businessman who has participated in a number of civic activities of considerable value to the community. Mr. K has been approached by the leaders of his political party as a possible congressional candidate in the next election. Mr. K's party is a minority party in the district, though the party has won occasional elections in the past. Mr. K would like to hold political office, but to do so would involve a serious financial sacrifice, since the party has insufficient campaign funds. He would also have to endure the attacks of his political opponents in a hot campaign.
>
> Imagine that you are advising Mr. K. Please check the lowest probability that you would consider acceptable for the risky play in question to be attempted.
>
> Mr. K should attempt the play if the chances are at least:
>
> ___1 in 10 that the play would succeed
>
> ___2 in 10 that the play would succeed

___3 in 10 that the play would succeed

___4 in 10 that the play would succeed

___5 in 10 that the play would succeed

___6 in 10 that the play would succeed

___7 in 10 that the play would succeed

___8 in 10 that the play would succeed

___9 in 10 that the play would succeed

___Mr. K should attempt the play only if it is certain (i.e., 10 in 10) that the play would succeed.27

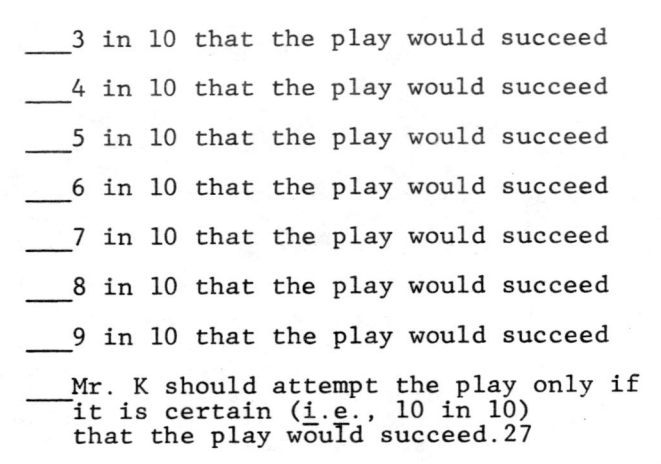

In the "re-test" part of the experiment (after the individual has made his choice on each dilemma) subjects are aggregated or pooled into small groups with an average of six people. The same scenarios are discussed as a group and after arriving at a group consensus with respect to a particular option, the group moves to the next scenario and the procedure is repeated until all scenarios are discussed and a decision is reached for each situation.

The "shift" for each group is calculated by summing the individual scores for a scenario, taking the mean, and subtracting this from the group decision. This process is repeated for all groups across all Choice Dilemmas. Using the previous political CDQ as an example, we might find something like the following:

GROUP 1 - POLITICAL DILEMMA

Individual	Pre-test Score	Mean	Group Decision (Post-test)	Shift
1	5			
2	4			
3	7	4.2	2	-2.2
4	2			
5	3			

In this example, the mean of the individual decisions is 4.2 (calculated by summing the individual scores and dividing by N, which is this case is 5). Subtract this score, 4.2, from the group decision, 2, and obtain a "shift-to-risk" of -2.2. Conversely, if the group decision were 6, a "shift" in the positive or cautious direction of +1.8 units would be obtained.

The Choice-Dilemma instrument that measures the risk-taking propensities of small decision-making units can not be effectively transcribed from the conventional social-psychological research that was previously described. International crises do not evoke a standardized set of probability responses as in the previously cited political dilemma. At best, a nation's options to a crisis can only be ordered on a scale of risk from alternatives which are perceived by an adversary to be non-threatening or least risky (for example, bilateral negotiations), to alternatives which are likely to evoke a like-minded response from the adversary (such as a military initiative against the enemy). It is assumed, then, that there approximates a natural ordering of national responses ranging from options which carry little risk (i.e., a high probability of success, but low pay-offs) to options which bring with them greater risk (low probability of success), but a potentially greater pay-off when compared to low-risk options.

Such a design necessitates a scale of options which range from low risk to high risk. The method of paired-comparison scaling produces a scale that reveals the relative intensity among the nation's options. This technique requires that all items be dyadically paired with every other item, using judges to select the more extreme item in each dyad, and calculating a frequency score for each option.[28] This yields a relative scale (of risk) among all items.[29]

In this research, the following national options were used to obtain a scale ranging from low risk to high risk:

1. Engage in bilateral negotiations or talks with the adversary to settle the crisis;

2. Call a meeting or special session of the United Nations Security Council;

3. Support (non-militarily) opposition elements in the area or nation in which the national interest and security of the US is threatened;

4. Discontinue diplomatic relations with the adversary and attempt to sway world public opinion to the side of the US;

5. Create economic turmoil in adversary's country to substantially weaken his war effort;

6. Send military advisors to the area that is threatening the US interests and security. These are non-combat personnel only;

7. Establish a military or naval blockade of adversary's country;

8. Use conventional ground forces to repel adversary's threat;

9. Engage in limited strategic bombing of non-civilian, military-oriented sites only; and

10. Use the nuclear capability of the US to eliminate the possibility of many American deaths and to bring the adversary to the point of negotiation.

University of Cincinnati Political Science faculty and graduate students (N=20) were used as judges to determine the scale quality of the options.

A further distinction between this research and earlier "risky-shift" studies is the incorporation of six hypothetical or contrived international crisis scenarios (see Appendix A). A thumbnail sketch of each crisis situation will illustrate the type of Choice Dilemma used in this research. Situation I involves the blocking of the Strait of Hormuz by the Soviet Union with the subsequent threat to the western world's oil supply. Situation II involves the downing of a US reconnaissance aircraft which strayed over the sovereign airspace of Cambodia. Its crew and highly secret equipment are captured with the likelihood that they will be spirited off to either Moscow or Peking. In <u>Situation III</u>, South Korean Army regulars along with 200 US military observers who broke across the North/South border are trapped and encircled by the North Koreans. <u>Situation IV</u> produces a dilemma in which the US discovers drastic violations of the SALT I agreement with the Soviet Union. In <u>Situation V</u>, the Panamanian Navy has detained and forcibly boarded a US cruiser at the entrance to the Panama Canal, thereby stopping all traffic until the US accedes to immediate steps toward nationalization of the Canal. And finally, in <u>Situation VI</u>, the US embassy in the Hague, Netherlands, has been seized by a militant faction of Arab nationalists who are holding the Ambassador hostage until the US agrees to a ransom demand and safe exit out of the country.

The sample used for this study was comprised of three unique groupings: Army Officers from the Fall 1976 Armored Officers Advanced course at the United States Army Armor School at Fort Knox, Kentucky (N=28);30 Army and Air Force Reserve Officer Training Corp Cadets (ROTC Cadets) of the University of Cincinnati (N=39);31 and graduate and undergraduate students enrolled in Political Science courses at the University of Cincinnati (N=56). In all, 123 persons or 26 small decisional groups participated in the experiment.

Many of the Officers had combat experience in Vietnam and/or served one or more tours of duty overseas. The advanced course is a regular career component for the Armored Officers and includes basic instruction in the principles of decision-making, leadership, and motivation.

The ROTC Cadets likewise received instruction in leadership and decision-making. The service level of the Cadets that were sampled varied. For some Cadets, this was their first year in the ROTC program; for others, this was their final year of ROTC instruction prior to graduation.

In both the Officer and Cadet sub-samples, potential national decision-makers were sampled. The students, by virtue of their enrollment in various political science courses, were heavily exposed to instruction in foreign policy decision-making.

The experimental design used here is a within-subjects or test - re-test design. Subjects are instructed to assume the role of National Security Advisors to the President of the United States whereupon they are presented with the six crises facing the nation. Under each of the crisis dilemmas, there appears the list of options that were derived from the paired-comparison technique. In the test portion, each subject is individually asked how far he would go down the scaled list of options for each crisis scenario in order to "bring about the desired outcome..." and "to protect the interests of the United States."

After the subjects complete the pre-test packet, they are randomly placed into small groups ranging in size from four to six people. In the post-test portion, the same crisis scenarios and accompanying scale of options are re-administered, but this time the group is instructed to reach a single group decision for each crisis. The individual's decision across the six scenarios and the collective group decision for each of the crises represent the degree of risk both isolated individuals and small groups are willing to assume for each of the dilemmas confronting the United States. It is then possible to compare individual levels of risk-taking to the degree of risk a group is willing to assume in bringing the crisis to its desired outcome. The shift, should it occur, is calculated by summing the individual pre-test scores of the group's members across the six scenarios, taking a mean for each situation, and subtracting this score from the group response for each crisis and across all crises.

Besides the individual and collective decisions of the groups on the six crisis scenarios, information on a host of individual level independent variables was also collected in the pre-test. These variables tap numerous psychological, political, and demographic characteristics of the respondent. Such individual attributes and personality variables include: the political belief or ideology of the respondent (PBS), the degree of a respondent's psychological flexibility (CPI), and the respondent's desire or willingness to see an active or interventionist role for US policy abroad (PIN). The Political Belief Scale profiles each subject's political ideology along a standard, seven-item forced identification scale which ranges from Extremely Liberal to Extremely Conservative. This variable is a conventional question asked bi-annually by researchers of the Center for Political Studies of the University of Michigan. A twenty-two item, true-false questionnaire from the California Psychological Inventory (CPI) measures a respondent's psychological flexibility or rigidity in accepting change. The Political Involvement Scale (PIN), first used by Campbell and his colleagues, "ranks persons along an attitude continuum of the desirable degree of United States intervention in international affairs."[32] In addition to these psychological and individual attribute variables, perceptual variables were included in the pre-test packets. Two such variables ask the subject which scenario he feels is the most (and least) threatening to the United States. Another set of variables asks for each crisis dilemma which option the subject feels others "at or above his 'rank'" would choose in solving or meeting this crisis. After the re-test instrument was collected, a post-experiment survey was given to each subject. This survey also included such perceptual variables as: group cohesion, group affinity, respondent's satisfaction with the group decision, perceived leadership within the subject's group, the factors leading the group to choose the particular decision it did for a given crisis, the type of decision-making process, the degree and intensity and extensity of "outside" political knowledge brought into the group decision-making process, and the existence of tension within the group.

Demographic variables profiling the subject's education, academic major, age, rank, commission source, combat months, etc., were obtained along with the already outlined psychological and perceptual variables. It is believed that these three types of variables will aid in explaining the dynamics of group interaction as related to group extremization in the crisis decision-making milieu. Along with these variables, the group discussions for three Student and six Officer groups were recorded on tape. This archiving procedure was done to facilitate a more intensive and detailed content analysis of group discussions. It is further believed that this type of data-- in addition to those variables already mentioned-- could help clarify the theoretical underpinnings of the group dynamic process with respect to small group decision-making.

Statistical Procedures

The experiment was constructed to test for individual and group decision-making behavior. The group extremization model guided the search for individual and group differences across the five (or six)[33] scenarios and the direction of the group decisional shift (either to risk or caution). Relatedly, this research is also interested in the factor(s) underlying or causing such behavior in the three dependent variables, pre-test, post-test, and shift scores. These dependent variables, to reiterate, are calculated as follows: the pre-test is the mean of the individual scores to each of the crisis scenarios (see page 90); the post-test score is the score of the group for each of the dilemmas; and the "shift" score is the difference between the group score and the mean of the individual scores for any particular crisis scenario. Eventually, this research seeks to discover which variables account for any extremization effects of group decision-making as opposed to individual choice selection.

To test whether the dependent variables are statistically significant across the three sub-samples, Officers, Cadets, and Students, and across the five (or six) crisis dilemmas, a 3x5(6)x1 repeated measures factorial Analysis of Variance (ANOVA) design was constructed.[34] The first factor, 3, represents the sub-samples; factor two, 5(6), represents the crisis dilemmas; and the last factor, 1, symbolizes each of the dependent variables, pre-test, post-test, and shift scores.

ANOVA can indicate if differences exist across the two decision responses (pre-test and post-test scores) and the difference between them (shift scores), i e., whether or not the dependent variables are statistically significant across the three sub-samples. It can not tell us either the magnitude of differences across the treatment variable, or the direction of the differences.

In other words, ANOVA can only tell us that there are important (i. e., statistically significant) differences arising from the three dependent variables across the three sub-samples. ANOVA basically:

> "seeks to determine the probability that a predictor variable could yield results different from simple random selection. This is, of course, the logic behind significance testing. Analysis of Variance, then, starts with a variable to be predicted-- measured on an interval or ratio scale-- and one or more predictor variables grouped according to some attribute."[35]

In order to account for the expected choice shifts among the 26 groups, several statistical techniques ranging from bivariate analysis (cross-tabulation) to multivariate analysis (multiple regression) will be employed. Those predictor variables suspected of explaining a large portion of the variance in the three decisional variables are: group membership, for example, Army Armor Officers, ROTC Cadets, or Students (GRNAME), the psychological flexibility of the group as measured by the California Psychological Inventory (CPI), the amount of international involvement prescribed for the US by the group (PIN), the group's profiled political belief index (PBS), and the decision rule employed (unanimity versus majority-vote; DECRULE). Other variables will be tested as well, but it is hypothesized that these variables will be most important in explaining the variance in the three dependent variables, pre-test, post-test, and shift scores.

In summary, the research procedure used in this study includes the following elements in testing for the group extremization effect in small foreign policy decision-making groups. First, a series of five or six international dilemmas or crises facing the United States were given to the three sub-samples: Fort Knox Officers, ROTC Cadets, and graduate and undergraduate students. Each individual was asked to respond to each dilemma on the basis of how he would resolve the particular crisis given the ascending scale of options from low risk to high risk. Next, the individuals were randomly assigned by identification numbers to the small group setting. Here, the same set of scenarios with the accompanying options were given to each group whereupon they were asked to reach a single group decision for each of the five or six dilemmas. Shift scores, either to risk or caution, were calculated by summing the pre-test scores of the individuals of a group for each of the dilemmas, taking a mean, and subtracting this score from the final group decision (post-test). A positive shift score denotes a shift to risk; a negative shift shows a shift to caution. Analysis of variance will be conducted to determine if the dependent variables-- pre-test, post-test, and shift scores-- are statistically significant across the three sub-samples and the crisis dilemmas. Multiple regression will be conducted to discern the relevant independent variables that account for the expected group shifts. Also, basic descriptive statistics such as percentages and gammas will be used to test the validity of the extremization and polarization models. Given the research technique of experimentation and the statistical procedures adopted, it is hoped that the relevant variables that contribute to individual and group choice-making behavior can be identified.

Conclusion

In structuring this research, it is believed that the cogent suggestions regarding decision-making research given by Kirkpatrick and his associates[36] have been incorporated. For example, this research ranges from the traditional boundaries and confines of the discipline such as psychology, sociology, and social-psychology to seek alternative hypotheses regarding group dynamics and decision-making behavior. Findings from sister disciplines, as well as political science itself, converge for what these authors refer to as "theoretical integration." In their words, "we should concern ourselves with synthesizing both the theoretical and empirical content of decision-making research."[37]

A second point which this research indirectly addresses is the employment of an alternative data generative approach to the study of political decision-making. Experimentation has not been a widely accepted method in the discipline of political science, but its use is increasingly important if political scientists wish to analyze such sub-systemic phenomena as the intersection of individual and group political behavior.

Traditionally, social scientists have been overly cautious in constructing their research designs to promote or maximize external validity or generalizability. While such concerns are indeed legitimate, this caution has inadvertently promoted survey research and aggregate statistical analysis as dominant research paradigms. Experimentation, however, allows analysts to observe and probe decision-making or choice-making behavior directly. By attempting to reconstruct reality through analogy or modeling, scientists can by-pass the many restrictions imposed by real-world political decision-making groups. Also, by adopting an experimental approach, analysts are forced to confront the conceptual and theoretical limitation of their frameworks. By establishing the research design's internal validity, replication-- a key scientific development-- is aided. The natural sciences, unlike many of the social sciences, have established their level of science by reproducibility, and not upon large-scale random sampling techniques.

Furthermore, this research finds its empirical anchor in many of the previously published accounts depicting the decision-making behavior of key governmental leaders who participated in an international crisis environment. By inspecting these case studies, it is believed that practical operationalization of the component concepts was greatly facilitated.38 The following two chapters are intended to illustrate these methodological contentions by analyzing the data collected in this experiment.

NOTES

1. C.f. Whiting (1960); Schlesinger (1965); Able (1966); Geyelin (1966); Martin (1966); Paige (1966); Sorenson (1966); Kennedy (1969); Allison (1971); inter alia.

2. Pool and Kessler (1965); Hermann (1965); Hermann and Hermann (1967); Hermann, et al. (1974).

3. Triska (1964).

4. Snyder (1962); Hermann (1963); Holsti (1965); Zinnes (1968); Hermann and Hermann (1967).

5. Holsti (1965a); Holsti (1972b).

6. Janis (1972).

7. Deutsch, et al. (1967); Dexter (1970).

8. North, et al. (1963); Holsti (1965); North (1967); Zinnes (1968); Holsti (1972).

9. Janis (1972).

10. Singer and Small (1968).

11. A. F. K. Organski (1972).

12. Semmel and Minix (1977:10).

13. Kirkpatrick, et al. (1976:56).

14. Kelman (1965); Singer (1965); De Rivera (1968); Jervis (1969).

15. Swanson (1951:351).

16. Glover (1976:1).

17. Raser (1969:X-XI).

18. Glover (1976:1-2).

19. Campbell and Stanley (1963:17).

20. Campbell and Stanley (1963:17).

21. Campbell and Stanley (1963:17).

22. Campbell and Stanley (1963:17).

23. Campbell and Stanley (1963:18).

24. Campbell and Stanley (1963:18).

25. Semmel and Minix (1977:12).

26. Marx and Wood (1975).

27. Myers and Lamm (1976:602).

28. Torgerson (1958); Smith, et al. (1976).

29. Mueller (1969, Chapter 8) is a valuable source regarding the use of judges to generate quantitative data. Zinnes (1968) offers a specific application of this method.

30. A great deal of appreciation is owed to those Officers of the United States Army Armor Advanced Training class at Fort Knox who participated in this experiment. Without their involvement, this research would be considerably less meaningful. Also, a large debt of gratitude is owed to Brigadier General Paul S. Williams, Assistant Commandant at Fort Knox, and to Captain Keith Titus of the Leadership department of the Advanced Course at Fort Knox. The above gave willingly of their time as volunteers. This experiment was not conducted for United States Army purposes.

31. Likewise, without the participation of the Air Force and Army ROTC Cadets, this research would not be as meaningful. Special thanks go to Captain James Connell and Captain Paul Sefrin, United States Army ROTC program, and to Captain Dennis Zack, Airforce ROTC program, University of Cincinnati, Department of Military Science. All Cadets were volunteers. The experiment was conducted neither for Army nor Airforce ROTC purposes.

32. Robinson, et al. (1968:296-97).

33. ROTC Cadets did not participate in Scenario 6, Hague Guerrillas.

34. Blalock (1972); Nie, et al. (1975); Iverson and Norpoth (1976).

35. Iverson and Norpoth (1976:1).

36. Kirkpatrick, et al. (1976:56-57).

37. Kirkpatrick, et al. (1976:56).

38. Kirkpatrick, *et al*. (1976:57).

CHAPTER VI

DECISIONAL POLARIZATION IN

SMALL FOREIGN POLICY-MAKING GROUPS

This experiment was designed to test a number of hypotheses related to individual and collective decision processes and behaviors during periods of international crisis. From the heterogeneous sample of Military Officers, ROTC Cadets, and College Students, twenty-six small decisional groups were formed to compare individual and group responses to a set of hypothetical crisis dilemmas posing in some degree: 1) high threat to the United States; 2) a short time in which to reach a decision; and 3) to a much lesser extent, a surprise to the decisional unit. Each of the subjects, as well as the small groups themselves, was profiled along several dimensions believed relevant to investigating rival choice-shift behaviors and hypotheses.

Essentially, this chapter raises similar questions as posed by Ole Holsti in his seminal volume, Crisis, Escalation, War. He asks:

> how do individuals and groups respond to the pressures and tensions of a crisis? Do we tend to approach such situations with high motivations, a keen sense of purpose, extraordinary energy and enhanced creativity? Is necessity, as Kahn suggests, the mother of invention? Or, is our capacity for coping with the problem impaired, perhaps even to the point suggested by Neustadt's phrase, "the paranoid reaction characteristic of crisis behavior?" When under intense pressure do we characteristically take the more cautious path, or are we more prone to taking high risks? Is our sense of what constitutes risk in any way altered?[1]

In this, and the following chapter, four broad research questions are posed to identify and unravel the choice-shift phenomenon believed common to small decision-making groups. Here, the first three questions are discussed. First, are there indeed differences across the various sub-samples with respect to the three decision or dependent variables: the pre-test, post-test, and shift scores? Are, for example, the military sub-samples (the Officers and the Cadets) more or less extreme in their individual and/or small group responses than the Students? Second, if there are differences across the sub-samples on the decision variables, what is the direction and the magnitude of the shift scores across the sub-samples? Relatedly, is there a decisional extremization/polarization effect underlying the hypothesized choice-shifts? Does the average of individual decisions offer a clue to the same small group decisions? If the polarization model is accurate, it is anticipated that individual predispositions which tend toward risk-taking (or caution-taking) would in all likelihood produce a group choice not only in the same direction, but also in an even more extreme direction than the average of the group membership's individual responses. Finally, if group polarization adequately explains the decisional behaviors of the twenty-six small groups, what factors or variables account for the effect? How can we best explain why small groups will further commit themselves to a course of action which is either riskier or more cautious than the average of individual predispositions? This last question is undoubtedly more difficult to answer than merely identifying the polarization effect itself. As such, an explanation will be attempted in the following chapter.

Some Over-Arching Sample Results

Generally, the data reveal that small group decision-making processes move the initial choice preferences of the group's membership in a direction that is more extreme than the average of the member's initial choices. This movement produced by the group's dynamics is not distinctly uni-directional, but bi-directional. That is, the sample groups are producing both riskier *and* more cautious decisions than individuals acting alone. There are but few instances where small group dynamics have had little or no effect in moving the group's final choice in either a more risky or a more cautious direction.

Table VI-1 compares the averages of the individual means (pre-test), the group responses (post-test), and shift scores (post-test minus pre-test) for all sample groups combined (N=26) as well as for each sub-sample. Overall, the average pre-test response across groups and scenarios was 4.42 (between discontinuing diplomatic relations-- option 4-- and creating economic turmoil-- option 5) and the average post-test response was 4.85. For all sample groups across the political dilemmas, an average (risky) shift of +0.43 units was recorded. Because of the unequal number of sub-sample groups, 6, 8, and 12 for the Officers, Cadets, and Students respectively, weighted averages were computed for the three decision variables (pre-test = 4.29; post-test = 4.52; and shift = +0.23). However, the weighting of these figures according to the number of sub-sample groups does not appreciably alter the results.

The data show that on average the Officers were generally more risky in their individual and group decisions than either the Cadets or Students. While the military professional generally began their group discussions with a moderate amount or risk (5.03-- creating economic turmoil), this attitude was further enhanced by group discussions (6.33-- send military advisors). These pre- and post-test averages gave the Officer sub-sample a rather robust shift average of +1.31 units is a risky direction.

Comparatively, the Army and Air Force ROTC Cadets on average preferred to adopt a less extreme individual and group response than their professional military counterparts. The Cadet's average pre-test score was 4.32; their final or group score was 4.72 (between discontinuing diplomatic relations and creating economic turmoil). The difference between the post-test and pre-test resulted in an average shift value of +.40 units is a risky direction.

The Student groups, on the other hand, generally were not so willing to adopt an initially "risky" position. Apparently, their group decision-making processes acted as a vehicle for a further intensification of this original caution-oriented calculus. Their average pre-test score was 3.90; their mean

TABLE VI-1

Average Pre-Test, Post-Test, and Shift Values Per Sample and Sub-Sample

	Officers N=6	Cadets N=8	Students N=12	All Groups* N=26
$\overline{X}$ Pre-Test	5.03	4.32	3.90	4.42 (4.29)
$\overline{X}$ Post-Test	6.33	4.72	3.47	4.85 (4.52)
$\overline{X}$ Shift	+1.31	+0.40	-0.43	+0.43 (+0.23)

*Numbers in parentheses indicate a weighted average due to the unequal number of sub-sample groups in the experiment.

post-test decision was 3.47 (between supporting non-military opposition elements and discontinuing diplomatic relations). Unlike the military and quasi-military sub-samples, the Students generally shifted downward to a more cautious position as a group. Their mean shift score was -0.43 units.

Table VI-2 compares the percentage of choice-shifts for all scenarios and for all groups across scenarios. By examining the number of shifts for all scenarios, $\underline{i}$. $\underline{e}$., at the group level (N=148), there were 53% (N=79) risky-shifts and 45% (N=66) cautious shifts. In only three cases (2%) were there no recorded shifts. There is a noticeable distinction between the military groups (the Armor Officers and the Cadets) on the one hand and the college Students on the other. Well over half the time, the military groups shifted to risk (72% for the Officers and 55% for the Cadets). By the same token, the Students were prone to elect more cautious or conservative group decisions (57%).

Using the sub-sample as the unit-of-analysis, though, is perhaps misleading when characterizing choice-shift behavior. Obviously, there were individual groups within each sub-sample that shifted in both risky and cautious directions. But, the contrast remains clear: some factor or factors are at work in the dynamics of the small groups of the military sub-samples (Officers and Cadets) which lend themselves to increased decisional extremization in the direction of increased risk-taking. While the evidence is mixed, the college Students exhibited a propensity to choose more conservative individual and collective choices.

Generally speaking, preliminary analysis appears to substantiate the group polarization hypothesis. On average, all sub-samples were pulled further to the preferred extreme by the internal dynamics of group discussion. The military groups, who initially endorsed risk-oriented options, further committed themselves to this risky extreme once in the milieu of the small decisional unit. The Students, likewise, were prone to continue their individual preferences along the lines of non-violence once in the small group. The group preferred pole of either risk or caution was generally detectable by simply looking at the average of individual opinions.

TABLE VI-2[*]

Percentage Choice-Shifts For All Scenarios and For All Groups Across Scenarios

	Shift: All Scenarios					Shift: Across Scenarios			
	% Shift to-Risk	% Shift-to Caution	% No Shift	N		% Shift to-Risk	% Shift-to Caution	% No Shift	N
Army Officers	72% (26)[a]	25% (9)	3% (1)	(36)		100% (6)[b]	0.0% (0)	0.0% (0)	(6)
ROTC Cadets	55% (22)[c]	40% (16)	5% (2)	(40)		100% (8)	0.0% (0)	0.0% (0)	(8)
College Students	43% (31)	57% (41)	0.0% (0)	(72)		42% (5)	58% (7)	0.0% (0)	(12)
Totals	53% (79)	45% (66)	2% (3)	(148)		73% (19)	27% (7)	0.0% (0)	(26)

[*]Table reproduced from Semmel (1976:22).

[a]The figures in parentheses indicate the number of shifts for all scenarios.

[b]The figures in parentheses indicate the number of groups that shifted in the set of scenarios.

[c]ROTC Cadets were asked to decide on five scenarios only.

Sub-Sample Differences

Aligned with the first research objective of identifying differences across the samples as to their response on the pre-test, post-test, and shift variables, the following hypothesis is posited:

H_1: The decision responses-- pre-test, post-test, and shift scores-- will be statistically significant (p=.05) across the three sub-samples.[2]

To test H_1, a repeated measures ANOVA program with a 3x5(6)x1[3] factorial design was used.[4] The first factor, "3," denotes each of the sub-samples in the experiment while the second factor "5(6)," represents the foreign policy crisis scenarios. Together, these two factors are repeated measures on the three decisional responses-- pre-test, post-test, and shift scores. Tables VI-3A, B, and C reveal the inter-sample F statistic and probability level across scenarios for each decision response. The three decision scores are all statistically significant at the .05 level or significance (pre-test: F=5.88; df=2, p <.01; post-test: F=17.01; df=2; p < .001; shift: F=11.44; df=2; p <.001).

Thus, the ANOVA-generated F statistics lend strong support to H_1 which states that there are significant differences in the pre, post, and shift scores across the sample populations for the five (or six) scenarios. However, as Iverson and Norpoth warn, F statistics can point only to statistical significance among the sample subjects. They can not point to either the direction or the magnitude of differences across the treatment variables.[5] These statistics do, nevertheless, suggest that there are important differences between and among the sample groups.

Direction and Magnitude of Shift Scores

The direction and size of the shift scores are of special importance. In preliminary research, it was discovered that the shift scores for all groups across

TABLE VI-3A

ANOVA for "Pre-Test" Responses for Three Experimental Groups

	Sum of Squares	Degrees of Freedom	Mean Square	F Ratio	Significance
Groups	23.79	2	11.89	5.88	0.009
Residual	46.49	23	2.02		

TABLE VI-3B

ANOVA for "Post-Test" Responses for Three Experimental Groups

	Sum of Squares	Degrees of Freedom	Mean Square	F Ratio	Significance
Groups	182.27	2	91.14	17.01	0.000
Residual	123.25	23	5.36		

TABLE VI-3C

ANOVA for "Shift" Scores for Three Experimental Groups

	Sum of Squares	Degrees of Freedom	Mean Square	F Ratio	Significance
Groups	74.49	2	37.24	11.44	0.000
Residual	74.86	23	3.25		

all scenarios (N=148) resulted in 80 (54%) "risky-shifts" and 65 (44%) "cautious shifts" with only 3 groups (2%) not registering any movement to risk or caution.6 However, when pre-test, post-test, and shift means were computed for each of the crisis scenarios, several hypotheses were suggested. These hypotheses were the result of the tendency of military and quasi-military groups to shift in a decidedly "risky" direction. The Students, though, presented a varied response pattern in terms of predicting either "risky" or "cautious" shift scores. Five of the twelve Student groups (42%) shifted toward risk; the other seven groups (58%) tended toward caution. However, the pattern in Table VI-2 is clear. The shift of the Army Officers and ROTC Cadets to risk <u>across</u> the set of scenarios is 100%; whereas the choice-shift of the College Students is more ambivalent-- less than 50% to risk and more than 50% to caution.

Several hypotheses pertaining to the magnitude and the direction of shift scores across the scenarios are presented below:

H_2: The Ft. Knox Officers group will shift-to-risk more often than the ROTC Cadets and the College Students;7

H_3: The ROTC Cadets will shift-to-risk more than the College Students, but less than the Ft. Knox Officers;8

H_4: The Military Officers will elicit choice preferences on both the pre-test and post-test decision responses which are higher than the ROTC Cadets and the College Students;9 and

H_5: The ROTC Cadets will elicit choice preferences on both the pre-test and post-test decision responses which are lower than the Military Officer groups and higher than the College Student groups.10

Hypotheses 2-5 implicitly point to socialization processes or group norms as a primary agent of influencing individual and collective choice-making behavior. Table VI-4 displays the average pre, post, and shift scores for each sample across the six hypothetical dilemmas. Generally speaking, the Officers elicited greater levels of risk on the pre- and post-test responses as well as greater shifts across the crises. The ROTC Cadets were generally more risky than the Students across the three decisional variables. Interestingly, in four of the six scenarios (Cambodia, SALT, Panama, and the Hague siege), the Student groups shifted in a negative or cautious direction whereas the Officers moved in a positive or risky direction. The same is true of the comparison between the Students and the Cadets. In the first five situations that were common to both samples, the Cadets shifted-to-risk in four instances; the Students only twice. As the Cadets shifted-to-risk in the Cambodian, SALT, and Panamanian dilemmas, the Students shifted downward to caution. Thus, there appears to be a similarity of thought between the Officers and the Cadets as to: 1) where the initial (i.e., individual) level of risk should be placed to resolve each of the crisis dilemmas; and 2) where they, as a group of either Officers or Cadets, should stop in terms of safeguarding US interests in each of the crises. The Students, conversely, show a pattern of response on neither the pre-test nor post-test scores which conforms to the Officer-Cadet response set.

Figures A, B, and C (Appendix B) illustrate the mean pre-test, post-test, and shift scores for each sample for each crisis dilemma (Table VI-1). In only one scenario, SALT, did the Officers fail to elicit a greater shift-to-risk than the Cadets or the Students (Officers: =.55; Cadets: +.74; Students: -.60). Moreover, the ROTC Cadets shifted-to-risk more frequently than the Students in three of the five scenarios common to both groups (Cambodia, SALT, and Panama). Thus, in all but three cases, the direction of the shift was as hypothesized (H_2 and H_3).

Hypotheses 4 and 5 direct us to look at pre-test and post-test scores for each group. Looking at these scores across the scenarios, the Officers held initially more risky individual choices and more risky group choices than both the Cadets and Students. The Cadets, on the other hand, were less risky as individuals and as a decision group than the Ft. Knox Officers, but they were more disposed toward force-

TABLE VI-4

Average "Pre-Test," "Post-Test," and "Shift" Decision Responses for Each Experimental Sub-Sample

Scenario	Officers (N=28) Pre	Officers (N=28) Post	Officers (N=28) Shift*	ROTC Cadets (N=39) Pre	ROTC Cadets (N=39) Post	ROTC Cadets (N=39) Shift*	Students (N=56) Pre	Students (N=56) Post	Students (N=56) Shift*
Persian Gulf	4.28	7.17	+2.89	3.11	2.13	-0.99	3.74	3.75	+0.01
Cambodia	3.66	5.00	+1.35	4.60	5.88	+1.28	3.75	1.92	-1.84
South Korea	6.79	8.33	+1.55	5.39	5.98	+0.59	4.37	5.17	+0.80
SALT	3.28	3.83	+0.55	2.89	3.63	+0.74	2.68	2.08	-0.60
Panama	6.89	7.83	+0.95	5.60	6.00	+0.40	4.91	4.25	-0.66
Hague**	5.27	5.83	+0.56	-	-	-	3.96	3.67	-0.29
$\bar{X}$	5.03	6.33	+1.31	4.32	4.72	+0.40	3.90	3.47	-0.43

*A positive shift value indicates a shift-to-risk and a negative shift value indicates a shift-to-caution.

**The N for the Hague Guerilla scenario is 18 since the ROTC groups did not participate in this dilemma.

related options than were the Students (Officers: pre $\bar{X}$ = 5.03; post $\bar{X}$ = 6.33; Cadets: 4.32; 4.72; Students: 3.90; .47).

Figure C pictures the mean shift scores for each group. The pattern of shifts for each sub-sample is unmistakably clear. Not only did the Officers shift-to-risk more than the Cadets or Students, but only once (SALT) did they dip below the ROTC Cadet groups who were generally more risky than the Students. The Cadets recorded lower shift scores than the Students on two scenarios, Persian Gulf and South Korea, but they elicited greater levels of risk in the Cambodian, SALT, and Hague Guerrilla dilemmas.

However, this is not to impute that shift scores are necessarily equal. For example, if the Officers and Students both shifted +1.50 units on the Persian Gulf scenario, the shift would indicate only that there was an identical degree of difference between the response of their respective groups and the average of their initial choice preferences. This does not indicate: 1) on what level of risk the respective groups began their group discussion; and 2) where they, as a group, concluded the appropriate level of risk on a given scenario should cease. The Students may have begun with an initial average recommendation at 2.5 (between multi-lateral negotiations and supporting opposition elements) and with a shift of +1.50 units endorsed option 4 (discontinue diplomatic relations). The Officers, on the other hand, may have begun their group deliberations with an average initial predisposition of 5.50 (between creating economic turmoil and sending military advisors) and with a shift of +1.50 units recommended a group decision of 7 (establish a military or naval blockade). This is obviously a far greater level of risk than what the Students elected-- discontinuing diplomatic relations. It is evident, nonetheless, that there are substantial differences between the groups with respect to: 1) the direction and the magnitude of the shifts; and 2) their response to pre-test and post-test scores. We can conclude, therefore, that hypotheses 2, 3, 4, and 5 are supported by the evidence presented.

Decisional Extremization and Polarization in Small Groups

The third research question seeks to identify decisional extremization and polarization in the small group decisions. As was stated earlier, much of the unwieldy accumulation of scientific literature, research findings, and competing explanations of the "choice-shift" and "risky-shift" studies have recently been recast into an "extremization" framework. Specifically, this states that groups will shift to a more extreme position (either to risk or caution) than the average of their individual predispositions. In this model, there is movement away from some psychological midpoint in either a more risky or a more cautious direction. With the extremization model, direction is not important; magnitude, though, is crucial.

A more specific elaboration of the extremization model is the group polarization model. This states that the average of the individual predispositions is a clue as to how the group will respond on a given decision dilemma. For instance, if the pre-test mean of a group was 7.5, and 7.5 was a militant option, then according to the polarization model, the group decision would also tend toward this same direction and would likely surpass the mean of the individual responses. Polarization is simply movement toward an already preferred pole.[11]

Given the first model, a basic <u>extremization</u> hypothesis is posited:

H_6: Group decisions will be more extreme-- either to risk or caution-- than the individual predecisional positions.

Other hypotheses which seek to identify the group <u>polarization</u> phenomena are:

H_7: Decision groups which shift-to-risk will have higher pre-test scores, on average, than those groups which shift-to-caution;[12] and

H_8: Decision groups which shift-to-caution will have lower pre-test scores, on average, than those grups which shift-to-risk.[13]

Supporting evidence for the more general hypothesis of group decisional extremization can be gleaned from re-examining Table VI-4. This table shows the mean pre-test, post-test, and shift scores for each sub-sample across the six hypothetical dilemmas. Of the seventeen pre-post dyads presented in this table, twelve (71%) post-test means are higher, i. e., riskier, than the pre-test means. The Officers had uniformly moved to higher post-test means across all scenarios, whereas the Cadets showed only one instance (Persian Gulf) of a pre-test mean being higher than a post-test mean. The Students, on the other hand, did not conform to the pattern presented by the military and ROTC samples. In four of the six scenarios, Cambodia, SALT, Panama, and Hague Guerrillas, the post-test means were lower than the pre-test means. Only on the Persian Gulf scenario was the post-test Student mean greater than the pre-test mean.

Table VI-5 (Appendix B) provides a more detailed look at the data by examining each group. In this table, pre-test, post-test, and shift scores are given for each group for each scenario. In only three cases (2%) was there no movement to a more extreme (either direction) group position. The movement on the part of the groups to either a more risky or more cautious position was roughly equal. In 66 cases (45%), there was a movement to a more cautious group decision. In 79 cases (53%), there was a movement of the groups to elect greater risk than the average of initial individual predispositions. Thus, it can be said rather assuredly that small group decisions are more extreme than individual positions (H_6).

To test the more narrowly defined phenomenon of group polarization (H7 and H8), Figure D visualizes the pre-test and post-test marginals of the sub-samples from Table VI-5. The Officers held initially higher (i.e., more risky) individual responses than either the Cadets or Students, but the Officers shifted dramatically upward and to the right (to risk) to higher group decisions than the other groups. The Cadets

FIGURE D

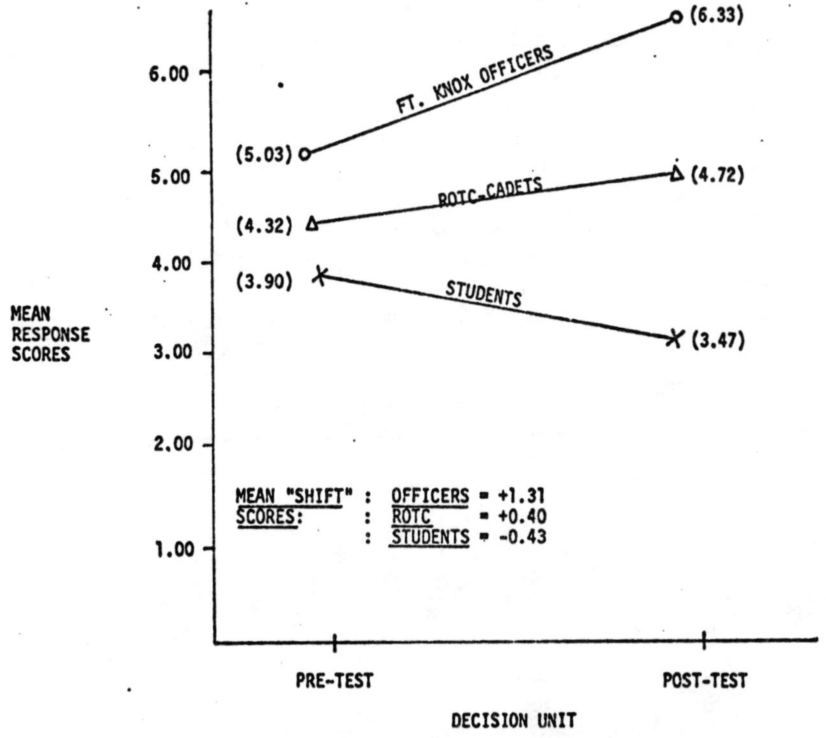

MEAN "PRE-TEST" AND "POST-TEST" RESPONSES PER SAMPLE

likewise shifted upward and to the right (to risk), but at less of a slope than the Officers. The Students, though, were less inclined to take risks as a group when compared to their average individual pre-test responses. Whereas risk-taking was enhanced in the small group discussions of the military and military-type groups, the Students showed a tendency to elect more cautious or conservative stances in the small group setting (see Figures E, F, and G, Appendix B).

Table VI-6 crosstabulates pre-test means with post-test scores. This table was constructed to visualize and test the polarization effect of small group decision-making. If the polarization model is valid, one would expect a high, positive Yule's Q resulting from the high number of entries in the diagonal that runs from cell A to cell D. In other words, for the data to support the polarization model, most of the cases would have to be concentrated in the low-lower and high-higher cells. Operationally, a diplomatic/ military breakpoint was used to differentiate between cautious or conservative choices (less than 4.5 on the ten-item scale) and risky or bellicose choices (4.5 or greater on the ten-item scale).

Those groups which chose a military (i.e., risky) option as indicated by the mean of the individual's pre-tests generally continued in the same direction as a small group (32%). Conversely, those groups who initially held diplomatic (i.e., cautious) crisis alternatives chose even more conservative diplomatic options (34%). Thus, the polarization effect among the Students, Cadets, and Officers is statistically substantiated by a strong, positive Yule's Q of .62 (Chi Square = 16.56; 1 df; p < .05).

What is not surprising, though, is the distribution of sample cases in the two cells low-lower, high-higher. As Figure D visualizes, the Officer and Cadet groups tended to select more risk-oriented options initially, while the Students (primarily) opted for diplomatic maneuvers. As a small homogenous group, the individuals within each of the three sub-samples provided an ambiance which apparently enhanced the pre-existing dominant values of the individuals. Assuming this is the case, the choice-shift among these sample groups may be attributable to two factors: the pre-existing value structure that individuals bring with them into each of the homogenous sub-sample groups; and an

TABLE VI-5

SHIFTS PER GROUP PER SCENARIO

	Persian Gulf	Cambodia	Korea	SALT	Panama	Hague Guerillas
9	GR = 6 IND.X = 6.6 Δ = -.6	GR = 3 IND.X = 5.0 Δ = -2.0	GR = 8 IND.X = 6.4 Δ = 1.6	GR = 1 IND.X = 2.2 Δ = -1.2	GR = 8 IND.X = 7.4 Δ = .6	GR = 2 IND.X = 4.4 Δ = -2.4
10	GR = 1 IND.X = 2.4 Δ = -1.4	GR = 1 IND.X = 3.2 Δ = -2.2	GR = 8 IND.X = 7.4 Δ = .6	GR = 1 IND.X = 3.4 Δ = -2.4	GR = 1 IND.X = 4.6 Δ = -3.6	GR = 1 IND.X = 2.8 Δ = -1.8
11	GR = 2 IND.X = 3.0 Δ = -1.0	GR = 1 IND.X = 2.6 Δ = -1.6	GR = 2 IND.X = 2.8 Δ = -.8	GR = 4 IND.X = 3.2 Δ = .8	GR = 2 IND.X = 4.2 Δ = -2.2	GR = 2 IND.X = 4.8 Δ = -2.8
12	GR = 3 IND.X = 2.4 Δ = .6	GR = 1 IND.X = 3.6 Δ = -2.6	GR = 7 IND.X = 3.4 Δ = 3.6	GR = 2 IND.X = 1.8 Δ = .2	GR = 7 IND.X = 4.8 Δ = 2.2	GR = 8 IND.X = 3.8 Δ = 4.2
13	GR = 5 IND.X = 1.75 Δ = 3.25	GR = 9 IND.X = 4.75 Δ = 4.25	GR = 6 IND.X = 5.0 Δ = 1.0	GR = 1 IND.X = 2.25 Δ = -1.25	GR = 1 IND.X = 7.0 Δ = -6.0	GR = 8 IND.X = 6.5 Δ = 1.5
14	GR = 4 IND.X = 2.5 Δ = 1.5	GR = 1 IND.X = 4.25 Δ = -3.25	GR = 7 IND.X = 5.5 Δ = 1.5	GR = 4 IND.X = 2.0 Δ = 2.0	GR = 1 IND.X = 2.0 Δ = -1.0	GR = 2 IND.X = 1.75 Δ = .25

STUDENT GROUPS

enhancement or re-enforcement of these values once in a small group setting by one, or possibly several, of the group dynamic attributes or processes-- social norms, contagion, rhetoric-or-risk, strong leader, etc.

Conclusion

In summary, it was shown that the three decision variables, pre-test, post-test, and shift scores, were statistically significant across the three sub-samples (H_1). Second, the Fort Knox Officers shifted to risk more than either the ROTC Cadets or the Students. The Cadets likewise shifted to risk more than the Students (H_2; H_3). Figure D illustrates the mean shifts for each sub-sample. On average, the Officers began their group deliberations with a score of 5.03; the Cadets 4.32; and the Students 3.90. There was a noticeable upward shift to risk, on average, by the Officers once the group had reached its final collective decision (6.33). Likewise, the Cadets exhibited a similar pattern of post-test decision responses; however, the student officers (Cadets) were a little less inclined to endorse collective decision responses that were as high (i.e., risky) as their professional counterparts (4.72). The Student groups were generally less risky, either deciding as individuals (3.90), or as a small decision-making unit (3.47). For this latter group, there was on average a decided shift downward to caution across the six crisis scenarios (H_4; H_5).

The general decisional extremization model of small group dynamics was convincingly supported by the experimental "crisis" groups. Of the seventeen pre-post dyads in Table VI-4, 71% (N=12) of the post-test means were higher than the pre-test means; 29% (N=5) were lower (H_6). To test the more specific form of group extremization, polarization, the ten-item risk scale accompanying each scenario was dichotomized into diplomatic (cautious) and military (risky) options. Sample groups were categorized into cells according to low/high pre-test means and post-test scores. The diagonal running from cell low-lower to high-higher (Table VI-6) produced a strong, positive Yule's Q of .62. Thus, these sub-sample groups who started their group deliberations with a cautious stance, generally enhanced this pre-group norm once in the context of the decisional unit. The converse is equally applicable. Those who were generally more inclined to pursue risky or militaristic alternatives as individuals were also so inclined as a small group (H_7; H_8). Not surprisingly, the distribution of sub-sample cases in each of the cells of Table VI-6 shows that the Student groups were the most frequent inhabitors of cell A-- low-lower (64%). Comparatively, the Army Officers were more inclined to settle in cell D-- high-higher (41%).

It is one thing to have identified the group extremization and polarization phenomena within and across the sample of subjects and crisis dilemmas. It is yet something else to offer an explanation for the occurrence of this effect. Chapter VII assumes that task.

NOTES

1. Holsti (1972:8).

2. This hypothesis was originally tested and confirmed in Semmel and Minix (1977:16).

3. The second factor, 5(6), represents the six crisis scenarios incorporated in the CDQ design. The ROTC Cadets, however, did not participate in six dilemmas. They participated in only the first five situations.

4. This ANOVA program was part of the Biomedical Statistical Package developed at the University of California at Los Angeles.

5. See Iverson and Norpoth (1976:7-11).

6. Semmel (1976:22).

7. This hypothesis was first tested and confirmed in Semmel and Minix (1977:18).

8. *Ibid.*, p. 18.

9. *Ibid.*, p. 19.

10. Ibid., p. 19.

11. Myers and Lamm (1976:603).

12. This hypothesis was first tested and confirmed in Semmel and Minix (1977:29).

13. Ibid., p. 29.

CHAPTER VII

AN EXPLANATION OF THE GROUP POLARIZATION PHENOMENA

In the previous chapter, three fundamental questions were posed regarding individual and collective decision behaviors. It was concluded that there were indeed statistically significant differences across the three sub-samples of Officers, Cadets, and Students on their pre-test, post-test, and shift scores (H_1). Furthermore, it was shown that the military sub-samples-- the Officers and the Cadets-- were generally more inclined to endorse higher individual and group risk levels across the crisis dilemmas than were the Students. Within the military groups, the Officers: 1) had higher pre-test and post-test responses which were, on average, higher than the Cadets; and 2) generally shifted to risk more than the Cadets (H_2 - H_5). Consequently, there appears to be hierarchical arrangement of the sub-samples along the degree of risk each grouping is willing to endorse. Finally, it was shown that a decisional polarization effect underlies the choice-shift behavior of the various groups. Not only are the small group foreign policy decisions generally more extreme than the individual pre-decisional positions (H_6), but also those groups which shift-to-risk (caution) will have higher (lower) pre-test scores on average than those groups which shift-to-caution (risk) (H_7, H_8). In addition, Table VI (Chapter VI) statistically confirmed the strong, positive relationship between the individual pre-test means and the group post-test scores.

Why Are Groups More Extreme Than Individuals?

The presence of decisional extremization and polarization among the Officer, Cadet, and Student groups leads to a series of hypotheses which seek to uncover why such small groups are committed to more extreme options than isolated individuals. The following hypotheses are divided between those based upon group processes, i. e., interactions, communications, etc., and those linked to the attributes of the individual members imported into the small group setting. The "process" hypotheses refer to such explanatory variables such as the information exchanged, the number and type of alternatives raised, decision rules, and so on. The "attribute" hypotheses seek explanations in such areas as: individual and group psychological rigidity, degree of world political involvement of the United States as advocated by the participants, their political beliefs, and finally, their individual and group norms. Conceptually, however, it does make sense to look at what happens within the group setting apart from the attributes that are imported into the deciding unit by members of the decisional body. The group process hypotheses are:

H_9: The magnitude and direction of the choice-shift is dependent upon the type of information exchanged within the group.1

H_{10}: When group members advocate several alternatives, the group will behave more conservatively than the average individual member. When the situation is such that only one (or a few) alternative(s) is advocated, then the group will take greater risks than the individual.2

H_{11}: The greater the use of historical analogies by a small group, the greater the choice-shift.

H_{12}: Subjects adopting more extreme positions initially will exert an influence upon the group so as to move the group closer to the subject's initial position.

H_{13}: Subjects who advocate extreme positions in the decision-making process will be perceived as the group leader.

H_{14}: Small decision groups in which there is a perceived group leader will gravitate toward the

position that is espoused
by that leader.

H_{15}: Small decision groups using a majority-vote <u>decision-making rule</u> will make riskier decisions than those groups who simply reach a consensus decision.

The <u>group attribute</u> hypotheses are:

H_{16}: Decision groups which have a great degree of <u>psychological flexibility</u> will elicit greater choice-shifts than groups that do not.

H_{17}: Decision groups which have a high <u>political involvement</u> score, i.e., are more internationalist, will elicit a higher shift-to-risk than groups that do not.

H_{18}: Decision groups which have a high <u>political belief</u> score, i.e., are more conservative, will shift-to-risk more than groups that do not.

H_{19}: The magnitude and direction of the choice-shift is primarily dependent upon <u>group norms and standards</u>.

Group Process Hypotheses

The first of the group process hypotheses, H_9, seeks an explanation of choice-shift behavior from the type of information exchanged with the group. It is assumed that the type of information exchanged will play a determining role in the decisional behavior or the degree of risk-taking within the group. This hypothesis, though, is not new. Its ancestral lineage is traceable to the early days of the "risky-shift" experiments where it encountered mixed results. For example, Lamm[3] and Wallach and Mabli[4] each conclude that information is a powerful determinant of the risky-shift. However, Kogan and Wallach[5] and Murdoch and his colleagues[6] found that information alone is insufficient to account for the risky-shift.[7] Accordingly, the hypothesis is formulated as:

> H_9: The magnitude and direction of the choice-shift is dependent upon the <u>type of information</u> exchanged within the group.

The type of data needed to test H_9 -- indeed H_{10} to H_{13} -- is difficult to gather and not readily available. Group discussions of five of the six Fort Knox Officer groups fortunately were recorded on tape.[8] With such fragmentary data, it is impossible to test adequately hypothesis 9-13. But, perhaps some of these hypotheses can be useful in directing this and other research to generate the necessary data for testing competing group process hypotheses.

The exchange of information within the small groups of the Fort Knox Officers was characterized by a considerable "rhetoric of risk."[9] Take, for example, this interchange between some of the Officers on the Persian Gulf scenario:

> "We're between the gap of (option) 1 (bilateral negotiations) and (option) 8 (use of conventional ground forces...."
>
> "Let's back up and see if we're talking the same language."
>
> "I'd go to number 8 initially and with a little more information, I could conceivably go to (option) 9 (limited strategic bombing of non-civilian, military-oriented cites) or 10 (use of nuclear capability of the United States...)."
>
> "Not all of these alternatives can apply."
>
> "Would you be willing to engage the

Soviet Union in a nuclear exchange?"

"Yeah."

"I wouldn't."

"Why would they do it? They're begging for some type of confrontation."

"You either throw in the towel or come out punching."

"Somewhere you're either going to have to fight or you're going to have to hang it up..."

"I'd go down as far as 8."

"Don't push the button unless you have to."

"I would go to 9."

"We don't have to ship the oil through the (Persian) Gulf. The oil is not the issue. It's what are the Soviets telling us when they throw up the blockade."

"Western Europe is going to be in an uproar!"

"If you're willing to use 9, then your're willing to go to 10."

"You cross the radical line of departure when you go up to nuclear."

"(option) 7 (establish a military or naval blockade...) is not feasible at all."

"How are you going to blockade Russia?"

"How long can they last?" They could sit there forever."

"I say 8."

"8."

"8 is an alternative."

This group of Officers finally decided on option 8-- use of conventional ground forces to repel the adversary's threat. To illustrate the choice shift or decisional extremization of this particular group, the average of the member's pre-test responses was 4.25. Their shift-to-risk on this crisis was 3.4.

Compare this discussion with another exchange by a different group of Officers. The scenario is Korea. The average of the member's pre-test is 8.0 (use of conventional ground forces...).

"We'll start at 8 on this one." (laughter).

"We are not the aggressors."

"I'd go to 9 (limited strategic bombing...)."

"I'd be willing to go to 9; then 10 (nuclear weapons)."

"I'd use 'tact' nukes."

"You're limited by being on a peninsula...."

"Good point."

"If we go to 8, much less 9, we can't afford not to win."

"That's right."

"I think 8 is a bare minimum."

"I agree."

"I'd use 'tact' nukes here, shoot."

"Boy, this is a tough one."

"Are we going to allow the South Koreans to force us into nuclear confrontation?"

(Analogy of the <u>USS</u> <u>Pueblo</u> was raised here.)

"The scenario approaches the point of being ludicrous."

"I'd go as far as 10."

"I'd say 10."

"Yeah - that's hoping you wouldn't automatically go that route."

"That's the limit. I'd go to 10."

"Why would you go to 10 in Korea and not in the Persian Gulf?"

"There are other alternatives there."

"If you start at 8, you don't have a helluva lot of options after that...."

"9."

"9."

"I've got to have that 'ace-in-the-hole' as far as nuclear capability - if nothing more than a threat."

"Based on what we've got here, I'd go with 10. Otherwise, I'd like to know what the Soviets - what the Chinese - were doing!"

"I can go with 10 based on this. Want to go with 10?"

"Uh huh."

    This group, while starting on average at option 8, concluded their deliberations by choosing option 10-- the use or threat of nuclear weapons. Their choice-shift was 2.0 options, but their <u>final group choice</u> was indicative of the decisional polarization found within all of the Officer groups as well as the rhetoric employed to justify risky military options to these crisis dilemmas. Furthermore, the selection of a military alternative to these hypothetical crises was expected. Perhaps this is an indicator of the military socialization process alluded to earlier. If one's job is to wage war or, as some prefer, to keep the peace, then in all likelihood one will use the methods and means for which he has been trained. In the case of the Officer and Cadet groups, these methods include the use of military force.

Though hypothesis 9 can not be confirmed (or disconfirmed) by the data presented here, these conversations of the two Officer groups are indicative of the "considerable rhetoric of risk" that flourished in their group discussions. This rhetoric appears to have been a factor in buttressing "relevant arguments" for the use of force. Likewise, the polarization of the ROTC Cadet and College Student groups was in all likelihood heavily influenced-- perhaps determined-- by an information exchange consisting of force-related or military initiatives. In the Military and Cadet groups, it led to a polarization toward risk. Thus, it appears to be the case that dominant individual values were further magnified in small group discussion.

Hypothesis 10 directs us to look at the number of options discussed within the group for a possible explanation of the choice-shift effect. Basically, it says that the more options discussed, the more moderate the final group outcome. Conversely, the fewer options raised, the riskier the final group choice. The striving for concurrence among group members may limit the possibility of discussing different alternatives; consequently, group members will not have the opportunity to correct the views and distortions of others which may force the group into adopting a premature and perhaps risky judgment. Put simply, individuals in a group situation may have a tendency to support their colleagues' positions in such a manner which may lead to increased risk-taking.

H_{10}: When group members advocate several alternatives, the group will behave more conservatively than the average individual member. When the situation is such that only

>one (or a few) alternative(s)
>is advocated, the group will
>take greater risks than the
>individual.

The Korean conflict vividly illustrates the latter portion of H_{10}. Joseph de Rivera, for example, recounts the thoughts of Truman, Acheson, and MacArthur concerning the crossing of the 38th parallel, where they reinforced each other's optimistic belief that the Chinese would not enter into the war. While each of the three leaders had different reasons for his optimism, the end result was that each was supporting the rationale of the other. Truman, for example, saw the Chinese Communists as puppets of Moscow. As such, he believed that the Soviet Union was not prepared for a war and would not unleash Peking. Acheson, though, came to the same conclusion, but by a different route. He felt the Chinese were neither puppets of Moscow nor would they be dissuaded by the bombing. Instead, he perceived the Chinese as independent communists and principally concerned with national development. Likewise, MacArthur firmly believed that US air superiority could destroy a large percentage of Chinese troops should they cross the Yalu, but even the time for them to do so had passed. As de Rivera states, "the result was a three-ring circus of the President looking toward his Commander, his Commander looking to the Chinese, and the Chinese looking to the President."[10] The concurrence-seeking tendency in this group did not permit voices of caution to be heard. Consequently, the "risk" option of crossing the 38th parallel was the only option discussed.

This apparently was not the case with one group of Officers who discussed virtually every option available to them concerning the Persian Gulf crisis.

>"I selected number five (create
>economic turmoil in the adversary's
>country)."
>
>"Initially we're looking at something
>for the United Nations Security
>Council (option 2). How far are
>we willing to go if this initial
>step doesn't go? I'd go along
>with the use of conventional
>forces (option 8) in the immediate

area. I think...strategic bombing (option 9) is too close to the use of nuclear weapons (option 10)."

"The question boils down to: are you willing to go to war over oil?"

"I think that based on the necessity of oil to the economy of the western world, that if negotiations don't work, ground forces or naval forces would be called for (option 8)."

"That would probably prompt war."

"Your choice of option 5 (economic turmoil)-- how would you do it? This one I'm more conservative on. I'd like to start with option 2 (UN Security Council)...Where do I start? Some of the ones down the road-- I'm ready to rip."

"How far would you be willing to go-- that's the ultimate question. I'd agree, maybe you'd start low and hope that would work."

"I agree; but can we take a look at some of these others, say (option) 6 (send military advisors)?"

"What about a naval blockade (option 7)?"

"What about 3-- put opposition elements in those countries?"

"That would be a reasonable one."

"That would be the next step-- start at 1; go to 2; if that doesn't work, go to 3. Would you go to 'nuking' them? I'd agree with the initial one-- 8. I wouldn't go much further than that."

"Their oil is not much good if they can't sell it."

"My way of thinking on option 4 (discontinue diplomatic relations)... world opinion, okay. Severing diplomatic relations won't do anything."

"Then 1, 2, 3, 5, and 8 are viable."

"We wouldn't have to worry about committing ground forces if we sent advisors (option 6). Would that work?"

"We're looking for the option that...as far as we're willing to go. I think we've got a consensus for conventional ground forces."

"If you go that far, you've essentially started a war. Are you willing to do that over Middle East oil?"

"Eventually we're going to have to probably maintain our industrial base."

"I'll give on this one."

This group of Officers touched all bases in deciding upon a solution to the Persian Gulf crisis. However, instead of being more conservative, as the hypothesis suggests, this group was willing to endorse option 8 (use of conventional ground forces) as a solution to the dilemma. Far from being more cautious, this group, at least, was more risky in their collective deliberations.

Hypothesis eleven suggests that there is a direct positive relationship between historical analogies in small group discussions and the size of the choice-shift. Drawing analogies from notable historic events to the uncertainty of the crisis at hand provides an intellectual or cognitive prescription for decision-makers. It is a way of reducing psychological stress caused by the pressures and uncertainty of the situation. It is a way of mastering cognitively complex problems with a ready-made decision calculus.[11] As Janis and Mann state:

> ...simple decision rules sometimes used by policy makers consist of relying on, as a guide for action, a general ideological principle-- e.g., "No appeasement of the enemy!"-- or an operational code-- e.g., "the best tactic for dealing with an ultimatum from an enemy is to respond promptly with a more drastic ultimatum."[12]

According to historian Ernest May[13] and political scientist Robert Jervis[14], the use of the historical analogy translates into the following simple decision rule: "Do what we did last time if it worked and the opposite if it didn't."[15] May says,

> Policy-makers ordinarily use history badly. When resorting to an analogy, they tend to seize upon the first that comes to mind. They do not search more widely. Nor do they pause to analyze the case, test its fitness, or even ask in what ways it might be misleading. Seeing a trend running toward the present, they tend to assume that it will continue into the future, not stopping to consider what produced it or why a linear projection might prove to be mistaken.[16]

The magnitude of the choice-shift with respect to the use of historical analogies may come about by reliance on a simple decision calculus. As George points out, "relying on a simple decision rule will lead to a premature choice that overlooks non-obvious negative consequences. Some of those consequences might be averted if the decision were delayed until a more thorough deliberation and evaluation were carried out after obtaining information from available intelligence sources."[17] Hypothesis eleven therefore states that:

H_{11}: The more references to historical analogies by a small group, the greater the choice-shift.

Use of historical analogy among the various Officer groups was the rule rather than the exception. Moreover, most analogies raised by the Officers were of the crisis genre-- indicating, perhaps, that crisis decision-making begets historical crisis examples. At least ten different <u>explicit</u> historical analogies were cited by the Officers:

1) Japanese attack on Pearl Harbor, 1941
2) Korean War, 1952-54
3) Berlin Blockade, 1948; Berlin Crisis, 1962
4) Soviet downing of a US U-2 reconnaissance plane (the "Gary Powers" incident), 1958
5) US blockade of Cuba, 1962
6) USS <u>Pueblo</u> incident, 1968
7) <u>Munich disaster</u>, 1972
8) Capture of the US merchant ship <u>Mayaquez</u> by the Cambodians, 1973
9) <u>Israeli</u> raid on Entebbe, Uganda, 1974; and
10) "DMZ tree incident" between North Korea, South Korea, and the United States, 1976

Take, for example, this reconstructed dialogue between several Officers:

"Cambodia has been rather uncivilized in the last year or so."

(<u>Mayaquez</u> and <u>Pueblo</u> analogy raised here)

"I'd go down as far as (option) 8 (use of conventional ground forces...)."

(Entebbe analogy raised here)

"Would you use the talks as a subterfuge knowing full well that you'll go in after the crew?"

"No. I'd start with bilateral talks."

"For $10 million we could replace all that technology."

"To me, 8 is where we're at in conventional war."

"...Pull a raid or something - I'd do that in a second."

"I just don't think that the US has been very...we talk of face... our Secretary of State, well, that's a bunch of baloney! The way we treat our ambassadors-- we go out and let them get kidnapped all over the world and get assassinated-- we don't do a damn thing about it. American nationals aren't safe out of the US. I think it's about time we stopped it."

"I'd go to war in a second for something that affects national interest, but situation two (Cambodia) isn't as extreme as situation one (Persian Gulf)."

"Initially, I don't think we should go as far as number 8."

"Agreed."

"I'd say 8."

"8."

"8."

"With that definition, I'd go to 8."

For this group of Officers, the mean of the group's pre-test responses was 4.0 (discontinue diplomatic relations with the adversary...). The final group decision was option 8 (use of conventional ground forces...) for a shift-to-risk of 4.0 options. In this exchange over Cambodia, there were three direct references to historical events-- the Mayaquez incident, the capture of the USS Pueblo by the North Koreans, and the raid on the Entebbe airport by the Israelis-- with some veiled references to recent US ambassadorial kidnappings.

The use of the simple decision rule, "do what we did last time...," appears operative in this case (as well as in other taped Officer discussions). Nor did the policy-makers, as May suggests, deviate from discussing any option other than number 8. Indeed, they did not search more widely. It is impossible though, since there is no correct response to the Cambodian crisis, to charge this, or any other group, with reaching a "premature choice that overlooks non-obvious negative consequences." The selection of a risky option in this case may mean defective judgment or, conversely, an appropriate level of response to the situation. It should also be noted that the raising of historical analogies can also produce the opposite type of decision-rule: "Let's not do what we (they) did last time." Two frequently cited cases in point are Munich, 1938 (the "appeasement principle") and Pearl Harbor, 1941. Indeed, the invocation of either of these decision maxims is a potential formula for premature closure and a contributor to a faulty decision-making calculus. For example, Robert Kennedy, during one of the meetings of the EXCOM in the 1962 Cuban missile crisis, emphasized his moral abhorrence to the bombing of Soviet missile installations in Cuba by saying that "he was against acting as the Japanese had in 1941 by resorting to a 'Pearl Harbor in reverse.'"[18]

However, the decision by this group of Officers does seemingly meet many of the symptoms of "defective decision-making," based upon the research conducted by Irving Janis in Victims of Groupthink.[19] These symptoms include: 1) an incomplete survey of alternatives; 2) an incomplete survey of objectives; 3) failure to examine risks of preferred choice; 4) poor information search; 5) selective bias in processing information at hand; 6) failure to reappraise alternatives; and 7) failure to work out contingency plans.[20]

Since these Officers were participants in an experiment where reality is imperfectly duplicated and simplified, it is unfair to be overly critical of this and other decision groups along the dimensions suggested by Janis. But taken from an overall perspective, it could well have been the case that the over-reliance on available historical analogies led this group to participate in a "defective decision-making" exercise which was conducive to their selection of option 8.

Hypothesis twelve, thirteen, and fourteen resemble two conventional rationales for the choice-shift phenomenon previously discussed: risk-as-value and the leadership hypothesis. These value and leadership hypotheses have received "mixed reviews" from the spate of research on the choice-shift phenomenon.[21]

Hypothesis twelve assumes that risk is a culturally prescribed and reinforced value-- much as youth, masculinity, strength, and physical beauty are culturally valued in Western society. Roger Brown, who is closely associated with the "value" research, once contended that individuals, in cultures which value risk-taking, will shift to risk in group discussions upon finding that others are greater risk-takers.[22] This explanation, however, soon ran aground because of its inability to account for cautious shifts. He later reframed this model in a broader light to include shifts-to-caution as well as shifts-to-risk. He states that "the group decision will be more extreme than the individual decision-- in the direction of the value engaged, whichever that direction may be."[23] As a second part to his reformulated model, Brown states that:

> Values are not specified, in advance, in terms of particular probabilities on the (traditional CDQ) story problems. On problems involving the value of risk we know that each individual before the discussion thinks himself at least as risky as the average person. We argued that the discussion served to make known the actual distribution and all those who were below the group average could no longer think of themselves

> as living up to the value on risk. So-- we have suggested-- they change to riskier decisions. Now we must predict in addition that for problems engaging the value of caution individuals will initially guess that "others like themselves" would adopt somewhat less cautious and so less ideal decisions. When the true distribution has been disclosed in discussion the subjects who find themselves riskier than the average of the group ought to shift to greater caution-- the direction of the value.[24]

Brown has essentially broadened the so-called "Walter Mitty" effect to include shifts-to-caution as well as shifts-to-risk in his two-part model of group extremization. Hypothesis twelve proposes that:

> H_{12}: Subjects adopting more extreme positions initially will exert an influence upon the group so as to move the group closer to the subject's initial position.

The leadership or persuasion hypothesis partially coincides with the above value hypothesis. It assumes that dominant forceful personalities exert undo influence over the group so as to draw reticent or cautious (assertive or risky) group members to the position of the group leader. Two hypotheses are suggested:

> H_{13}: Subjects who advocate extreme positions in the decision-making process will be perceived as the group leaders.

> H_{14}: Small decision groups in which there is a perceived group leader will gravitate toward the position that is espoused by that leader.

It is difficult, without a systematic content analysis of the tapes, to discern whether a leader(s) emerged within the group discussions to move the group closer to that person's preferred position. Throughout most of the taped discussion, though, someone in the group tended to dominate the conversation by offering reasons why his preferred option should be adopted (frequently by citing statistics and bringing in "outside" or tangential information) and citing reasons why another person's position was untenable. For example, one group's discussion on the SALT dilemma seems to indicate that there was a group leader (PL = Perceived Leader).

        "I'd initially say...not too much success could be expected... I'd go with (option) 2 (call a special session of the UN Security Council...)."

PL: "I disagree. I'd go as far as (option) 5 (create economic turmoil...)."

"What?"

PL: "The enemy doesn't have a very sound economic system. We've given him grain, industrial plants, technology, we're alowing him to trade on a world-wide basis. We have the power to bring havoc to his economy."

(irrelevant dialogue)

PL: "You've got a group of people who'll use this situation to their best advantage...You can upset their schedule without actually taking an overt act of aggression..."

(irrelevant dialogue)

PL: "I'm saying if they want grain, we don't sell it to them...We embarrass them internationally...We don't give them the industrialization they are counting on."

"Can you tell Great Britain not to sell them things?"

PL: "We're exporting technology to them ever since the (Russian) Revolution."

"I'll go to 5."

"Would we substantially weaken his war effort."

PL: "Yes, we would, because his war effort is predicated on a very weak economy. It's almost like one-third of his total economy is geared to the war effort."

"What's it going to do to our economy?"

PL: "Not that much...That wheat is coming from the US. As soon as that wheat reaches the dock, it's stamped with a hammer and sickle, so they aren't aware of the fact that it's imported goods. Supposedly they don't believe in inflation, supposedly they don't believe in trading with foreign countries-- that's a lot of bullshit."

"You have a fairly convincing argument. I could probably go with 5."

PL: "We've tried negotiations. Now it's time to take a somewhat more active stance."

"I agree. He's won me over. The most drastic is 5."

"Yeah."

"I go with 5."

"I think 5 also."

The unanimous final choice of this group was option 5. The perceived leader tended to dominate the discussions with a low, forceful monotone. His long, articulate discourses were filled with statistics and historical analogies. At the end of the tape, the "leader" acted like a defense attorney summing up his client's case before a jury. It is obvious from the tape, but perhaps not so clear from the transcript, that once the "leader" won-over or persuaded the primary dissenter of the group to adopt his option, the other members of the group fell into agreement with the perceived leader.

Another possible explanation of the choice-shift phenomenon resides in examining the decision-rule employed in the choice-making procedure. In laboratory groups where there are no fixed decision rules, groups generally opt for an "equiprobability" scheme whereby "each strategy advocated by a member has an equal probability of being selected."[25] However, some researchers have suggested that "a social decision scheme of majority-rule predicts shift toward the dominant pole when the majority favors that direction and when there is skewness in the distribution of initial choices..."[26] None of these analysts, however, point to the majority-rule scheme as being a monistic explanation for the polarization effect. But, Myers and Lamm point out the plausibility of such a contributory explanation. As posited, hypothesis fifteen reads that:

H_{15}: Small decision groups using a majority-vote decision-making rule will make riskier decisions than those groups who simply reach a consensus decision.

The potential explanation is intuitively appealing (as are most of the proferred explanations), but it too has met with numerous contradictory findings. With mixed evidence, however, a decision was made to test the validity of the decision-rule hypothesis with the three sub-samples.

Results from the one-way Analysis of Variance for the group responses to the six crisis dilemmas (GRESP 1-6) and the decision-rule (DECRULE) employed in the groups' decision-making calculus lend little support for Hypothesis 15. Of the 26 experimental groups, 18 were instructed to reach a unanimous decision and 8 were told to reach a decision by majority-vote procedures. For the six scenarios, there was no statistical significance (p = .05) between the final group choice and the decision rule employed to teach that decision (F probabilities for GRESP 1-6, respectively, are: .82; .58; .61; .86; .61; and .17).

This research, then, supports those findings which indicate that the type of decision-rule used by small groups has little bearing upon the group polarization phenomenon. Hypothesis fifteen, therefore, is not confirmed.[27]

The set of seven Group Process hypotheses (9-15) examined here are those which operate under the assumption that group decision-making will become more extreme when compared to individual decision-making because of the internal behavioral dynamics of the group. This is apprently attributable to the collectivity's increased rational capacities based upon the type of information exchanged and to the arguments raised by group discussion.[28] Here, there is sufficient support to confirm tentatively H_9 - H_{14}; however, H_{10} failed to achieve such documentation and is consequently classified as "leaning against confirmation" (see Table VII-2).

Group Attribute Hypotheses

Unlike the qualitative data used for the group process hypotheses, the group attribute hypotheses are more rigorously tested because of the quantitative nature of the data used. For example, Pearson r values and the related F scores are consistently used to test the variables mentioned in hypotheses sixteen to nineteen.

Hypothesis sixteen suggests that decision groups

which have a high psychological flexibility will elect greater choice-shifts than groups that do not.[29] Underlying this hypothesis is the assumption that "flexible" members of the group may be persuaded to take a more extreme stand for any number of reasons, e.g., a strong, forceful group leader, the rhetoric of the discussion, "relevant arguments," and the like. To test this notion, two dependent variables were used: ASHIFT and ABSHIFT. ASHIFT is the sum of the absolute values for scenarios 1-5 (N=26); ABSHIFT is the sum of the absolute shift values for scenarios 1-6 (N=18). These variables account for the net shift by ignoring the signs (i.e., psychologically flexible) answers. In hypothesis form, Hypothesis 16 suggests that:

H_{16}: Decision groups which have a greater degree of psychological flexibility will elicit greater choice-shifts than groups that do not.

Both ASHIFT (N=26) and ABSHIFT (N=18), however, are not significant at the .05 level when the predictor variable, CPI, is used. Thus, with respect to magnitude of shift, there is no significant statistical relationship that exists when using a group's psychological score as a predictor. Consequently, hypothesis sixteen is not confirmed.

Hypothesis seventeen suggests a relationship between a group's degree of internationalism (PIN) and its propensity for electing risky crisis alternatives. PIN is measured on an ordinal scale ranging from low internationalism to high internationalism. Unlike hypothesis 16, this hypothesis predicts direction toward the risk-oriented end of the scale. Since over 50% of the sample groups are military or military-oriented, this hypothesis is a partial test of Huntington's assertion that the military mind is "usually assumed to be disciplined, rigid, logical, scientific, inflexible, intolerant, nonintuitive, and non-emotional, with a tendency towards bellicosity and authoritarianism."[30] Given this proposed relationship, hypothesis seventeen states that:

H_{17}: Decision groups which have a high political involvement score, i.e., are more internationalist, will elicit

a higher shift-to-risk than
groups that do not.

The dependent variables used to test this hypothesis are the sums of the shift values for situations 1-5 (N=26) and 1-6 (N=18), respectively. Since direction is a significant factor here, the net shift will not be calculated by using absolute values as in hypothesis 16. These variables will instead utilize a summing procedure which accounts for both risky and cautious shifts.

The political involvement variable is significant at both the .05 and .01 levels. However, the Pearson r's reveal both a weak positive and a weak negative relationship between the group's degree of internationalism and the total group shift. Apparently, knowing a group's position on the degree of U.S. involvement in world affairs is of little value in predicting its move to a more extreme or risky choice. There is a very slight indication that the two variables are inversely related (as predicted); that is, the more isolationist the group is, the less inclined it will be to opt for a force-related alternative. Hypothesis seventeen, however, can not be confirmed on such marginal statistical evidence.

Hypothesis eighteen looks to a group's political belief score (PBS), i.e., whether the group is composed of predominantly liberal, middle-of-the-road, or conservative members, for a possible link to group risk-taking behavior. This is a test of the belief that conservatism "correlates positively with activism abroad or with the use of more coercive instruments of foreign policy."[31] The "shift" variables retain the same operationalization as in hypothesis seventeen. The independent variable, political belief, is a measure based on the conventional seven point self-identification scale which ranges from extremely liberal to extremely conservative. In hypothesis form, hypothesis eighteen states that:

H_{18}: Decision groups which have a high political belief score, i. e., are more conservative, will shift-to-risk more than groups that do not.

The F statistic shows that the group political belief variable is statistically significant at the .05 level with shift variables. The Pearson r's, while not exceedingly high, are both positive (.33 and .22, respectively). Subsequently, there is a slight tendency for a more politically conservative group to adopt a more risky alternative. Hypothesis eighteen is therefore confirmed.

The final group attribute hypothesis seeks an explanation of choice-shift behavior in the predominant norms and standards of the group membership. As stated, hypothesis nineteen examines the possibility that:

H_{19}: The magnitude and direction of the choice-shift is primarily dependent upon the content of group norms and standards.

Though the type of data to test the above hypothesis is not readily available, hypothesis nineteen is in many respects the primary test of the model of small group dynamics which was explicated in Chapter III. The establishment and adherence to group norms is speculated to be the prime variable in fostering the group's commitment parallel to that underlying norm established by the individual's acting alone. Group norms, in turn, promote greater group homogeneity/conformity which commits the group to bolster their beliefs by pursuing only relevant arguments. This may have an effect of driving away outsiders or dissidents which in turn completes the circle by drawing the group even closer together. These tautological statements find considerable support in the experimental literature on small group behavior. The norms of the group, as Hare says, "are standards which set limits for present behavior, while goals are standards to be achieved. There is no basis for organized interaction until group members reach some agreement about each of these kinds of expectations."[32]

Since the three homogenous sub-samples of Officers, Cadets, and Students were never integrated with one another in the small group sessions, it would not be at all surprising to see an already preferred set of norms operating within each of the sub-sample groups. In other words, it is anticipated that the

Officers, for example, would bring with them into the group setting a pre-established set of standards and goals pertinent to the conduct of U.S. foreign policy. Likewise, the Cadets, undergoing a process of military socialization, would in all likelihood present themselves in such a manner acceptable to their ROTC peers. The Students, while not being trained for military combat, were actively engaged in the study of political science and hence may operate on an entirely different set of assumptions and principles that are appreciably different from the conduct standards generally achieved through military socialization. While this may indeed be the case, it should be strongly emphasized that no *a priori* measure of the concept group norm existed.

If the proposed polarization model is valid, and if there is a hierarchy of sub-samples willing to use force-related (risky) crisis alternatives, then it should not be at all surprising to see the results discussed in the previous chapter. It is anticipated that the group membership variable (GROUP) will be highly correlated with the three decision variables, Pre-test, Post-test, ahd Shift scores. Concomitantly, it is expected that the Pearson Correlation coefficients will be particularly strong for both the Post-test and Shift variables where group interaction provided the ambiance for polarization.

TABLE VII-1

Pearson Correlation Coefficients Between "GROUP" and "Pre," "Post," and "Shift" Variables

Pre-test		Post-test		Shift	
(N=26)	(N=18)	(N=26)	(N=18)	(N=26)	(N=18)
.58	.66	.77	.78	.71	.66

The Pearson r values of Table VII-1 solidly confirm the anticipated relationship between group norms and the three decisional variables. While all r coefficients show strong, positive relationships across the three dependent variables, this relationship is predictably the "weakest" with the Pre-test scores (.58; .66) which is probably due to the absence of other group members to bolster or reinforce the dominant set of group values of beliefs. For the Post-test and Shift variables, however, the small group environment apparently provided a rich and fertile base for the enhancement and promotion of these preconceived individual norms. The Post-test correlational coefficients are .77 and .78; the Shift values are .71 and .66.

The findings from both the preceding group *process* and group *attribute* hypotheses-- plus the findings from the previous chapter-- point to several factors which influence group decisional polarization in foreign policy crisis deliberating groups. Foremost among these factors is group membership. The confirmation of Hypotheses 2-5 and 19 lend empirical support to the contentions that: 1) who makes foreign policy-- military or civilian personnel-- is highly related to the kinds of options chosen in such critical policy situations as international crises; and 2) how this policy is derived--whether individually or in a small group-- is greatly associated with an enhanced commitment to individually derived choices. In well over half of all cases (66%), the individual commitment to the crisis alternative was further enhanced in the same direction by the small decision-making group.

These findings lead to the conclusion that there is generally an attitudinal difference between the Military (Officer and Cadet) and Student sub-samples which allows the former groups to adopt more bellicose national options in times of crisis compared to their civilian counterparts. This conclusion is consistent with the conclusion expressed by Bernard Mennis when he states that:

> political-military Officers and political Foreign Service Officers (FSOs) may be distinguished attitudinally, and that the direction of the differences between them consists of the military manifesting a more hard-line perspective (*i. e.*, one with anti-Communism - absolutist idea elements) than FSOs.[33]

Group Process versus Group Attribute Hypotheses

Two rather general categories of hypotheses were constructed to examine the relationship between individual and group decision-making behavior on the one hand and the choice-shift behavior of the collectivity on the other. However, from the previous discussion, can it be ascertained which set of hypotheses-- process or attribute-- are better predictors of the choice-shift behavior of small groups?

It must be remembered that there is a distinct difference in the data used for each of these hypothetical groupings. With respect to the group process hypotheses, the data that were used were decidedly qualitative, making it more difficult to confirm or disconfirm the hypotheses. Because of the nature of the data collected for the group attribute hypotheses, quantitative verification was possible which enabled and facilitated a more structured, rigorous analysis.

In terms of the two previously discussed and highly touted polarization hypotheses, interpersonal comparison and information exchange, this research would give a slight edge to those hypotheses which seek an explanation to this effect in the <u>attributes</u> of those individuals comprising the group (interpersonal comparison). This is evidenced by the confirmation of "attribute" hypotheses 18 and 19 (see Table VII-2). While these two hypotheses were the only ones labeled "confirmed," the remaining three hypotheses in this category were oppositely labeled "disconfirmed." In addition, most of the group <u>process</u> hypotheses (9, 11, 12, 13, 14) were categorized as "leaning towad confirmation." Hypothesis 10, though, fits into the "leaning against confirmation" category, while hypothesis 15 was disconfirmed.

Thus, the findings of this research argue forcefully for a conceptual integration of these two hypothetical approaches for explaining the group dynamic phenomena referred to as polarization. Instead of bifurcating social motivations and group dynamics and seeking an explanation in one area to the exclusion of the other, linking both analytical perspectives would apparently provide analysts with a clearer picture of reality. The conceptual scheme offered by Myers and Lamm attempts to provide this linkage.

These researchers state that:

> ...social motivation (a desire to perceive and present oneself favorably relative to others) may change an attitude through the interpersonal comparison process, but it also motivates the person to express socially desirable arguments. This verbal commitment may enhance the attitude, and it also serves a cognitive rehearsal function for the listeners. Thus, the effects of social motivation may be partly mediated by the learning and rehearsal that accompanies the hearing and speaking of discussion arguments.[34]

TABLE VII-2

Hypotheses which are:

Confirmed

H_{18}: Decision groups which have a high <u>political belief</u> score, <u>i. e.</u>, are more conservative, will shift-to-risk more than groups that do not.

H_{19}: The magnitude and direction of the choice-shift is primarily dependent upon <u>group norms and standards</u>.

Leaning Toward Confirmation

H_9: The magnitude and direction of the choice-shift is dependent upon the <u>type of information</u> exchanged within the group.

H_{11}: The greater the use of <u>historical analogies</u> by a small group, the greater the choice-shift.

H_{12}: Subjects adopting more <u>extreme positions</u> initially will exert an influence upon the group so as to move the group closer to the subject's initial position.

H_{13}: Subjects who advocate extreme positions in the decision-making process will be perceived as the <u>group leader</u>.

H_{14}: Small decision groups in which there is a perceived <u>group leader</u> will gravitate toward the position that is espoused by that leader.

TABLE VII-2 continued

Leaning Against Confirmation

H_{10}: When group members advocate several alternatives, the group will behave more conservatively than the average individual member. When the situation is such that only one (or a few) alternative(s) is advocated, the group will take greater risks than the individual.

Disconfirmed

H_{15}: Small decision groups using a majority-vote decision-making rule will make riskier decisions than those groups who simply reach a consensus decision.

H_{16}: Decision groups which have a great degree of psychological flexibility will elicit greater choice-shifts than groups that do not.

H_{17}: Decision groups which have a high political belief score, i. e., are more internationalist, will elicit a higher shift-to-risk than groups that do not.

Summary: Risk-as-a-Value?

Roger Brown, in setting forth his hypothesis on group extremization (though he does not use the term), argues that there is a "Walter Mitty" effect of sorts that compels each individual within the group to be as cautious or as risky as the next person. Brown notes, however, that the direction of the discussion to either risk or caution is largely circumstantial. That is to say that certain scenarios or dilemmas will have a tendency to evoke a risk-oriented response, while others may have the totally opposite effect.[35] While he is no longer adhering to the "risk-as-value" hypothesis, Brown seems to be saying that, depending upon the circumstances either a risky or cautious response will be selected according to the particular set of group norms at hand.

Through this reasoning, the importance of intra-group dynamics diminishes somewhat as a purveyor of extreme choices. Group deliberations serve primarily as a vehicle for identifying others' views on the dilemma-- in other words, to establish the perceived group norm. This is particularly evident from a cursory gleaning of the opening remarks of the transcribed tapes. Invariably, the group would begin its deliberations with one extroverted member querying his colleagues as to where they stood individually. By doing this, group discussions have a tendency to promote conformity and homogeneity. The reduced range of options is achieved, says Brown, by bolstering the perceived group norm with <u>relevant information</u>. In relation to Asch's conformity experiments, he says that:

> the strength of the conformity effect increases as the number of confederates increases only up to a majority of three. Beyond that value, increasing the size of the majority results in no further significant increments in conformity....Three-agreed is, it would appear, the clotting point.[36]

With increased homogeneity, there can result a reduced range of policy options, premature closure, bolstering, and so on, until group decisional polarization is a likely outcome. The group, in short, has further committed the membership in the direction already preferred by most of the members as individuals.

Though the results of this research are not at all incompatible with Roger Brown's proposal, the data suggest that one additional pre-condition for polarization be appended. Given the rather disparate results stemming from the dichotomous sample groups of military and civilian personnel, it is highly probably that the prior norms resulting from secondary socialization processes would lead the Officer and Cadet subjects to be at least as risky as the rest of their colleagues. As Brown himself states with respect to Stoner's original experiments:

> one must argue, therefore, that the value of the role is more salient, more firmly engaged, when the management student is talking with his peers....The student alone would be less concerned to manifest ideal role behavior than would the student in the presence of other students....37

In the case of the more cautious students, it is possible that a different set of socialization experiences led them to seek out less belligerent, hence more cautious, crisis alternatives.

Because very risky or ultra conservative members are not necessarily influential within the group discussion, the intuitively appealing leadership thesis gives way to a more complex, but potentially more rewarding, explanation. It is posited, then, that socialization processes establish individual values which, when socially compared in the context of the small group, arouse relevant arguments which effectively silence dissenting members, increase group solidarity and result in an increased commitment on the part of the group to the dominantly held individual values.

Why should this be so if values are internally engaged? Again, the answer apparently lies in the realm of socialization and the relevant arguments which prop up the engaged value. And second, the "Walter Mitty" effect compels those in the group to be as risky or as cautious as the next fellow depending upon the norms engaged. Roles, particularly in those military sub-samples, seem to enhance this process by "setting the stage" for those relevant norms.

If this conceptualization is accurate, it would be anticipated that the military's counter-part, for example, the political FSOs, would have a tendency to err on the side of caution in such crisis deliberations. Such comparisons, however, await empirical verification.

NOTES

1. See Semmel and Minix (1977:29).

2. De Rivera (1968:150).

3. Lamm (1967).

4. Wallach and Mabli (1970).

5. Kogan and Wallach (1967).

6. Murdoch, *et al*. (1970).

7. See Campbell (1974:15).

8. Because of a mechanical malfunction, one group's tape was lost.

9. See Semmel and Minix (1977:31).

10. De Rivera (1968:149).

11. See Shapiro and Bonham (1973).

12. Janis and Mann (1977:28). See also Leites (1953); Lindbloom (1965); and George (1974).

13. May (1973).

14. Jervis (1975).

15. Janis and Mann (1977:28).

16. May (1973:XI). See also Thomson (1968).

17. George (1974) as cited in Janis and Mann (1977:28).

18. Janis (1972:157).

19. Janis (1972).

20. The "defective decision-making symptoms" are based on Janis (1972), but taken from Janis and Mann (1977:32).

21. See Chapter 3.

22. Brown (1965:679-708).

23. Brown (1965:705). See also Madras and Bem (1968:350-65) and Vinokur (1971:234).

24. Brown (1965:705).

25. Hare (1976:356).

26. Myers and Lamm (1976:611).

27. Myers and Lamm (1976:611-12) provide three reasons which support this finding. In abbreviated form, they are:

    1) group-induced shift appears to be internalized; not a temporary group product;

    2) when the opportunity for combining pre-test decisions according to a decision-rule is eliminated, shift still occurs; and

    3) skewness can not account for group polarization.

28. Pages 68-71 discuss the group polarization phenomena. Particular attention should be given to pages 70-71, which refer to the information-exchange hypothesis as a principal explanation for such group dynamic behavior.

29. Garnham (1974) also uses the California

Psychological Inventory (CPI) to measure rigidity in the beliefs of Foreign Service Officers. He concludes that "Foreign Service psychological flexibility is homogeneous and high and as such, does not explain conservative conformist behavior in the Department of State".

30. Huntington (1959) as quoted in Raser (1966:169).

31. Semmel and Minix (1977:24). See also Raser (1966) and McCloskey (1967).

32. Hare (1976:57).

33. Mennis (1971:168).

34. Myers and Lamm (1976:619).

35. Brown (1965:702-06). Though the literature amply confirms the choice-shift effect, there remains no precise formula for generating either risky or cautious situations.

36. Brown (1965:673).

37. Brown (1965:698).

CHAPTER VIII

CONCLUSION

Introduction

This exploratory study of small group decisional polarization and crisis decision-making has resulted in several interesting and intriguing findings. Like the tangled morass of the early "risky-shift" studies, this work is comparably long on description and somewhat short on explanation. In an attempt to minimize this deficiency, this chapter is designed to amplify upon the analysis provided in Chapter VII and to identify additional avenues of social-psychological research in the area of small group foreign policy decision-making behavior after briefly summarizing the study's major findings.

The Study's Findings: A Compendium

The analysis provided in Chapter VI and VII clearly supports the following contentions:

1) small group decision-making is generally more extreme than individual decision-making;

2) the direction of this group decisional extremization (either to risk or caution) is generally predictable by examining the mean of the individual's pre-test scores;

3) the Officers, and to a lesser extent, the Cadets, generally opted for increased force-related responses to the six international crises while the Student groups, on average, moved in a decidedly different direction toward increased caution; and

4) this effect is believed attributable to the primacy

of group norms which are
further enhanced by the social
dynamics of inter-personal
communication.

Clearly, the type of group membership-- military or civilian-- is a highly significant factor in determining the general direction and tone of a nation's crisis response. Since the military sub-sample (Officers and Cadets combined) enhanced their individual predispositions by further committing themselves in the group context toward greater military action, it is perhaps consistent for the Student groups, who generally lacked this requisite intensity for force-related options, to counterbalance the military sub-sample by moving toward increased caution.

Apparently, the nature of the decision placed in the context of the group's norms significantly determines the type of response a group will adopt. Subjects generally move toward the manipulated norm. Because most political situations-- especially crises-- are typically ambiguous, the influence of other group members on the judgment of another can be substantial.[1] Situations which lack precise referents or historical precedents create a tendency within the person(s) to adopt readily the group's standards or norms in order to cope with the situation's uncertainty. This has the effect of reducing anxiety and psychological conflict. The need for a psychological anchor is great, and the group may provide the requisite interpersonal guidance in coping with the uniqueness and fluidity of the crisis.[2] As a result, the combatting of personal ambiguity tends to increase the spirit of group solidarity or cohesiveness. If "three is a clotting point" as Brown suggests, and given the allegedly operable "Walter Mitty" effect, then it would appear that only a few individuals promoting an emerging or dominant group norm could convince the remainder of the collectivity to adopt a similar posture.

The social influence of the group tends to mold individual behavior through the process of identification. Identification is the process by which one adopts the group perspective because "it puts him in a satisfying self-defining relationship to the person or persons with whom he is identifying" rather than because it is "intrinsically satisfying."[3]

In principle, then, the composition of the foreign policy elite is presumably correlated with the level of response (risky or cautious) issued by a nation. Furthermore, the "who" represents not only the level-of-analysis, individual or small group, but also the _type_ of individual or small group. In the words of several authors:

> The manipulation of the norms present in the individual and group situations enabled us to counteract the forces accounting for increased risk-taking in groups. This suggests that norms play an important role in group decisions and that they may be critical...There is, in a word, social support for the person who exercises caution or takes risks. The support, however, is related to the circumstances involved or specifically to the problem under discussion. The group's discussion of these varied circumstances would seem to allow the discussants to bring information to bear which supports the socially favored norm.[4]

The social support discussed above by Rabow and his associates parallels closely the results obtained by Milgram in his experimental studies of group effects on the obedience to authority.[5] As a variation to his original experimental design, Milgram placed a naive subject in the lab with two "peers" (_i. e._, confederates). The peers (at designated successive shock intervals) refused to comply with the experimenter, thereby leaving the naive subject to shock the victim. In this experiment, 36 of the 40 subjects defied the experimenter (while the corresponding number in the absence of group pressure is 14). As he states, "the effects of peer rebellion are very impressive in undercutting the experimenter's authority."[6] Milgram's research on group conformity/obedience bolsters the notion that an emerging group consensus (demonstrated in this case by the "peers") can successfully convince the remainder of the group (the subject) to adhere to the emerging group consensus by terminating the experiment.

Though there are obvious disparities between the actual crisis deliberations conducted by military and civilian leaders and the participants in these experiments, the intention is only to demonstrate that there are some significant parallels from the laboratory to the real world along the dimensions discussed. Higbee's warnings concerning generalizations that are drawn from experimental data and extended to governmental circles are important. As he suggests, the potential gain and loss in real-world decision-making is real, therefore greater, whereas laboratory studies involve only hypothetical gains and losses. Additionally, the personal involvement of actual decision-makers is greater than the involvement of either volunteer or remunerated subjects. Finally, "the uncertainty of gain or loss in the real world is based on interacting multiple determinants, rather than on a single determinant, such as the role of a die or the choosing of a known probability outcome."[7] Though this experimental design has liabilities that should not be overlooked, neither should they be over-emphasized. Officers, Cadets, and Students acted as surrogates for actual foreign policy decision-makers in modeled crisis situations. They rendered responsible individual and collective decisions in an aura of experimentally contrived uncertainty that provided sufficient evidence to confirm a small group decision-making polarization effect during such critically fluid international crises.

Alternative Small Group Decisional Structures

The shortcomings of small group decision-making have been especially well documented. At the same time, though, analysts have not been willing to accede to the costs of the group decision-making structure by casting it aside. Instead, there have been several alternative organizational techniques which attempt to utilize and promote those valuable group qualities while simultaneously minimizing the costs of collective decision-making. Three alternative decisional structures-- multiple advocacy, the nominal group technique (NGT), and Delphi-- are analyzed with repsect to their applicability in foreign policy decision-making. Later, several prescriptions will be offered as suggestions for improving the quality of the crisis deliberation process.

The System of Multiple Advocacy

One alternative organizational structure which seeks to maximize the efficiencies of group deliberations is the system of multiple advocacy. Multiple advocacy is a system "whereby competition and disagreement among different participants is structured and managed in order to achieve the benefits of diverse points of view."[8] This system, as its name may imply, does not encourage a free play of internal organizational processes and bureaucratic politics. Nor does it allow the chief executive or president to assume simply a passive role in the decision-making process. Rather, it transcends the devil's advocate approach and requires that the chief executive become firmly enmeshed within the decision-making system. According to Alexander George, "multiple advocacy is neither a highly centralized or decentralized system. It is a mixed system which requires executive initiative and centralized coordination of some of the activities of the participants."[9] The premise of this system is to "improve the quality of information search and appraisal and illuminate better the problems the executive must decide and his options for doing so."[10] In short, multiple advocacy is a carfully controlled attempt to bolster the rational considerations of policy and decision-making.

Traditional criticisms of bureaucratic politics center upon the frequently fierce conflict among high level government participants. But as Joseph Bower notes, "conflict can be an important factor motivating constructive thought and analysis."[11] Therefore, under certain conditions, conflict promulgated by bureaucratic tensions can lead to heightened search and analysis. The objective of multiple advocacy, then, is to "indicate how much the policy-making system might be structured and managed so that internal disagreements might contribute to improving the quality of search and evaluation activities associated with the choice of policy."[12]

George and proponents of this type of decisional

system are quick to point out that this decision-making organization is not a panacea for poor policy-making. The system will not function effectively if it finds an uncongenial president who spurns face-to-face combat. Nor is it likely to function well if the senior players are uneducated concerning the functioning of the system or if they are uninterested in its success. Moreover, the system of multiple advocacy is a time consuming process-- a high cost item to be seriously considered in periods of crisis. In short, multiple advocacy is an imperfect attempt to bridge the benefits of collective decision-making with some additional safeguards for more productive information searches and analyses.

There are few perfect applications of the system of multiple advocacy in the foreign policy formation of the United States. Wilfrid Kohl, though, cites the definition of the Presidential National Security Advisor that McGeorge Bundy brought to his job early in the Kennedy Administration as approaching the neutral custodial concept of multiple advocacy.[13]

Nominal Group Technique

Another technique for improving the quality of information generation and processing by small groups is the nominal group technique (NGT). The proponents of this technique, Andre Delbecq and his colleagues, promote NGT as a process that involves judgmental or creative decision-making like that associated with crises-- as well as most decisional activity in general. NGT is not concerned with "routine" decisions like negotiation or bargaining. The three objectives of the nominal group technique are:

1) To assure different processes for each phase of creativity;
2) To balance participation among members; and
3) To incorporate mathematical voting techniques in the aggregation of group judgment.[14]

The processes by which these objectives are fulfilled are unique in comparison with the previously discussed technique of multiple advocacy. Instead of using conflict as a catalyst in enhancing group decision-making, NGT attempts to minimize verbal communication among participants by requiring that they silently generate ideas in writing. Next, there is "round robin" feedback from the group to record each idea in a terse phrase. Phase three involves discussion of each recorded idea for clarification and evaluation. Finally, group members vote on the priority of ideas with group decision-making being mathematically calculated through ranking or rating.[15]

Nominal groups, who adopt the processes just described, are allegedly better than interactive groups (e. g., multiple advocacy) in generating relevant information to a problem. Interactive groups, it is believed, tend to inhibit creative thinking because of the "give and take" among group members which frequently leads to conflict. But, for other purposes, such as attitude change, team building, and consensus generation, interactive groups are believed superior.[16]

The obvious gravamen with the NGT (in terms of its applicability to crisis decision-making) lies in its rigidity. Seldom, if ever, are critical policy-making deliberations conducted under an aura of simple majority-rule decision-making that deletes the saliency of political leadership. Moreover, it is doubtful that this technique could function effectively at the very highest levels of government because of the inherent pulling and hauling of senior administrative officials who have parochial/bureaucratic interests to defend and who must operate under severe pressures due to the stress of international crises. Undoubtedly, these constraints contribute to the fact that this alternative small group technique has not been employed by high-level policy-makers.

Delphi

Other techniques of decision-making seek to eliminate the dynamics (and hazards) of small group interaction altogether. One such technique is Delphi. While decision-making can be bifurcated into two critical phases, fact-finding and evaluation, Delphi is concerned principally with the latter. Delphi, developed by Olaf Helmer and Norman Dalkey at the

Rand Corporation in the late 1940's, systematically seeks to "elicit, combine, and improve opinions from a group of experts on a given subject."[17] Its salient points are:

> 1) formulation of the problem under investigation in quantitative terms;
>
> 2) interrogation of a diverse group of experts individually by questionnaire or interview, and presentation of the results anonymously; and
>
> 3) controlled iteration of the procedure, in which the aggregated results are presented statistically (usually) stressing the median and inter-quartile range) and participants are allowed to refine or justify their opinions.[18]

Like NGT, however, Delphi creates several disadvantages to decision-making during crises. Face-to-face contact under this method is eliminated; consequently, tensions and intra-group conflict are reduced, but the absence of such conflict also retards creative suggestion-making. This technique is highly sensitive to the administrator of the program who, because of his unaccountability, may engender numerous misperceptions which may go undetected. Delphi is used most successfully as a forecasting technique. Its utility as a reactive decision-making process to a crisis is altogether questionable. Because of these qualities, Delphi is a principal tool for government agencies involved in long-range forecasting. Like the Nominal Group Technique, Delphi has seldom, if ever, been applied by top-level executives in the resolution of a crisis.

Some Prescriptions

Despite the universality of the group decision-making technique in political (especially crisis) situations, several potential pitfalls are frequently cited by both the organizers and the participants of such groups. For example, there have been claims of:

1) Personality effects-- where strong, dominant personalities move the discussion toward their preferred goal or position;

2) Bandwagon effects-- a striving for consensus by group members;

3) Dissonance effects-- the discussion of irrelevant and tangential points;

4) Productivity-- high on manual tasks; somewhat lower on intellectual tasks; and

5) Information and Recall-- fewer, but more accurate facts-- generally better recall because of better "storage."

Given these potential weaknesses though, most crisis decisions are consummated by small groups of individuals because the complexity inherent in the situation requires diverse specializations and considerable expertise to initiate policy options. If, for example, the U.S. were faced with formulating a national response to a crisis involving the Soviet Union, several factors such as Soviet history, economics, political-military structure, cognitive structures of leadership, inter alia, must be evaluated and considered. Seldom is there a single individual with the necessary depth and breadth to encompass these as well as other factors. Consequently, the executive charged with promulgating a response to the crisis will undoubtedly engage colleagues both inside and outside of government to produce the nation's response. The task for the organizer or convenor of such generally ad hoc groups is to combine collectively the individuals' talents so as to insure maximum productivity and creativity without loss of effort and time. In order to guard against these potential pitfalls or pathologies of group information processing, Professors Janis, George and Hermann, among others, have suggested several tentative prescriptions aimed at promoting efficiency and quality in deliberations where any group of executives meet with their chief executive.[19]

Janis identifies the central paradox in effective group information processing when he states that: 1) groups must have a high degree of like-mindedness and mutual respect; and 2) group members must forego trying to score points in a power struggle or to obtain ego gratification by defeating rivals.[20] Implicit in this is the need for cohesion. But, cohesion, or rather excessive cohesion, is the core ingredient in Janis' identified decision-making pathology called groupthink. Therefore, the dilemma is how to foster cohesion without inadvertently promoting conformity, premature closure, and other attendant symptoms. To guard against this collective decision-making malaise, several prescriptions, of sorts, are offered. Though this list is drawn largely from Professor Janis' volume, <u>Victims of Groupthink</u>, these suggestions pertaining to enhanced group performance are a synthesis from the scholarly literature encompassing small group decision-making.[21]

1. The chief executive of the policy deliberating group should appoint a <u>critical evaluator</u> who encourages the group to express freely their doubts and misgivings about the recommendations discussed. The chief executive must reinforce this point by showing that he can accept criticism and be persuaded by it. However, protracted debates-- especially during crises-- are particularly costly. Criticism, too, must be "diplomatic" or it will otherwise be labelled as a personal attack upon the individual. "Feelings of rejection, depression, and anger might be evoked so often when this role assignment is put into practice that it could have a corrosive effect on morale and working relations within the group."[22]

2. Those charged with organizing such <u>ad hoc</u> policy planning groups should exercise great caution in protecting their <u>impartiality</u> regarding the scope of the problem and the proposals that he should like to see adopted. The practice obviously has the advantage of not giving the group a built-in norm or position from which to begin deliberating. One of the perceived benefits of group discussions rests in the group's ability to generate more, and better ideas to the problem. This should not be undermined.

"Among the hazards, however, is a potential cleavage between the leader and the members, which could become a disruptive power struggle if the chief executive regards the merging consensus among the members as an anathema to him."[23]

3. *Parallel groups* should be established to work independently on the same problem. These groups should be conducting their deliberations under different leadership. The advantage of this proposal is to generate new initiations within the policy-proposing apparatus. However, in the security conscious environment accompanying crisis decision-making, this proposal may be too costly in time, efficiency, morale, and security. And, multiple groups may engender yet another collective decision-making malaise-- bureaucratic politicking-- which is a virulent offspring of groupthink. Safeguards, such as delineating the roles and responsibilities of each group, would be essential. Finding politically disinterested group leaders whose only goal is to bring forth a sound recommendation to the crisis, is a highly probabilistic, though necessary, goal if this proposal is to be effective.

4. The chief executive should periodically divide the primary policy-making group into two or more *sub-units* who meet under different chairmen. This recommendation assumes that further dividing the primary group into smaller units will decrease the possibility of concurrence-seeking behavior and will give an opportunity for a critical evaluation of policy alternatives before the final judgment is reached by the larger group. This recommendation was utilized in 1962 by the EXCOM during the Cuban missile crisis and, as Janis states, "it appears to have contributed to the effectiveness of that group's critical appraisals."[24]

5. Members of the group should engage in *interpersonal discussion* with close associates of the member's own bureaucratic organization, political party, etc. Also, the advice and counsel of these outside confidants should be reported back to the policy planning group should the advice run contrary to the emerging group norm. Again, it is assumed that the farther the security net is cast (with the same amount of security and secrecy as before), the more limited the number of participants. This

assumption is a tenuous one, but the potential pay-
offs regarding the blockage of foreign policy fiascos
are worth considering. Could, for example, the
Bay of Pigs fiasco have been averted if McNamara
or Rusk had asked for advice and counsel from the
Defense or State Departments? Chester Bowles expressed
shock and dismay over the planned invasion to Secretary
Rusk, but Rusk did not allow Bowles' memorandum
to be shown to Kennedy or anyone else. Would Rusk
or anyone else be less likely to assume the role
of a mind guard if he were to encounter stiff opposition
within his respective bureaucracy?

    6. The chief executive should import into
the group, on a rotating basis, disinterested but
trustworthy associates who can function as __anti-
mind guards__ for the group. Ideally, these individuals
would be able to catch quickly hidden flaws in logic
and judgment, be able to transmit criticisms judicious-
ly, and most importantly, be a quick study to the
issues and complexities outside the normal focus
of their duties. Janis also suggests that:

    A) Visitors who are likely to
raise debate-worthy objections
should be invited long before
a consensus has been reached,
not after most of the core
members have made up their
minds as was the case when
Senator Fulbright was invited
to participate in the Bay
of Pigs deliberations.

    B) Second, each visitor should
be asked to speak out about
his qualms and not brood
silently, as Bowles felt
constrained to do when he
attended a Bay of Pigs planning
session; and

    C) Third, after the visitor
speaks his piece, the chairman
should call for open discussion
of his objectives instead
of moving on to other business,
as President Kennedy did
after Senator Fulbright

gave his rousing speech at
the final planning session
about the undesirable political
and moral consequences of
the Bay of Pigs invasion
plan.[25]

7. The chairman should assign the role of a <u>devil's advocate</u> to one or two group members. Whenever it is impossible or unfeasible to assign the role of a critical evaluator to someone in the group (prescription 1), then the use of a devil's advocate may be pursued as a fallback position. However, there are some potential drawbacks to this recommendation despite the seemingly inherent logicality of it. President Johnson, it will be recalled, had an institutionalized devil's advocate in George Ball. But, Ball's dissent over Vietnam policy was permitted only within the accepted parameters established by Johnson and his inner-council. George Reedy, Johnson's press secretary, recalls that "(the official devil's advocate's) objections and cautions are discounted before they are delivered. They are actually welcomed because they prove for the record that decision was preceded by controversy."[26] Alexander George cautions that the ritualized use of a devil's advocate may engender a false sense of security to the group because of the sense that all sides of an issue have been seriously and impartially considered.[27]

8. The group should <u>survey all warning signals from adversarial governments</u> and organizations and construct alternative scenarios of the rival's intentions. This suggestion will hopefully combat complacency and a shared illusion of invulnerability that may be present if the group ignores various danger signals from the environment. Also, the group should select a special sub-committee or utilize existing security structures in re-writing and re-analyzing "canned" scenarios. The rationale here is to avoid the decision maxim: "do what we (they) did last time...." Historical analogizing has a place in foreign policy decision-making, but all too often it is relegated to a position of primacy in determining a nation's response to an international crisis. Decision-makers, under the extreme stress of a crisis, are likely to see a high degree of isomorphism or "fit" between past national victories (or defeats)

and the current crisis at hand.

9. After a preliminary choice, the group should hold a "<u>second chance meeting</u> in which all members express residual doubts and frustrations. This "second chance," or perhaps "last chance," meeting is designed to "prevent premature consensus based on unwarranted expectations or invulnerability, stereotypes about the enemy, and other unexamined assumptions shared by members of the group...."[28] In sum, this session should be a virtual free-for-all in attempting to dislodge any lingering doubts, frustrations, and misgivings about the future of the policy proposed.

If the phenomena of decisional extremization and groupthink are to be avoided, then these suggestions as gleaned from Professor Janis and others are worth considering. Even more than that, they are worthy of the classification of hypotheses which await empirical verification. It is worth reiterating, though, that even if these so-called decisional safeguards were enacted, there is the possibility of producing low quality decisions which result in foreign policy fiascos. Decisional quality, again, refers to the <u>process</u> of deliberation; by ferreting out poor <u>decisional</u> procedures, the likelihood is greater that the quality of foreign policy outputs will be greater.

Further Research Goals

With the results obtained from this experimental study, a series of comparative experiments (using the same CDQ's and crisis responses) should be undertaken to determine if higher educational levels and different ranks within the Officer corps would yield a similar set of results. The reader will recall that the Officer groups used in this experiment were composed of Captains and senior First Lieutenants-- most of whom had obtained a Bachelor's degree and many of whom had some field or combat experience (generally in Vietnam). However, it is unclear whether the polarization toward risk would have occurred if senior Officers (from the level of Major on up) had participated in the same deliberation along with lower ranking or junior officers. Given the generally higher levels of education and varied position assignments of the former group, it is worth pondering whether their individual and group responses would have been any different.

The same is true for the civilian segment of the sample. Would political Foreign Service Officers from the Department of State respond in a similar vein as the college students? What would be the impact of higher educational levels as well as varied work-related experiences in the State Department on individual and group choices to a series of foreign policy crises?

Bernard Mennis' research, for example, concludes that there are attitudinal differences between political FSO's and their political counterparts in the Department of Defense. Political-military officers tend to be more hard-line, more bellicose, in their attitudes compared to their State Department colleagues.[29] Would this translate, though, into an intensification of bellicosity for a small group of political-military officers? Concomittantly, if political FSO's are less hard-line, would a homogeneous grouping of these officers further polarize in this same preferred direction? Research is unavailable in which to answer these questions, but there is experimental evidence available which suggests that political beliefs and behavior are linked. Daniel Lutzker, for example, conducted a series of experiments in which the general hypothesis was whether "performance in an experimental situation in which both cooperation and competition were possible could be predicted on the basis of the subject's views regarding international cooperation. It was predicted that the subjects who were internationally oriented would tend to be cooperative, where isolationists would tend to be competitive."[30] Lutzker reports that "a scale of political opinions can be used to predict behavior in a decision-making situation....Evidence (was) presented...to show that internationalists differ from isolationists in at least two important ways: 1) they are more cooperative, and 2) they are more reluctant to abandon efforts at cooperation."[31]

Most importantly, however, what would a mix of these upper eschelon personnel produce? These experiments were conducted within the "homogeneous" sub-samples with no mixing of Officers - Cadets - Students in the small groups. However, in most crisis-deliberating groups, there is a mix of civilian, governmental, and military personnel who participate in these deliberations. Given the norm-based explanation of this study, what would be the result of the supposed clash of several different norms? Mennis is apparently accurate when he says that "if beliefs and behavior in fact are significantly correlated, then our findings suggest that the organizational composition of foreign policy 'decisional units' that include military officers and FSOs must be taken into consideration when the behavioral outcomes of such interactions are examined."[32]

Each of these sample variations would tend to effect the external validity of the experimental results. In addition to these experimental variations, several technical devices should be implemented to test for the emergent norm explanation. For example, all experimental groups should be videotaped and their conversations and mannersims analyzed to test for this anticipated norm effect. Since only two of the Choice Dilemma Questionnaires dealt with non-communist adversaries (Panama and the Hague Guerrilla scenarios), several other crises dealing with the disruption of the international system from a non-military strategic perspective should be devised to determine whether force-related (military) options would be induced. Would, for example, an attack by several of the "frontline" African states on South Africa yield a more "risky" or more "cautious" decision? These are but a few of the additional research projects that are necessary in empirically attempting to resolve this complex and intertwined phenomenon of small group decisional polarization.

Social-Psychology and International Relations:
The Question of Relevance

In Chapter I, the question was posed: can international politics/foreign policy be fruitfully studied from a social-psychological perspective? The answer would be a qualified "yes." International politics in its broadest sense can be studied social-psychologically because such a focus can highlight the necessary concepts and methods for the intricate study of the processes that are central to such inter-personal dynamics as decision-making and negotiations. However, qualifications arise when analysts assume that the social-psychological focus is the focus or the sole focus for studying such political phenomena. There are, indeed, multiple productive avenues and alternative methodologies available for research. The social-psychological level-of-analysis is but one. The nature of the question to be probed and explored remains the most important determinant in the selection of a theoretical perspective.

To study those individuals and organizations which participate in the decision-making processes of government requires the analyst to confront the dilemma of accessibility. Participation or observation of important government deliberations is rarely obtained, hence the problem of access is one reason for turning to an experimentally-based social-psychological focus in the area of decision-making and negotiations. By assuming that the same dynamics can be studied at a lower or more available level, studies can be conducted which may yield valuable insights to supplement those observations made from direct observations.[33] Methods such as the observation of labor management negotiations, mathematical gaming of inter-personal and inter-group relations (e.g., the Prisoner's Dilemma matrix), simulation (e.g., Harold Guetzkow's Inter-nation Simulation), and experimentation are salient examples of the possible methods available to investigate higher level, inaccessible phenomena. The method of experimentation, for example, provides increased accessibility, an environment in which to study the interaction of prime variables, a data base from which to predict likely behaviors and suggest additional hypotheses, and perhaps most importantly, a means for controlling the effects of extraneous factors on the phenomena being measured.

The major criticism of such a technique arises from the question of external validity. Can the results obtained experimentally from the laboratory be generalized to the real world setting of political decision-makers? No firm answer can be given. An experiment is constructed, however, to test the effects of one or more variables on a certain outcome or process. Consequently, total isomorphism with the real-world structure or process being studied is not needed. As Verba points out, "the experimental model does not need to 'look like' the real world.

What is important is the question of whether it *operates like the real-world in the respects that are relevant to the study at hand.*"[34]

Experimentation, then, is not a panacea. As Kelman notes, "there is no laboratory situation that can have universal validity."[35] This technique has several potential pay-offs besides those already described. "Relationships observed in experimental studies can cut into commonly held assumptions about international relations by demonstrating the *possibility of the impossible and the questionableness of the obvious.*"[36] The question investigated by this study, the so-called "choice-shift," is an example of using experimentation to dislodge firmly held convictions concerning interpersonal group dynamics and their propensity to elect risky or cautious decisions.

Given the many published accounts of the choice-shift effect, additional research on group decisional polarization in small foreign policy-making groups needs to be continued by those analysts who believe that much of the variance in a nation's behavior can be explained by a social-psychological framework. It is anticipated that this exploratory experimental study will contribute to the literature used by those analysts and to the level of understanding among those who share or do not share this analytic perspective on foreign policy and international politics.

NOTES

1. Hare (1976:25).

2. Freedman and Freedman (1975:90) state that several factors influence the degree of control a group maintains over an individual. These include: the person's affinity for the group or members of the group; the number of persons taking a specific stand within the group; one's expectations regarding future interaction with the group; trust in the group's expertise and prestige; the necessity of making a public rather than a private commitment; the penalties and sanctions used against non-conformists; the explicitness of the group's expectations; and the nature of the individual's motives, personalities,

and goals.

3. Freedman and Freedman (1975:90). Like the Freedmans, Janis and Smith (Kelman, 1965:201) cite several factors which predict members' adherence to group norms. They are: 1) affection, friendship, and other positive ties toward the group's leaders and fellow members; 2) a desire for prestige and self-esteem; 3) a desire to escape from social isolation; and 4) restraints that act to keep the person within the group regardless of his desires in the matter. These analysts contend that the first two affective motives are the strongest factors in contributing to one's internalization of the group's norms "so that they are maintained even in the absence of external sanctions." Thus, the internalization can be regarded as a case of identification.

4. Rabow, et al. (1966:25).

5. Milgram (1974).

6. Milgram (1974:118).

7. Higbee (1972:55).

8. George (1975:95). For a full treatment of this system, see George (1972).

9. George (1975:95).

10. George (1975:95).

11. Bower (1965) as in George (1972:758).

12. George (1972:758). George (1975:95-96) posits three conditions for this system to work effectively. In abbreviated form, they are:

    A. No major maldistribution among the various actors in the policy-making system of the following intellectual and bureaucratic resources:

        Intellectual resources:

        1. Competence relevant to the policy issues.
        2. Information relevant to the

        policy issues.
     3. Analytic support (e. g., staff,
        technical skills).

   Bureaucratic resources:

     1. Status, power, and standing
        with the president.
     2. Persuasion and bargaining
        skills.

  B. Presidential-level participation in order
     to monitor and regulate the workings of
     multiple advocacy.

  C. Time for adequate debate and give-and-take.

13. Kohl (1974:2). Kohl says, however, that there were important exceptions to Bundy's initial self-conceived role as National Security Advisor when Bundy himself became a Vietnam policy advocate.

14. Delbecq, et al. (1975:9).

15. Delbecq, et al. (1975:8).

16. See Delbecq, et al. (1975:17).

17. Schweitzer (1977:4).

18. The author appreciates Nicholas Schweitzer's and the Central Intelligence Agency's permission to quote the above references to the Delphi technique.

19. Janis (1972); Janis and Mann (1977); George (1972; 1975); Hermann and Hermann (1975).

20. Janis (1972:207).

21. Janis offers his list only as tentative suggestions, for most, if not all, of these points are, in fact, untested hypotheses. See Janis (1972:209-24). Also, see Janis and Mann (1977), George (1972; 1975) and Hermann and Hermann (1975).

22. Janis (1972:210).

23. Janis (1972:211).

24. Janis (1972:213).

25. Janis (1972:214).

26. Janis (1972:215).

27. Janis (1972:215).

28. Janis (1972:218).

29. Mennis (1971:180).

30. Lutzker (1960:429-30).

31. Lutzker (1960:429-30). It should be noted that Lutzker's operationalization of the concepts isolationism and internationalism are not synonymous with this analyst's operationalization of the same concepts in Chapters V and VII.

32. Mennis (1971:185).

33. Kelman (1965:595).

34. Verba (1964:502).

35. Kelman (1965:599).

36. Kelman (1965:600).

APPENDIX A

Scenarios

Questionnaire

APPENDIX A

The following is the scenario format used in the test and re-test packets. The question at the bottom of each scenario was deleted in the group or re-test packet. Note, also, that the directions and options are not included for scenarios II-VI in the Appendix, but were included in the test and re-test packets.

Situation I

The Persian Gulf, the heartline of the western world's oil supply, is connected to the Indian Ocean by the tiny stretch of water known as the Strait of Hormuz. The Soviet Union, which is the most prominent naval power in the area, has decided to block the Strait and deprive the western world of its vital energy source. As a member of the National Security Council, your recommendation to the President would be to:

A number of alternatives for action have been made. Some are more decisive and involve more risk to the U.S., but are also more likely to bring about the desired outcome. If necessary, how far down the list of options below would you be willing to go in order to protect the interests of the United States?

Note that the alternatives are listed in the order of the extremity of the action involved. The first item is the least extreme and the last the most extreme. CHECK ONLY ONE ITEM!

1. ___ Engage in bilateral negotiations or talks with the adversary to settle the crisis.

2. ___ Call a meeting or special session of the United Nations Security Council.

3. ___ Support (non-militarily) opposition elements in the area or nation in which the national interest and security of the U.S. is threatened.

4. ___ Discontinue diplomatic relations with the adversary and attempt to sway world public opinion to the side of the U.S.

5. ___ Create economic turmoil in adversary's country to substantially weaken his war effort.

6. ___ Send military <u>advisors</u> to the area that is threatening the U.S. interests and security. These are non-combatant personnel only.

7. ___ Establish a military or naval blockade of adversary's country.

8. ___ Use conventional ground forces to repel adversary's threat.

9. ___ Engage in limited <u>strategic</u> bombing of non-civilian, military cites only.

10. ___ Use the nuclear capability of the U.S. to eliminate the possibility of many American deaths and to bring the adversary to the point of negotiation.

What option do you think most officers at or above your rank would be likely to recommend? (#___).

Situation II

A U.S. reconnaissance aircraft recently strayed over the sovereign airspace of Cambodia. The plane was shot down with a Soviet made surface-to-air missile and its highly secret, sophisticated technology and its two man crew captured. Now, the government of Cambodia has secretly demanded that the U.S. commit itself to a $10 billion economic aid program over the next five years or risk the execution of the U.S. airmen as spies and the transfer of the secret aerial technology to the Soviet Union or China. As a member of the National Security Council, what is your recommendation to the President?

Situation III

Three days ago, an ally of the United States-- South Korea-- thrust across the fortified border separating itself from North Korea. At the time, South Korea said that its military action was begun to prevent an attack from the North Koreans. This morning, it was learned that nearly 90,000 South Korean regulars have been encircled just north of the border. Included among the South Korean army are 200 U.S. military observers who followed the northward incursion. If the South Korean army is wiped out or forced to surrender, it would leave open a gap through which the North Koreans could push southward and threaten the safety of some 50,000 U.S. nationals in South Korea. As a member of the National Security Council what is your recommendation to the President?

Situation IV

The Strategic Arms Limitation Talks (SALT) between the Soviet Union and The United States have attempted to produce an acceptable balance in the number, size and capacity of missiles and bombers of the two countries. Such an agreement is based on the belief that both sides will abide by its provisions. If, upon learning of drastic violations by the Soviets of this agreement, what would your National Security Council recommendation to the President be?

Situation V

The Panamanian Navy has detained and forcibly boarded a United States cruiser at the entrance to the Panama Canal. Its action has stalled all commercial

and military traffic trhough the canal.
Moreover, the Panamanian Government
is holding the cruiser as "hostage"
in order to compel the U.S. to yield
to its demands for immediate nationalization of the Canal Zone. As a
member of the National Security Council,
your recommendation to the President
would be:

Situation VI

The U.S. Embassy in the Hague, Netherlands,
has been seized since early this morning
by a militant faction of Arab nationalists who are a splinter group
of a Chinese communist-supported organization that is headquartered in Damascus,
Syria. Since the occupation, the
guerrillas have killed four and wounded
two in a violent attempt to establish
their credibility. The U.S. Amabassador
to the Netherlands is also a captive,
but before his release, the guerrillas
are demanding $10 million in cash,
$3 million in medical supplies, and
a safe exit out of the country via
a Swiss airliner. AS a member of
the National Security Council, what
is your recommendation to the President?

APPENDIX A

Your number _____

Group number _____

    This questionnaire is designed to elicit information about the foreign policy exercise you just participated in. Feel free to be off the record. If you need more space, use the back of this sheet or attach another sheet.

1. What factor(s) in your opinion led the group to decide on the options it did?

2. Describe the decision-making process used by your group (*e. g.*, majority-rule; unanimity; averaging; coin-flips; bargaining, etc.

3. a) How much "outside or new knowledge" was brought up during the group discussion?

    b) Describe the contents of this "outside or new or new knowledge" in general terms.

    c) Did it, in any way, influence your final decision? How?

4. Did everyone in the group participate equally?
   _____Yes; _____No
   If not, briefly explain.

5. Was there anyone in your group that you perceived as a "leader?" _____Yes; _____No

Did his behavior influence the group's final decision? _____Yes; _____No

Explain how.

6. Overall, how satisfied were you in your group's final decisions?

   1. Very satisfied
   2. Satisfied
   3. Neutral
   4. Not Satisfied
   5. Very Unsatisfied

7. How cohesive was your group?

   1. Very Cohesive
   2. Cohesive
   3. Mixed
   4. Not Cohesive
   5. Very Non-Cohesive

8. How would you describe your feelings toward all other members of your group?

   1. Very Favorable
   2. Favorable
   3. Neutral
   4. Unfavorable
   5. Very Unfavorable

   Explain.

9. a) How did your group deal with disagreements over option selection?

   b) Was this accomplished by any tension in the group?

10. Did you find the scenarios credible?

Comments: Please feel free to append any comments you would like to make.

APPENDIX B

Figures A - G

Table VI-5

FIGURE A
COMPARATIVE PRE-TEST RESPONSES OF SUB-SAMPLES ACROSS DILEMMAS

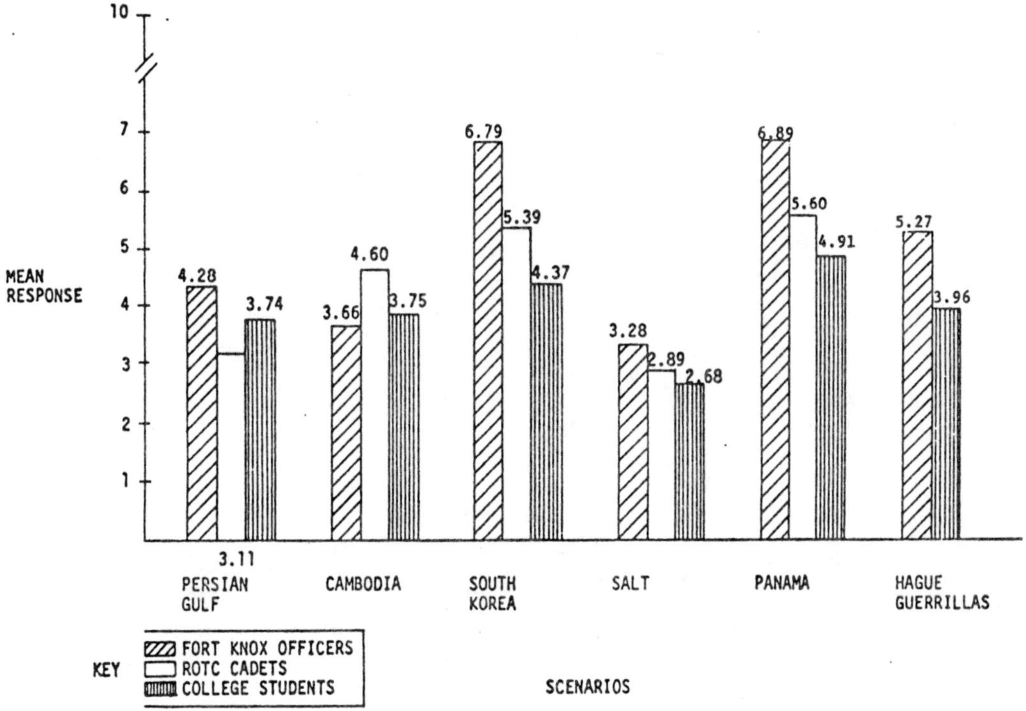

FIGURE B

COMPARATIVE POST-TEST RESPONSES OF SUB-SAMPLES ACROSS DILEMMAS

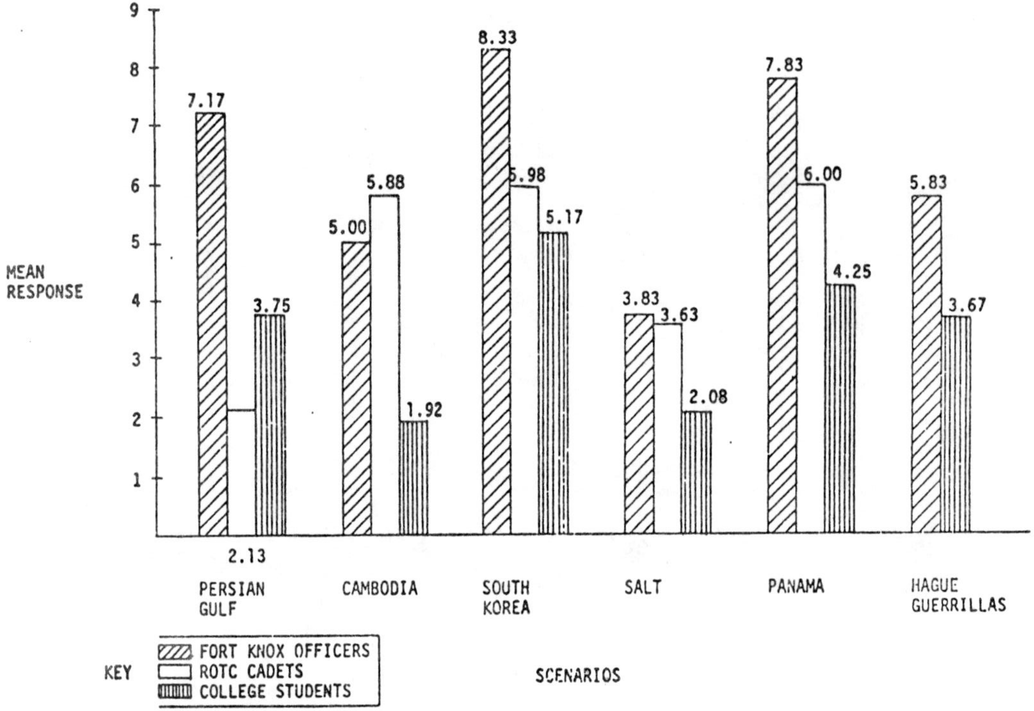

SCENARIO	FORT KNOX OFFICERS	ROTC CADETS	COLLEGE STUDENTS
PERSIAN GULF	7.17	2.13	3.75
CAMBODIA	5.00	5.88	1.92
SOUTH KOREA	8.33	5.98	5.17
SALT	3.83	3.63	2.08
PANAMA	7.83	6.00	4.25
HAGUE GUERRILLAS	5.83		3.67

190

FIGURE C

COMPARATIVE DECISION "SHIFT" SCORES FOR SUB-SAMPLES ACROSS DILEMMAS

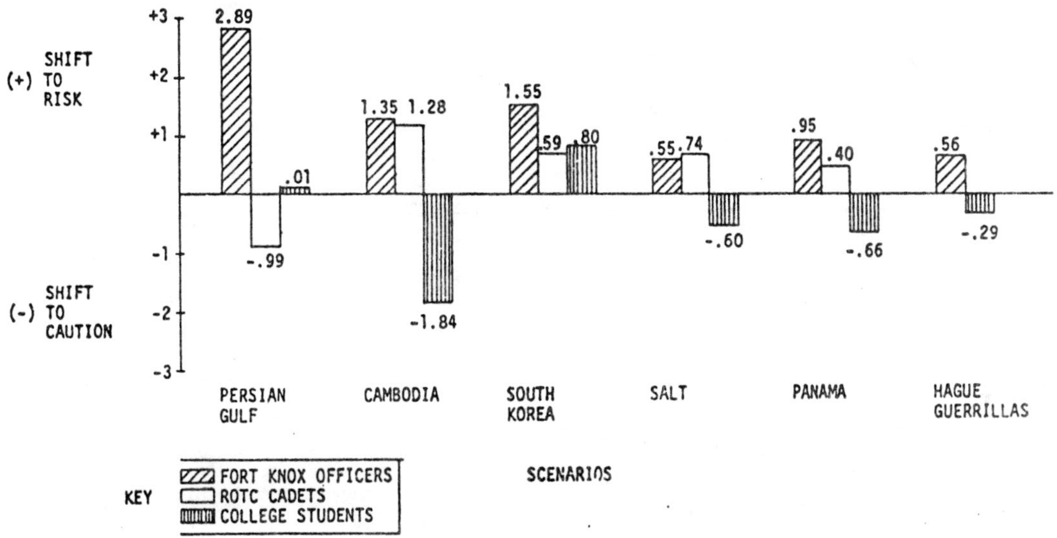

FIGURE E

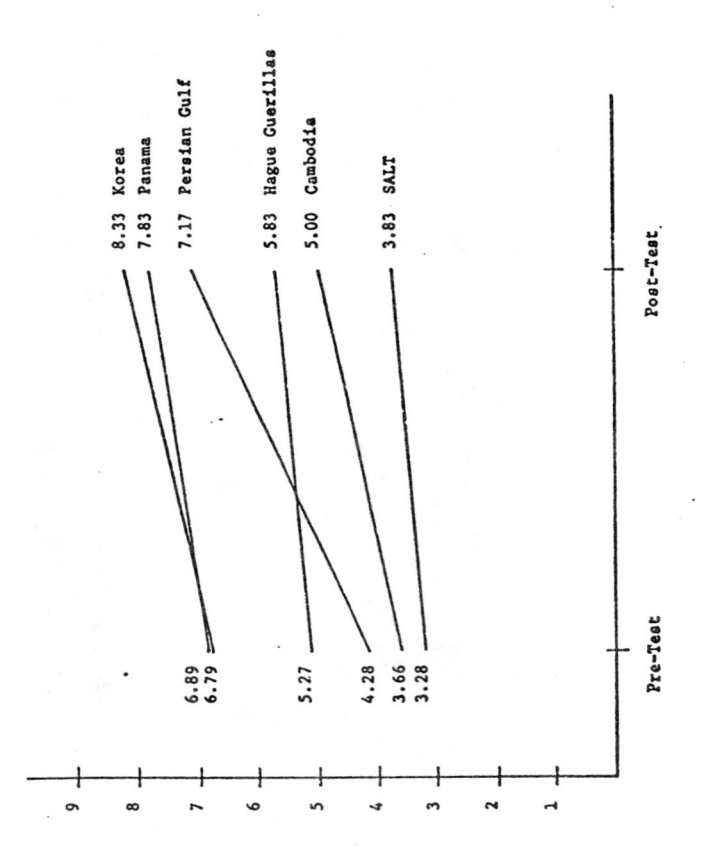

9		
8		8.33 Korea
		7.83 Panama
7	6.89	7.17 Persian Gulf
	6.79	
6		5.83 Hague Guerillas
5	5.27	5.00 Cambodia
4	4.28	3.83 SALT
3	3.66	
	3.28	
2		
1		

Pre-Test   Post-Test

OFFICERS

FIGURE F

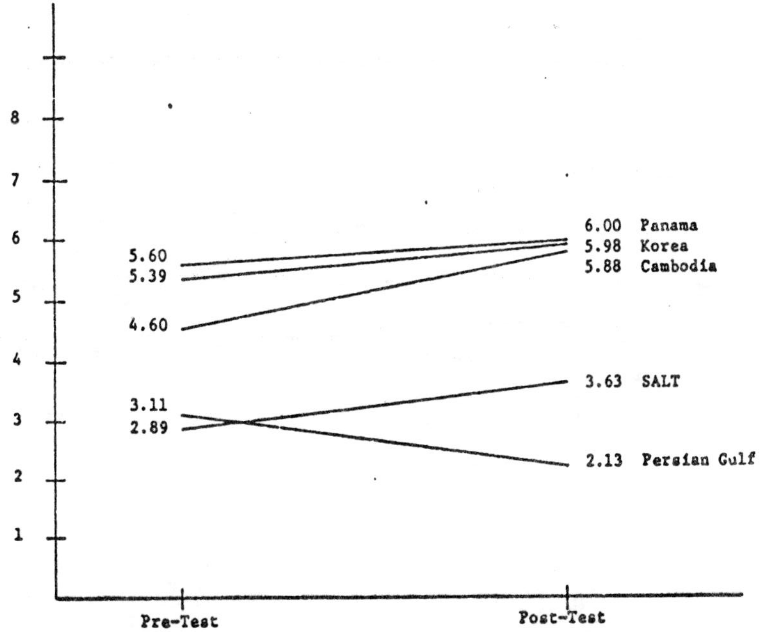

```
8 -|
7 -|
6 -|        6.00 Panama
    5.60    5.98 Korea
    5.39    5.88 Cambodia
5 -|
    4.60
4 -|
            3.63 SALT
3 -| 3.11
    2.89
            2.13 Persian Gulf
2 -|
1 -|
    Pre-Test         Post-Test
```

ROTC Cadets

FIGURE G

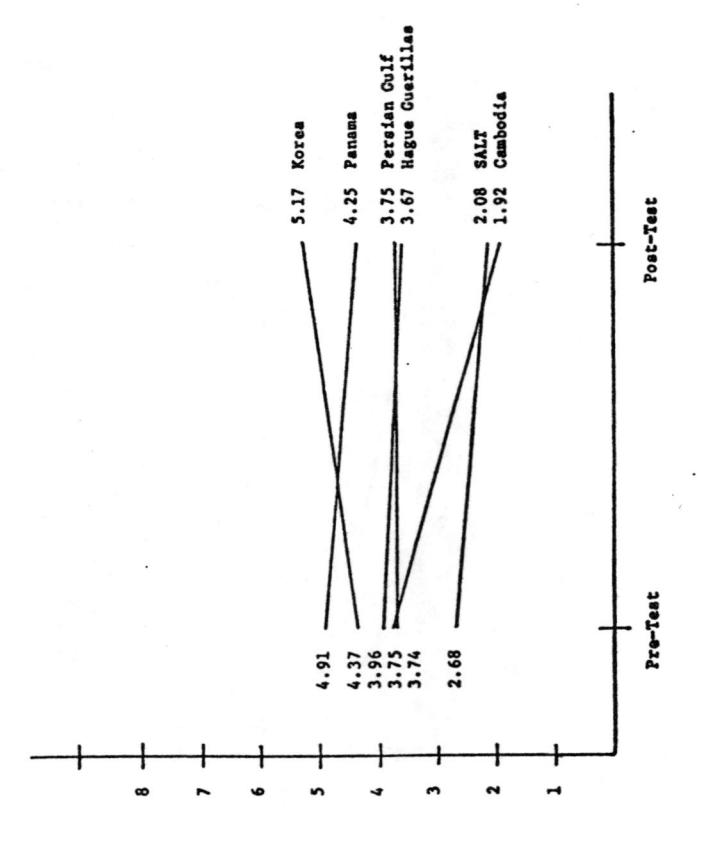

Pre-Test — Post-Test

Pre-Test	Post-Test
4.91	5.17 Korea
4.37	4.25 Panama
3.96	3.75 Persian Gulf
3.75	3.67 Hague Guerillas
3.74	
2.68	2.08 SALT
	1.92 Cambodia

STUDENTS

TABLE VI-6

Cross Tabulation of Pre-Test Means by Post-Test Scores Per Group Per Scenario

*Pre-Test Means

	Low (Diplomacy)	High (Military)	
Post-Test Scores Lower (Diplomacy)	Students - 32 ROTC - 12 Officers - 6 Σ = 50	Students - 9 ROTC - 4 Officers - 4 Σ = 17	67
Higher (Military)	Students - 16 ROTC - 10 Officers - 6 Σ = 32	Students - 15 ROTC - 12 Officers - 19 Σ = 46	89
	82	63	145 = N

$\chi^2 = 16.56$, 1df, $p < .05$

Yule's Q = .62

*Breakpoint: ≥ 4.5 = Military Options
             < 4.5 = Diplomatic Options

**Three groups had identical pre-test and post-test scores; consequently the original N of 148 is reduced to 145.

STUDENT GROUPS (cont.)	Persian Gulf	Cambodia	Korea	SALT	Panama	Hague Guerillas
15	GR = 4 IND.X = 4.6 Δ = -.6	GR = 2 IND.X = 4.5 Δ = -2.5	GR = 8 IND.X = 6.6 Δ = 1.4	GR = 2 IND.X = 2.8 Δ = -.8	GR = 8 IND.X = 7.6 Δ = .4	GR = 6 IND.X = 5.2 Δ = .8
22	GR = 7 IND.X = 5.75 Δ = 1.25	GR = 1 IND.X = 2.75 Δ = -1.75	GR = 2 IND.X = 1.75 Δ = .25	GR = 1 IND.X = 2.25 Δ = -1.25	GR = 7 IND.X = 5.5 Δ = 1.5	GR = 1 IND.X = 2.75 Δ = -1.75
23	GR = 5 IND.X = 3.0 Δ = 2.0	GR = 1 IND.X = 4.25 Δ = -3.25	GR = 2 IND.X = 1.5 Δ = .5	GR = 5 IND.X = 4.25 Δ = .75	GR = 7 IND.X = 6.0 Δ = 1.0	GR = 3 IND.X = 3.5 Δ = -.5
24	GR = 1 IND.X = 2.2 Δ = -1.2	GR = 1 IND.X = 5.8 Δ = -4.8	GR = 3 IND.X = 3.2 Δ = -.2	GR = 2 IND.X = 2.6 Δ = -.6	GR = 1 IND.X = 3.4 Δ = -2.4	GR = 8 IND.X = 3.6 Δ = 4.4
25	GR = 5 IND.X = 4.2 Δ = .8	GR = 1 IND.X = 3.2 Δ = -2.2	GR = 7 IND.X = 5.2 Δ = 1.8	GR = 1 IND.X = 4.2 Δ = -3.2	GR = 6 IND.X = 4.2 Δ = 1.8	GR = 1 IND.X = 3.8 Δ = -2.8
26	GR = 2 IND.X = 6.5 Δ = -4.5	GR = 1 IND.X = 1.75 Δ = -.75	GR = 2 IND.X = 3.75 Δ = -1.75	GR = 1 IND.X = 1.25 Δ = -.25	GR = 2 IND.X = 2.25 Δ = -.25	GR = 2 IND.X = 4.25 Δ = -2.25

	Persian Gulf	Cambodia	Korea	SALT	Panama	Hague Guerillas
AIRFORCE & ARMY ROTC CADETS 1	GR = 1 IND.X = 2.8 △ = -1.8	GR = 1 IND.X = 5.4 △ = -4.4	GR = 8 IND.X = 4.2 △ = 3.8	GR = 5 IND.X = 3.2 △ = 1.8	GR = 8 IND.X = 5.4 △ = 2.6	GR = IND.X = △ = NA
2	GR = 1 IND.X = 2.3 △ = -1.3	GR = 8 IND.X = 4.8 △ = 3.2	GR = 8 IND.X = 3.8 △ = 4.2	GR = 4 IND.X = 2.7 △ = 1.3	GR = 1 IND.X = 3.0 △ = -2.0	GR = IND.X = △ = NA
3	GR = 2 IND.X = 2.0 △ = -	GR = 7 IND.X = 3.0 △ = 4.0	GR = 2 IND.X = 4.5 △ = -2.5	GR = 4 IND.X = 4.0 △ = -	GR = 8 IND.X = 5.8 △ = 2.2	GR = IND.X = △ = NA
4	GR = 1 IND.X = 4.2 △ = -3.2	GR = 8 IND.X = 6.8 △ = 1.2	GR = 2 IND.X = 3.0 △ = -1.0	GR = 5 IND.X = 3.0 △ = 2.0	GR = 8 IND.X = 6.2 △ = 1.8	GR = IND.X = △ = NA
5	GR = 2 IND.X = 3.8 △ = -1.8	GR = 7 IND.X = 3.8 △ = 3.2	GR = 8 IND.X = 7.8 △ = .25	GR = 2 IND.X = 2.3 △ = -.25	GR = 8 IND.X = 7.5 △ = .50	GR = IND.X = △ = NA
6	GR = 1 IND.X = 2.6 △ = -1.6	GR = 7 IND.X = 5.0 △ = 2.0	GR = 8 IND.X = 7.6 △ = .4	GR = 5 IND.X = 2.8 △ = 2.2	GR = 7 IND.X = 6.6 △ = .4	GR = IND.X = △ = NA

FT. KNOX OFFICERS (cont.)

	Persian Gulf	Cambodia	Korea	SALT	Panama	Hague Guerillas
19	GR = 7 IND.X = 5.8 Δ = 1.2	GR = 1 IND.X = 1.2 Δ = -.2	GR = 8 IND.X = 7.8 Δ = .2	GR = 5 IND.X = 3.2 Δ = 1.8	GR = 8 IND.X = 6.2 Δ = 1.8	GR = 3 IND.X = 5.6 Δ = -2.6
20	GR = 4 IND.X = 4.2 Δ = -.2	Gr = 8 IND.X = 5.0 Δ = 3.0	GR = 8 IND.X = 5.2 Δ = 2.8	GR = 2 IND.X = 2.6 Δ = -.6	GR = 8 IND.X = 6.2 Δ = 1.8	GR = 2 IND.X = 6.6 Δ = -4.6
21	GR = 8 IND.X = 2.5 Δ = 5.5	GR = 4 IND.X = 4.0 Δ = -	GR = 8 IND.X = 6.75 Δ = 1.25	GR = 2 IND.X = 3.0 Δ = -1.0	GR = 7 IND.X = 6.75 Δ = .25	GR = 6 IND.X = 4.5 Δ = 1.5

Key:

GR = Group Response
IND.X = Individual Mean
Δ = Shift Score

Note:

Positive values are a "risky-shift"; negative values are a cautious shift.

FT.KNOX OFFICERS (cont.)	Persian Gulf	Cambodia	Korea	SALT	Panama	Hague Guerillas
19	GR = 7 IND.X = 5.8 Δ = 1.2	GR = 1 IND.X = 1.2 Δ = -.2	GR = 8 IND.X = 7.8 Δ = .2	GR = 5 IND.X = 3.2 Δ = 1.8	GR = 8 IND.X = 6.2 Δ = 1.8	GR = 3 IND.X = 5.6 Δ = -2.6
20	GR = 4 IND.X = 4.2 Δ = -.2	Gr = 8 IND.X = 5.0 Δ = 3.0	GR = 8 IND.X = 5.2 Δ = 2.8	GR = 2 IND.X = 2.6 Δ = -.6	GR = 8 IND.X = 6.2 Δ = 1.8	GR = 2 IND.X = 6.6 Δ = -4.6
21	GR = 8 IND.X = 2.5 Δ = 5.5	GR = 4 IND.X = 4.0 Δ = -	GR = 8 IND.X = 6.75 Δ = 1.25	GR = 2 IND.X = 3.0 Δ = -1.0	GR = 7 IND.X = 6.75 Δ = .25	GR = 6 IND.X = 4.5 Δ = 1.5

Key:

GR = Group Response
IND.X = Individual Mean
Δ = Shift Score

Note:

Positive values are a "risky-shift"; negative values are a cautious shift.

BIBLIOGRAPHY

Abel, Elie
1966   THE MISSILE CRISIS. New York: Bantam.

Allison, Graham T.
1971   ESSENCE OF DECISION: EXPLAINING THE CUBAN MISSILE CRISIS. Boston: Little-Brown.

Allison, Graham T. and Halperin, Morton H.
1972   "Bureaucratic Politics: A Paradigm and Some Policy Implications." WORLD POLITICS, Spring, 40-79.

Appelwhite, Phillip B.
1965   ORGANIZATIONAL BEHAVIOR. Englewood Cliffs, New, Jersey: Prentice Hall.

Asch, S. E.
1951   "Effects of Group Pressure Upon the Modification and Distortion of Judgement." W. H. Guetzkow (ed.). GROUPS, LEADERSHIP, AND MEN. Pittsburg: Carnegie Press.

Asch, S.
1952   SOCIAL PSYCHOLOGY. New York: Prentice Hall.

Atthowe, J. M. Jr.
1961   "Interpersonal Decision-Making: The Resolution of a Dyadic Conflict." JOURNAL OF ABNORMAL AND SOCIAL PSYCHOLOGY. 62:114-19.

Axelrod, Robert (ed.)
1976   STRUCTURE OF DECISION: THE COGNITIVE MAPS OF POLITICAL ELITES. Princeton, New Jersey: Princeton University Press.

Bachrach, P. and Baratz, M. S.
1963   "Decisions and Nondecisions: An Analytic Framework." AMERICAN POLITICAL SCIENCE REVIEW. 57:632-42.

Baddely, A. D.
1972   "Selective Attention and Performance in Dangerous Environments." BRITISH JOURNAL OF PSYCHOLOGY. LXIII, 537-46.

Baker, Robert A., Ware, Roger J., Spires, G.H., and Osborn, W. C.
1966 "The Effects of Supervisory Threat on Decision-Making and Risk-Taking in a Simulated Combat Game." BEHAVIORAL SCIENCE. XI, 167-76.

Bales, Robert F.
1950 INTERACTION PROCESS ANALYSIS Reading, Massachussetts: Addison-Wesley.

Bales, R. F. and Borgatta, E. F.
1966 "Size of Group as a Factor in Interaction Profile." SMALL GROUPS: STUDIES IN SOCIAL INTERACTION. A. P. Hare, E. F. Borgatta, and R. F. Bales (eds.). New York: A. A. Knopf, 495-512.

Barber, James David
1972 THE PRESIDENTIAL CHARACTER: PREDICTING PERFORMANCE IN THE WHITE HOUSE. Englewood Cliffs, New Jersey: Prentice Hall.

Baron, R. S., Monson, T. C. and Baron, P. H.
1973 "Conformity Pressure as a Determinant of Risk-Taking: Replication and Extension." JOURNAL OF PERSONALITY AND SOCIAL PSYCHOLOGY. 28:405-13.

Baron, P. H., Baron, R. S., and Roper, G.
1974 "External Threats and the Risky Shift: Emotional Threats and Theoretical Implications." JOURNAL OF PERSONALITY AND SOCIAL PSYCHOLOGY. 32:95-103.

Bateson, N.
1966 "Familiarization, Group Discussion, and Risk Taking." JOURNAL OF EXPERIMENTAL SOCIAL PSYCHOLOGY. 2:119-29.

Bauer, Raymond A., Pool, Ithiel De Sola, and Dexter, Lewis A.
1972 AMERICAN BUSINESS AND PUBLIC POLICY. Chicago: Aldine-Atherton.

Baur, R. H. and Turner, J.
1974 "Betting Behavior in Sexually Homogeneous and Heterogeneous Groups." PSYCHOLOGICAL REPORTS 34:251-58.

Bell, P. R. and Jamieson, B. D.
1970 "Publicity of Initial Decisions and the Risky-Shift Phenomenon." JOURNAL OF EXPERIMENTAL SOCIAL PSYCHOLOGY 6:329-45.

Belovica, M. A. and Finch, F. E.
1971 "A Critical Analysis of the Risky-Shift Phenomena." ORGANIZATIONAL BEHAVIOR AND HUMAN PERFORMANCE 6:150-68.

Bem, Daryl J., Wallach, M. A. and Kogan, N.
1965 "Group Decision-Making under Risk of Aversive Consequences." JOURNAL OF PERSONALITY AND SOCIAL PSYCHOLOGY 1:453-60.

Bennett, Stephen E.
1971 "Modes of Resolution of a 'Belief Dilemma' in the Ideology of the John Birch Society." JOURNAL OF POLITICS v 33, August, 735-72.

Berkowitz, L.
1953 "Sharing Leadership in Small Decision-Making Groups." JOURNAL OF ABNORMAL AND SOCIAL PSYCHOLOGY V. 48, 231-38.

Berkowitz, M., Bock, P. G., and Fuccillo, V.
1977 THE POLITICS OF AMERICAN FOREIGN POLICY. Englewood Cliffs, New Jersey: Prentice Hall.

Betts, R. K.
1978 "Analysis, War, and Decision: Why Intelligence Failures are Inevitable." WORLD POLITICS, XXXI, 1, October, 61-89.

Blake, D., and Walters, R.
1976 THE POLITICS OF GLOBAL ECONOMIC RELATIONS. Englewood Cliffs, New Jersey: Prentice Hall.

Blalock, H. M., Jr.
1972 SOCIAL STATISTICS. New York: McGraw Hill.

Blascovich, J.
1972 "Sequence Effects of Choice Shifts Involving Risks." JOURNAL OF EXPERIMENTAL SOCIAL PSYCHOLOGY 8:260-65.

Blascovich, J. and Ginsburg, G. P.
1974 "Emergent Norms and Choice Shifts Involving Risk." SOCIOMETRY 37:205-18.

Bonham, G. M.
1975 "Cognitive Process Models and the Study of Foreign Policy Decision-Making." Presented to the International Studies Association, Washington.

Bonham, G. M. and Shapiro, M. J.
1976 "Explanation of the Unexpected: The Syrian Intervention in Jordan in 1970." In Axelrod, 1976:113-41.

Borgatta, E. F. and Bales, R. F.
1953 "Interaction of Individuals in Reconstituted Groups." SOCIOMETRY v. 16:302-20.

Borgatta, E. F., Couch, A. S., and Bales, R. F.
1954 "Some Findings Relevant to the Great Man Theory of Leadership." AMERICAN SOCIOLOGICAL REVIEW v. 19:755-59.

Borgatta, E. F., and Lambert, William W. (eds.)
1968 HANDBOOK OF PERSONALITY THEORY AND RESEARCH. Chicago: Rand McNally.

Bower, J.
1965 "The Role of Conflict in Economic Decision-Making Groups: Some Empirical Results." QUARTERLY JOURNAL OF ECONOMICS, 79, May, 263-77.

Brecher, M.
1977 "Toward a Theory of International Crisis Behavior: A Preliminary Report." INTERNATIONAL STUDIES QUARTERLY 21/1 March, 39-74.

Brem, O.D., and Cohen, D.
1964 "Re-evaluation of Choice Alternatives as a Function of Their Number and Qualitative Similarity." DIMENSIONS IN SOCIAL PSYCHOLOGY. Vinacke (ed.). Chicago: Scott-Foresman.

Brem, O. D., Glass, C., Laven, D. E., and Goodman, N.
1962 PERSONALITY AND DECISION PROCESSES. Stanford: Stanford University Press.

Brenner, M. J.
1973 "The Problem of Innovation and the Nixon-Kissinger Foreign Policy." INTERNATIONAL

STUDIES QUARTERLY 17:255-94.

Broadbent, D. E.
1971   DECISION AND STRESS. London: Academic Press.

Brown, Roger
1965   SOCIAL PSYCHOLOGY. New York: Free Press.

Brown, R.
1974   "Further Comment on the Risky-Shift."
        AMERICAN PSYCHOLOGIST 29:468-70.

Buchan, A.
1966   CRISIS MANAGEMENT. Boulogne-sur-Seine,
        France: Atlantic Institute.

Burgess, P. M.
1967   ELITE IMAGES AND FOREIGN POLICY OUTCOMES.
        Columbus: Ohio State University Press.

Burnstein, E. and Katz, S.
1971   "Individual Commitment to Risky and Conservative Choices as a Determinant of Shifts in Group Decisions. JOURNAL OF PERSONALITY AND SOCIAL PSYCHOLOGY 39:564-80.

Burnstein, E., Miller, H., Vinokur, A., Katz, S., and Crowley, J.
1971   "Risky Shift is Eminently Rational."
        JOURNAL OF PERSONALITY AND SOCIAL PSYCHOLOGY 20:462-71.

Burnstein, E. and Vinokur, A.
1973   "Testing Two Classes of Theories About Group-Induced Shifts in Individual Choice."
        JOURNAL OF EXPERIMENTAL SOCIAL PSYCHOLOGY 9, 123-37.

Burton, J. W., Groom, A. G. R., Mitchell, C. R. and DeReuck, A. V. S.
1974   "The Study of World Society." International Studies Association. Occasional Paper No. 1.

Campbell, D. R. and McCormack, T. H.
1957   "Military Experience and Attitudes towards Authority." AMERICAN JOURNAL OF SOCIOLOGY March, 62:482-90.

Campbell, D. and Stanley, J. C.
1963   EXPERIMENTAL AND QUASI-EXPERIMENTAL DESIGNS
        FOR RESEARCH. Chicago: Rand McNally.

Campbell, J.
1974   "The Risky Shift." Unpublished seminar paper.
        University of Cincinnati.

Caporaso, J. A., and Roos, L. L., Jr. (eds.)
1975   QUASI-EXPERIMENTAL APPROACHES. Evanston:
        Northwestern University Press.

Carlson, J. A. and Davis, C. M.
1971   "Cultural Values and the Risky Shift: A
        Cross Cultural Test in Uganda and the United
        States." JOURNAL OF PERSONALITY AND SOCIAL
        PSYCHOLOGY 20:361-76.

Carter, L., Haythorn, W., Shriver, B. and Langetta, J.
1950   "The Behavior of Leaders and Other Group
        Members." JOURNAL OF ABNORMAL SOCIAL
        PSYCHOLOGY v. 46:589-95.

Cartwright, D.
1971   "Risk-Taking By Individuals and Groups: An
        Assessment of Research Employing Choice
        Dilemmas." JOURNAL OF PERSONALITY AND
        SOCIAL PSYCHOLOGY 20:361-78.

Cartwright, D.
1973   "Determinants of Scientific Progress: The
        Case of Research on the Risky Shift."
        AMERICAN PSYCHOLOGIST 28:222-316.

Cartwright, D. and Sander, A.
1960   GROUP DYNAMICS RESEARCH AND THEORY. New
        York: Harper and Row.

Castore, C. J.
1972   "Group Discussion and Pre-Discussion: An
        Assessment of Preferences in the Risky Shift."
        JOURNAL OF EXPERIMENTAL SOCIAL PSYCHOLOGY
        8:161-67.

Clark, R. D., III
1971   "Group-Induced Shift toward Risk" A Critical
        Appraisal." PSYCHOLOGICAL BULLETIN 76:251-70.

Clark, R. D., III, Crockett, W. H. and Archer, R. L.
1971   "Risk as Value Hypotheses: The Relation Between Perception of Self, Others, and the Risky Shift." JOURNAL OF PERSONALITY AND SOCIAL PSYCHOLOGY 20:425-29.

Cobb, R. W.
1973   "The Belief-System Perspective: An Assessment of a Framework." JOURNAL OF POLITICS 35:121-53.

Cohen, B.
1973   THE PUBLIC"S IMPACT ON FOREIGN POLICY. Boston: Little Brown.

Collins, B. E. and Guetzkow, H.
1964   A SOCIAL PSYCHOLOGY OF GROUP PROCESSES FOR DECISION-MAKING. New York: John Wiley.

Converse, P. E.
1964   "The Nature of Belief Systems in Mass Publics." D. Apter (ed.) IDEOLOGY AND DISCONTENT. New York: Free Press.

Cooper, C. L.
1972   THE LOST CRUSADE. Greenwich: Fawcett.

Corning, P. A.
        "The Biological Bases of Behavior and Some Implications for Political Science." WORLD POLITICS 23 (Ap):321-70.

Cyert, R. M. and March, J. G.
1963   A BEHAVIORAL THEORY OF THE FIRM. Englewood Cliffs, New Jersey: Prentice Hall.

Dahl, Robert A.
1961   WHO GOVERNS? New Haven: Yale University Press.

Davis, D. F.
1976   "Search Behavior of Small Decision-Making Groups: An Information Processing Perspective." R. T. Golembiewski (ed.). THE SMALL GROUP IN POLITICAL SCIENCE: THE LAST TWO DECADES OF DEVELOPMENT. Athens: University of Georgia Press.

Delbecq, A., Van de Van, A. H., and Gustavson, D.
1975   GROUP TECHNIQUES FOR PROGRAM PLANNING.
       Dallas: Scott-Foresman.

De Palma, G. and McCloskey, H.
1970   "Personality and Conformity: The Learning of
       Political Attitudes.: AMERICAN POLITICAL
       SCIENCE REVIEW, December, 1054-73.

De Rivera, J.
1968   THE PSYCHOLOGICAL DIMENSION OF FOREIGN POLICY.
       Columbus: Merrill.

Destler, J. M.
1972   PRESIDENTS, BUREAUCRATS, AND FOREIGN POLICY.
       Princeton University Press.

Deutsch, K. M., Edinger, Lewis, Macredis, R. and
         Merritt, R.
1967   FRANCE, GERMANY AND THE WESTERN ALLAINCE.
       New York: Charles Scribners.

Dexter, L.
1970   ELITE AND SPECIALIZED INTERVIEWING. Evanston:
       Northwestern Press.

Dion, K.
1970   "Why do Groups Make Riskier Decisions than
       Individuals?" ADVANCES IN EXPERIMENTAL
       SOCIAL PSYCHOLOGY, U.S., New York: Academic
       Press. 305-77.

Dion, K. L., and Miller, N.
1971   "An Analysis of the Familiarization Explana-
       tion of the Risky Shift." JOURNAL OF
       EXPERIMENTAL SOCIAL PSYCHOLOGY 7:524-33.

Dion, K. L., Miller, N., and Magnam, M. A.
1971   "Cohesiveness and Social Responsibility as
       Determinants of Group Risk-Taking."
       JOURNAL OF PERSONALITY AND SOCIAL PSYCHOLOGY
       20:400-406.

Doise, W.
1969   "Inter-Group Relations and Polarization of
       Individual and Collective Judgements."
       JOURNAL OF PERSONALITY AND SOCIAL PSYCHOLOGY
       12:136-43.

Doise, W.
1971 "An Apparent Exception to the Extremization of Collective Judgements." EUROPEAN JOURNAL OF OF SOCIAL PSYCHOLOGY 1:511-518.

Dougherty, J. E. and Pfaltzgraff, R. L., Jr.
1971 CONTENDING THEORIES OF INTERNATIONAL RELATIONS. New York: J. B. Lippincott.

Dyson, J.
1975 "Political Experimentation: Some Theoretical Fragments Pertinent to Experimental Research." Presented at the Annual Meeting of the American Political Science Association. San Francisco, September.

East, M., and Hermann, C.
1974 "Do Nation-Types Account for Foreign Policy Behavior?" in James Rosenau, ed., COMPARING FOREIGN POLICIES: THEORIES, FINDINGS, AND METHODS. New York: Wiley.

Edwards, W.
1961 "Behavioral Decision Theory." ANNUAL REVIEW OF PSYCHOLOGY 12:473-98.

Etheredge, L. S.
1978 "Personality Effects on American Foreign Policy, 1898-1968: A Test of Interpersonalization Generalization Theory." AMERICAN POLITICAL SCIENCE REVIEW 72/2, June, 434-51.

Etzioni, A.
1969 "Social-Psychological Aspects of International Relations." In G. Lindzey and E. Aronson (eds.). THE HANDBOOK OF SOCIAL PSYCHOLOGY (2nd ed.), Vol. 5, Reading, Massachussetts: Addison-Wesley.

Eulau, H.
1969 "Logics of Rationality in Unanimous Decision-Making." In H. Eulau, ed. MICRO-MACRO POLITICAL ANALYSIS. Chicago: Aldine, pp. 23-46.

Farquharson, R.
1969 THEORY OF VOTING. New Haven: Yale University Press.

Fenno, Richard F.
1959　THE PRESIDENT'S CABINET. Cambridge, Massachussetts: Harvard University Press.

Ferguson, D. A. and Viomar, N.
1971　"Effects of Group Discussion on Estimates of Culturally Appropriate Risk Levels." JOURNAL OF PERSONALITY AND SOCIAL PSYCHOLOGY 20: 436-45.

Festinger, Leon
1957　A THEORY OF COGNITIVE DISSONANCE. Evanston, Illinois: Row, Peterson.

Festinger, Leon, et al.
1964　CONFLICT, DECISION, AND DISSONANCE. Stanford: Stanford University Press.

Fiorina, M.
1975　"Axiomatic Models of Risk and Decision: An Epository Treatment." Presented at the Annual Meeting of the International Studies Association, Washington, D. C.

Fisher, B. A.
1974　SMALL GROUP DECISION-MAKING. New York: McGraw Hill.

Flanders, J. P. and Thistlewaite, D. L.
1967　"Effects of Familiarization and Group Discussion Upon Risk Taking." JOURNAL OF PERSONALITY AND SOCIAL PSYCHOLOGY 5:91-97.

Frank, J. D.
1967　SANITY AND SURVIVAL: PSYCHOLOGICAL ASPECTS OF WARS AND PEACE. New York: Vantage Press.

Frankel, J.
1963　THE MAKING OF FOREIGN POLICY: AN ANALYSIS OF DECISION-MAKING. London: Oxford University Press.

Fraser, C.
1970　"Group Risk Taking and Group Polarization." Presented at the European Association of Social Psychology Conference, Konstanz.

Freedman, A. E. and Freedman, P. E.
1975   THE PSYCHOLOGY OF POLITICAL CONTROL. New York: St. Martin's.

French, E.
1955   "Interrelation Among Some Measures of Rigidity Under Stress and Non-Stress Conditions." JOURNAL OF ABNORMAL SOCIAL PSYCHOLOGY. July, 51:114-118.

Galtung, J.
1968   "Small Group Theory and the Theory of International Relations." In M. Kaplan (ed.), NEW APPROACHES TO INTERNATIONAL RELATIONS. New York: St. Martin's.

Garnham, D.
1974   "State Department Rigidity: Testing a Psychological Hypothesis." INTERNATIONAL STUDIES QUARTERLY, 18/1, March, p. 31-40.

George, A. L.
1969   "The 'Operational Code': A Neglected Approval to the Study of Political Leaders and Decision-Making." INTERNATIONAL STUDIES QUARTERLY, 13/2, June, p. 190-222.

George, A. L.
1972   "The Case of Multiple Advocacy in Making Foreign Policy." AMERICAN POLITICAL SCIENCE REVIEW 66 September, p. 751-85.

George, A. L.
1974   "Adaptation to Stress in Political Decision-Making." In G. V. Coelho, D. A. Hamburg, and J. Adams, (eds.), COPING AND ADAPTATION. New York: Basic Books.

George, A. L., et al.
1975   Appendices: Commission on the Organization of the Government for the Conduct of Foreign Policy. Vol. 2, Washington: GPO.

Geyelin, P.
1966   LYNDON B. JOHNSON AND THE WORLD. New York: Praeger.

Glover, Maryline
1976   "Experimental Laboratory Analogs." Unpublished

seminar paper. University of Cincinnati.

Glover, Maryline
1977 "Toward an Integrated Approach to Choice (Group-Induced) Shifts in Groups." Unpublished seminar paper. University of Cincinnati.

Gorman, R. A.
1970 "On the Inadequacies of Non-Philosophical Political Science: A Critical Analysis of Decision-Making Theory." INTERNATIONAL STUDIES QUARTERLY, 14/4, December, p. 395-411.

Graham, W. K. and Harris, S. G.
1970 "Effects of Group Discussion on Accepting Risk and On Advising Others to be Risky." PSYCHOLOGICAL RECORD 20:219-24.

Green, D. and Connolley, E.
1974 "Groupthink and Watergate." Presented to the American Psychological Association.

Greenstein, F. I.
1967 "The Impact of Personality on Politics." AMERICAN POLITICAL SCIENCE REVIEW. September.

Greenstein, F. I.
1969 PERSONALITY AND POLITICS. Chicago: Markham.

Guetzkow, H. and Gyr, J.
1954 "An Analysis of Conflict in Decision-Making Groups." HUMAN RELATIONS 7:367-81.

Guthman, E.
1971 WE BAND OF BROTHERS. New York: Harper and Row.

Halberstam, D.
1972 THE BEST AND THE BRIGHTEST Greenwich, Conn.: Fawcett.

Haley, J. and Rule, B. G.
1971 "Group Composition Effects on Risk Taking." JOURNAL OF PERSONALITY 39:150-161.

Halper, T.
1971 FOREIGN POLICY CRISES: APPEARANCE AND REALITY ON DECISION-MAKING. Columbus: Charles Merrill.

Halperin, M.
1974   BUREAUCRATIC POLITICS AND FOREIGN POLICY.
       Brookings Institution.

Hamlin, R.
1968   "Leadership and Crises." In Darwin Cart-
       wright and A. Fander (eds.), GROUP DYNAMICS,
       3rd ed., New York: Harper and Row.

Hare, A. P.
1976   HANDBOOK OF SMALL GROUP RESEARCH, 2nd edition.
       New York: Free Press.

Hare, A. Paul, Borgatta, E. F., and Bales, R. F. (eds.)
1965   SMALL GROUPS: STUDIES IN SOCIAL INTERACTION.
       New York: Alfred A. Knopt.

Harsanyi, John C.
1969   "Rational-Chioce Models of Political Behavior
       vs Functionalist and Conformist Theories."
       WORLD POLITICS. July, 513-38.

Hazelwood, Leo, Hayes, J. J., and Brownell, J.R. Jr.
1977   "Planning for Problems in Crisis Management."
       INTERNATIONAL STUDIES QUARTERLY. 21/1,
       March, p. 75-106.

Hempel, C. G.
1966   PHILOSOPHY OF NATURAL SCIENCE. Englewood
       Cliffs, New Jersey: Prentice Hall.

Herder, F.
1958   THE PSYCHOLOGY OF INTERPERSONAL RELATIONS.
       New York: John Wiley.

Hermann, Charles F.
1963. "Some Consequences of Crisis Which Limit
       the Viability of Organization." ADMINISTRATIVE
       SCIENCE QUARTERLY. VIII, 61-82.

Hermann, Charles F.
1965   CRISIS IN FOREIGN POLICY MAKING: A SIMULATION
       OF INTERNATIONAL POLITICS. China Lake,
       California: Project Michelson. Contract
       N123 (60530) 32779A.

Hermann, Charles F. (ed.)
1972   INTERNATIONAL CRISIS: INSIGHTS FROM BEHAVIORAL
       RESEARCH. New York: Free Press.

Hermann, Charles F.
1972   "Threat, Time, and Surprise: A Simulation of International Crisis." In Hermann (ed.) 187-214.

Hermann, Charles F.
1975   "Research Tasks for International Crisis Avoidance and Management." Report for the Advanced Research Office in the Office of Naval Research.

Hermann, Charles F.
1977   "What Decision Units Shape Foreign Policy: Individual, Group, Bureaucracy?" Presented to the International Studies Association. St. Louis.

Hermann, Charles F. and Hermann, Margaret G.
1967   "An Attempt to Simulate the Outbreak of World War I." AMERICAN POLITICAL SCIENCE REVIEW. LXI 400-16.

Hermann, Charles F. and Brady, Linda
1972   "Alternative Models of International Crisis Behavior," In Hermann, ed.

Hermann, Charles F., Hermann, Margaret G., and Cantor, R. A.
1974   "Counterattack or Delay" Characteristics Influencing Decision-Makers Responses to the Simulation of an Unidentified Attack." JOURNAL OF CONFLICT RESOLUTION, 18/1, March, 75-106.

Hermann, Margaret G.
1966   "Testing a Model of Psychological Stress." JOURNAL OF PERSONALITY, 34/3, September, 381-96.

Hermann, Margaret G. and Hermann, Charles F.
1975   "Maintaining the Quality of Decision-Making in Foreign Policy Crisis: A Proposal." In Appendices: Commission on the Organization of the Government for the Conduct of Foreign Policy. Vol. 2, Appendix, D. Washnigton: GPO.

Higbee, K. L.
1972   "Group Risk-Taking in Military Decisions."

JOURNAL OF SOCIAL PSYCHOLOGY, 88, October, 55-64.

Hilsman, Roger
1959 "The Foreign Policy Consensus: An Interim Research Report." JOURNAL OF CONFLICT RESOLUTION, December.

Hinton, B. L. and Reitz, H. J.
1971 GROUPS AND ORGANIZATIONS. Belmont, California: Wadsworth Company.

Hoffman, L. and Maier, Norman R. F.
1961 "Quality and Acceptance of Problem Solutions by Members of Homogeneous and Heterogeneous Groups." JOURNAL OF ABNORMAL AND SOCIAL PSYCHOLOGY, LXII, 401-17.

Hollander, E. P.
1954 "Authoritarianism and Leadership Choice in a Military Setting." JOURNAL OF ABNORMAL AND SOCIAL PSYCHOLOGY, 49, 365-70.

Holsti, Ole R.
1962 "The Belief System and National Images: A Case Study." JOURNAL OF CONFLICT RESOLUTION, 6:244-52.

Holsti, Ole R.
1965a "The 1914 Case." AMERICAN POLITICAL SCIENCE REVIEW, LIX, 365-378.

Holsti, Ole R.
1965b "Perception of Time, Perception of Alternatives, and Patterns of Factors in Crisis Decision-Making." Peace Research Society Papers, 3, 79-86.

Holsti, Ole R.
1971 "Crisis, Stress and Decision-Making." INTERNATIONAL SOCIETY SCIENCE JOURNAL, November, 53-67.

Holsti, Ole R.
1972a "Time, Alternatives, and Communications: The 1914 and Cuban Missile Crises." In Hermann (ed.) 58-80.

Holsti, Ole R.
1972b CRISIS, ESCALATION, WAR. Montreal: McGill

Queens.

Holsti, Ole R.
1974 "The Study of International Politics Makes Strange Bedfellows: Theories of the Radical Right and Radical Left." AMERICAN POLITICAL SCIENCE REVIEW, LXVIII 1, March, 217-242.

Holsti, Ole R.
1976 "Cognitive Process Approaches to Decision-Making: Foreign Policy Actors Viewed Psychologically." AMERICAN BEHAVIORAL SCIENTIST. 20/1, 11-32.

Holsti, Ole R., Brady, Richard A., and North, R. C.
1964 "Measuring Affect and Action in International Reaction Models: Empirical Materials from the 1962 Cuban Crisis." JOURNAL OF PEACE RESEARCH, 170-90.

Holsti, Ole R. and George, Alexander
1975 "The Effects of Stress on the Performance of Foreign Policy Makers." POLITICAL SCIENCE ANNUAL: AN INTERNATIONAL REVIEW, Vol. 6. Cornelius P. Cotter (ed.). Indianapolis: Bobbs-Merrill.

Hoopes, Townsend
1969 THE LIMITS OF INTERVENTION. New York: David McKay.

Hopkins, Terrence K.
1964 THE EXERCISE OF INFLUENCE IN SMALL GROUPS. Totowa, New Jersey: Bedminster Press.

Horelick, Arnold L.
1964 "The Cuban Missile Crisis." WORLD POLITICS 16:363-89.

Horne, W. C. and Long, G.
1972 "Effect of Group Discussion of Universalic-Particularistic Orientation." JOURNAL OF EXPERIMENTAL AND SOCIAL PSYCHOLOGY 8:236-46.

Hoyt, G. C. and Stoner, J.
1968 "Leadership and Group Decisions Involving Risk." JOURNAL OF EXPERIMENTAL AND SOCIAL PSYCHOLOGY 4:275-84.

Hull, R. K. and Peter, L. J.
1969   THE PETER PRINCIPLE. New York: William Morrow.

Huntington, S.
1959   THE SOLDIER AND THE STATES. Cambridge: Belknap-Harvard University Press.

Inglehart, R.
1967   "An End to European Integration." AMERICAN POLITICAL SCIENCE REVIEW 61:91-105.

Iverson, Gudmund and Norpoth, Helmut
1976   ANALYSIS OF VARIANCE. Beverly Hills, California: Sage Publications, Inc.

James, J.
1951   "A Preliminary Study of the Size Determinant in Small Group Interaction." AMERICAN SOCIOLOGICAL REVIEW 16.

Jamieson, B. D.
1968   "The Risky-Shift Phenomena with a Heterogeneous Sample." PSYCHOLOGICAL REPORT 23:203-06.

Janis, Irving L.
1959   "Decisional Conflict: A Theoretical Analysis." JOURNAL OF CONFLICT RESOLUTION III, 6-27.

Janis, Irving L.
1972   VICTIMS OF GROUPTHINK. New York: Houghton-Mifflin.

Janis, Irving L.
1973   STRESS AND FRUSTRATION New York: Harcourt, Brace, Jonovich.

Janis, Irving L. and Leventhal, Howard
1968   "Human Reaction to Stress." In Borgatta and Lambert, 1973:1041-85.

Janis, Irving L. and Mann, Leon
1977   DECISION MAKING" A PSYCHOLOGICAL ANALYSIS OF CONFLICT, CHOICE, AND COMMITMENT. New York: Free Press.

Jaros, Dean
1972   "Biochemical Desocialization: Depressants

and Political Behavior." MIDWEST JOURNAL OF
POLITICAL SCIENCE, February, 1-28.

Jeffers, K., Dyson, J., and Davis, D.
1976 "An Experimental Investigation of Uncertainty
Reduction and Policy Shifts by Small
Decision-Making Groups." Presented to the
Midwest Political Science Association, Chicago
April 29 - May 1.

Jellison, J. M. and Davis, D.
1973 "Relationships between Perceived Ability and
Attitude Extremity." JOURNAL OF PERSONALITY
AND SOCIAL PSYCHOLOGY 27:430-36.

Jellison, J. M. and Riskind, J.
1973a "A Social Comparison of Abilities: Interpretation of Risk Taking." JOURNAL OF PERSON-
ALITY AND SOCIAL PSYCHOLOGY 22:175-90.

Jellison, J. M. and Riskind, J.
1973b "A Social Comparison of Abilities: Interpretation of Risk Taking." JOURNAL OF
PERSONALITY AND SOCIAL PSYCHOLOGY 25:375-90.

Jensen, Lloyd
1966 "American Foreign Policy Elites and the
Prediction of International Events." Peace
Research Society: Papers, V, Philadelphia.
199-209.

Jervis, Robert
1968 "Hypothesis on Misperception." WORLD POLITICS
20:454-79.

Jervis, Robert
1969 "The Costs of the Quantitative Study of
International Relations." In K. Knorr and
James Rosenau (eds.).

Jervis, Robert
1976 PERCEPTION AND MISPERCEPTION IN INTERNATIONAL
RELATIONS. Princeton, New Jersey: Princeton
University Press.

Johnson, Charles
1970 RISK TAKING DECISION" STRATEGY AND PERSON-
ALITY. Ann Arbor: University Microfilms.

Johnson, Norris
1974 "Collective Behavior as Group-Induced Shift."
SOCIOLOGICAL INQUIRY. 44:2, 105-110.

Johnson, Norris, Stemler, James, and Hunter, Deborah
1977 "Crowd Behavior as 'Risky Shift': A Laboratory Experiment." SOCIOMETRY 40:2, 183-87.

Johnson, Norris and Glover, Maryline
1977 "Individual and Group Shifts to "Risk':
Two Laboratory Experiments on Crowd Polarization." Paper submitted to the annual
meeting of the North Central Sociological
Association, May 12-14.

Johnson, Norris and Feinberg, William
1977 "A Computer Simulation of the Emergence of
Consensus in Crowds." AMERICAN SOCIOLOGICAL
REVIEW 42:505-21.

Joll, James
1968 1914: THE UNSPOKEN ASSUMPTION. London:
Werdenfield and Nicholson.

JOURNAL OF PERSONALITY AND SOCIAL PSYCHOLOGY, Vol. 20,
No. 3, December 1971. Special "Risky-Shift"
Issue.

Kahn, Herman
1965 ON ESCALATION. New York: Praeger.

Kalven, H. G. and Feisel, H.
1966 THE AMERICAN JURY. Boston: Little Brown.

Kaplan, M.
1957 SYSTEM AND PROCESS IN INTERNATIONAL POLITICS.
New York: John Wiley.

Katz, Daniel and Kahn, Robert L.
1966 THE SOCIAL PSYCHOLOGY OF ORGANIZATIONS. New
York: John Wiley.

Kelly, H. H. and Thibant, J.
1965 "Group Problem Solving." In G. Lindzey and
E. Aronson (eds.). 1969, v. 4:1-101.

Kelman, Herbert C.
1965   INTERNATIONAL BEHAVIOR. New York: Holt Rinehart.

Kelman, Herbert C.
1970   "The Role of the Individual in International Relations: Some Conceptual and Methodological Considerations." JOURNAL OF INTERNATIONAL AFFAIRS No. 1, p. 1-17.

Kennedy, R. F.
1969   THIRTEEN DAYS. New York: Norton.

Keohane, R. and Nye, J.
1977   POWER AND INTERDEPENDENCE. Boston: Little Brown.

Kirk, Elizabeth
1976   "Group, Organizational and Crisis Models of Decision-Making in the Formulation of Foreign Policy." Presented to the International Studies Association, Toronto.

Kirkpatrick, Samuel A.
1975a   "Psychological Views of Decision-Making." POLITICAL SCIENCE ANNUAL. C. P. Cotter, ed., Vol. VI, Indianapolis: Bobbs-Merrill.

Kirkpatrick, Samuel A.
1975b   "Problems of Risk-Taking in Bureaucracies." Presented at the annual meeting of International Studies Association. Washington, D. C., February.

Kirkpatrick, Samuel A.
1975c   "Epistemological Perspectives on the Social-Psychological Study of Political Decision-Making." Presented at the annual meeting of the American Political Science Association, San Francisco, September.

Kirkpatrick, Samuel A., Bernick, E. L., Thompson, R. J., and Rycroft, R. W.
1975   "Risks in Political Decision-Making: An Experimental Analysis of Choice Shifts." EXPERIMENTAL STUDY OF POLITICS, January, 4:55-92.

Kirkpatrick, Samuel A., and Robertson, Roby D.
1976a "Choice Shifts in Political Decision-Making: An Experimental Test of Value Theory." Presented at the annual meeting of the Midwest Political Science Association. Chicago, Ill. April 29 - May 1, 1976.

Kirkpatrick, Samuel A., Davis, Dwight, F., and Robertson, Roby D.
1976b "The Process of Political Decision-Making in Groups: Search Behavior and Choice-Shifts." AMERICAN BEHAVIORAL SCIENTIST. September-October, 20, 1, p. 33-64.

Kirkpatrick, Samuel A. (ed.)
1976c AMERICAN BEHAVIORAL SCIENTIST. September-October, 20/1. Beverly Hills, Calif.: Sage Publications. Special issue devoted to: "Political Decision-Making: Interdisciplinary Developments from a Microanalytic Perspective."

Knorr, K. and Rosenau, J.
1969 CONTENDING APPROACHES TO INTERNATIONAL POLITICS. Princeton: Princeton University Press.

Knutson, J. N.
1972 THE HUMAN BASIS OF THE POLITY: A PSYCHOLOGICAL STUDY OF POLITICAL MEN. Chicago: Aldine, Atherton.

Kogan, N. and Wallach, M. A.
1964 RISK-TAKING: A STUDY IN COGNITION AND PERSONALITY. New York: Holt, Rinehart and Winston.

Kogan, N. and Wallach, M. A.
1967a "Effects of Physical Separation of Group Members Upon Group Risk-Taking." HUMAN RELATIONS 20:41-48.

Kogan, N. and Wallach, M. A.
1967b "Group Risk-Taking as a Function of Member's Anxiety and Defensiveness Levels." JOURNAL OF PERSONALITY AND SOCIAL PSYCHOLOGY 35:50-63.

Kogan, N. and Wallach, M. A.
1967c "The Risky-Shift Phenomena in Small Decision-Making Groups." A Test of the Information Exchange Hypothesis." JOURNAL OF EXPERIMENTAL SOCIAL PSYCHOLOGY 3:65-85.

Kogan, N. and Zalleska, M.
1969 "Level of Risk Selected by Individual and Groups When Deciding for Self and Others." Proceedings of the 77th Annual Convention of the American Psychological Association 4:423-24.

Kogan, N., Lamm, H. and Trommsdorff, G.
1972 "Negotiation Constraints in the Risk-Taking Domain: Effects of Being Observed by Partners of Higher or Lower Status." JOURNAL OF PERSONALITY AND SOCIAL PSYCHOLOGY 23:143-56.

Kohl, Wilfred
1974 "The Nixon-Kissinger Foreign Policy System and U.S.-European Relations: Patterns of Policy-Making." Presented to the American Political Science Association, Chicago.

Lamm, H.
1967 "Will an Observer Advise High Risk Taking After Hearing a Discussion of the Problem?" JOURNAL OF PERSONALITY AND SOCIAL PSYCHOLOGY 6:467-71.

Lamm, H. and Kogan, N.
1970 "Risk-Taking in the Context of Intergroup Negotiations." JOURNAL OF EXPERIMENTAL AND SOCIAL PSYCHOLOGY 6:351-63.

Lamm, H., Schaude, E., and Trommsdorff, G.
1971 "Risky-Shift as a Function of Group Member's Value of Risk and Need for Approval." JOURNAL OF PERSONALITY AND SOCIAL PSYCHOLOGY 20:430-35.

Lamm, H., and Trommsdorff, G.
1974 "Group Influences on Probability Judgments Concerning Social and Political Changes." PSYCHOLOGICAL REPORTS 35:987-96.

Lane, R. E.
1972   POLITICAL MAN. New York: Free Press.

Lasswell, H.
1960   PSYCHOPATHOLOGY AND POLITICS. New York: Viking.

Lazarus, Richard S.
1966   PSYCHOLOGICAL STRESS AND THE COPING PROCESS. New York: McGraw-Hill.

Lazarus, R. S., Averill, J. R., and Opton, E. M., Jr.
1974   "The Assessment of Coping," in G. V. Coelho, D. A. Hamburg, and J. Adams, eds., COPING AND ADAPTATION. New York: Basic Books.

Leege, D. and Francis, W.
1974   POLITICAL RESEARCH. New York: Basic Books.

Leites, N.
1953   A STUDY OF BOLSHEVISM. New York: Free Press.

Lenter, H.
1972   "The Concept of Crisis as Viewed by the United States Department of State," In Hermann (ed.), 112-35.

L'Etang, H.
1970   THE PATHOLOGY OF LEADERSHIP. New York: Hawthorne.

Levinger, G. and Schneider, J.
1969   "A Test of the Risk as Value Hypothesis." JOURNAL OF PERSONALITY AND SOCIAL PSYCHOLOGY 11:165-69.

Lewin, Kurt
1951   FIELD THEORY IN SOCIAL SCIENCE. New York.

Lindbloom, C. E.
1965   THE INTELLIGENCE OF DEMOCRACY. New York: Free Press.

Lindzey, G. and Aronson, E. (eds.)
1969   THE HANDBOOK OF SOCIAL PSYCHOLOGY (2nd ed.). Reading, Mass.: Addison-Wesley. V. 1-4.

Lowi, T. J.
1964 "American Business, Public Policy, Case Studies, and Political Theory." WORLD POLITICS 16:677-715.

Lowi, T. J.
1967 "Making Democracy Safe for the World: National Politics and Foreign Policy." In Rosenau (ed.).

Lutzker, D.
1960 "Internationalism as a Predictor of Cooperative Behavior." JOURNAL OF CONFLICT RESOLUTION 4, 429-30.

McClelland, C.
1961 "The Acute International Crisis." WORLD POLITICS, 14 (October) 182-204.

McClelland, C.
1962 "Decisional Opportunity and Political Controversy in the Quemoy Case." JOURNAL OF CONFLICT RESOLUTION, September.

McClelland, C.
1966 THEORY AND THE INTERNATIONAL SYSTEM. New York: McMillan.

McClelland, C.
1968 "Field Theory and System Theory in International Politics," mimeo, Los Angeles: University of Southern California.

McClelland, C.
1972 "The Beginning, Duration and Abatement of International Crises: Comparisons on Two Conflict Arenas," in Hermann (ed.), 83-108.

McCloskey, H.
1967 "Personality and Attitude Correlates of Foreign Policy Orientation." In Rosenau (ed.). DOMESTIC SOURCES OF FOREIGN POLICY, New York: Free Press. 51-109.

McConahay, J. B.
1973 "Experimental Research," in J. N. Kruitson (ed.). HANDBOOK OF POLITICAL PSYCHOLOGY, Vol. 3, Reading, Mass.: San Francisco: Jossey-Bass.

McCormick, J. M.
 1975 "Evaluating Models of Crisis Behavior: Some Evidence from the Middle East." INTERNATIONAL STUDIES QUARTERLY, 19/1, March, 17-45.

McGinnis, S.
 1976 "Belief Systems and Foreign Policy: Basic Values and Consistency." Presented to the International Studies Association, Toronto.

McGrath, J. E. (ed.)
 1970 SOCIOLOGICAL AND PSYCHOLOGICAL FACTORS IN STRESS. New York: Holt, Rinehart.

McWhirter, D. A.
 1974 "Testing for Groupthink: The Effects of Anticipated Group Membership on Individual Decision-Making." Presented at the Annual meeting of the American Political Science Association, Chicago.

Madaras, G. and Bem, D.
 1968 "Risk and Conservation in Group Decision-Making." JOURNAL OF EXPERIMENTAL SOCIAL PSYCHOLOGY 4:350-65.

Madron, Thomas W.
 1969 SMALL GROUP METHODS AND THE STUDY OF POLITICS. Evanston: Northwestern University Press.

Maier, N. R. F.
 1963 PROBLEM-SOLVING DISCUSSIONS AND CONFERENCES. New York: McGraw-Hill.

Maier, Norman R. F.
 1970 "Problem Solving and Creativity in Individuals and Groups." Belmont, California: Brooks-Cole.

March, James G. and Simon, H. A.
 1965 ORGANIZATIONS. New York: John Wiley.

Marquis, P. G.
 1962 "Individual Responsibility and Group Decisions Involving Risk." INDUSTRIAL MANAGEMENT REVIEW, 3, 8-23.

Martin, J. B.
1966 OVERTAKEN BY EVENTS: THE DOMINICAN CRISIS FROM THE FALL OF TRUJILLO TO THE CIVIL WAR. New York: Doubleday.

Marx, S. and J. Wood.
1975 "Strands of Theory and Research in Collective Behavior." In A. Inkeles (ed.), ANNUAL REVIEW OF SOCIOLOGY. Palo Alto: Annual Review, Inc. 363-428.

May, Ernest
1973 LESSONS OF THE PAST. New York: Oxford University Press.

Mennis, B.
1972 AMERICAN FOREIGN POLICY OFFICIALS. WHO THEY ARE AND WHAT THEY BELIEVE REGARDING INTERNATIONAL POLITICS. Columbus: Ohio State University Press.

Middleton, M. A. and Warren, L.
1972 "Risk-Taking Effects on Group Decision-Making." JOURNAL OF PSYCHOLOGY 82:89-96.

Milburn, T.
1972 "The Management of Crisis." In C. F. Hermann (ed.) 259-80.

Milburn, T. and Billings, R. S.
1976 "Decision-Making Perspective from Psychology: Dealing with Risk and Uncertainty." AMERICAN BEHAVIORAL SCIENTIST, 20/1, 111-26.

Milgram, S.
1974 OBEDIENCE TO AUTHORITY. New York: Harper and Row.

Miller, Kent and Iscoe, Ira
1963 "The Concept of Crisis: Current Status and Mental Health Implications." HUMAN ORGANIZATION 22:195-201.

Miller, N. and Dion, K.
1970 "An Analysis of the Familiarization Explanation of the Risky-Shift." Proceedings, Annual Convention of the American Psychological Association, 337-38.

Minix, Dean A.
1975 "A Literature Review of the 'Risky-Shift' Phenomenon." Unpublished seminar paper, University of Cincinnati.

Minix, Dean A.
1976 "The Role of the Small Group In Foreign Policy Decision-Making: A Potential Pathology in Crisis Decisions?" Presented to the Southern Political Science Association, Atlanta.

Moore, Peter
1972 RISK-TAKING IN BUSINESS DECISION. London: Toryman.

Morganthau, Hans
1970 POLITICS AMONG NATIONS. 4th ed., New York: Random House.

Moscovici, S. and Neve, P.
1973 "Studies of Polarization of Judgments: III. Majorities, Minorities and Social Judgments." EUROPEAN JOURNAL OF SOCIAL PSYCHOLOGY 3:479-84.

Moscovici, S. and Zavalloni, M.
1969 "The Group as a Polarizer of Attitudes." JOURNAL OF PERSONALITY AND SOCIAL PSYCHOLOGY 12:125-35.

Mueller, John E.
1969 "The Use of Judges to Generate Quantitative Data." In Mueller, APPROACHES TO MEASUREMENT IN INTERNATIONAL RELATIONS. New York: Appleton, Century, Crofts.

Murdoch, P., Myers, D. G. and Smith, G. F.
1970 "Information Effects on Cautions and Risky Shift Items." PSYCHONOMIC SCIENCE 20: 97-98.

Murphy, W. F.
1966 "Courts as Small Groups." HARVARD LAW REVIEW 79:1565-72.

Myers, D. and Aronson, S. J.
1972 "Enhancements of Dominant Risk Tendencies in Group Discussion." PSYCHOLOGICAL REPORTS 30:615-23.

Myers, D. G. and Murdoch, P. H.
1972　"Is Risky-Shift Due to Disproportionate Influence by Extreme Group Members?" BRITISH JOURNAL OF SOCIAL AND CLINICAL PSYCHOLOGY 11:109-114.

Myers, D. G. and Lamm, H.
1975　"The Polarizing Effect of Group Discussion." AMERICAN SCIENTIST. May-June, v. 63, no. 3, 297-303.

Myers, D. G. and Lamm, H.
1976　"The Group Polarization Phenomena." PSYCHOLOGICAL BULLETIN 83/4:602-27.

Myers, D. G., Schrieber, E. G. and Veil, D.
1974　"Effects of Discussion on Opinions Concerning Illegal Behavior." JOURNAL OF SOCIAL PSYCHOLOGY 92:77-84.

Nalven, F. B.
1961　DEFENSE PREFERENCE AND PERCEPTUAL DECISION-MAKING. Ph.D. Dissertation, Boston: Boston University.

Nathan, James A.
1975　"The Missile Crisis: His Finest Hour Now." WORLD POLITICS, January, 27, 256-81.

Nie, N., Hull, C. H., Jenkins, J. G. Steinbrenner, K. and Best, D. H,
1970　STATISTICAL PACKAGE FOR THE SOCIAL SCIENCES. New York: McGraw-Hill, Inc.

Nixon, Richard M.
1962　SIX CRISES. New York: Doubleday.

North, R. C.
1967　"Perception and Action in the 1914 Crisis."

North, R. C., Holsti, O. R., Zaninovich, M. G. and Zinnes, D. A.
1963　CONTENT ANALYSIS: A HANDBOOK WITH APPLICATIONS FOR THE STUDY OF INTERNATIONAL CRISIS Evanston, Ill: Northwestern University Press.

Paige, G. D.
1966　THE KOREAN DECISION. New York: Free Press.

Paige, Glenn D.
1972   "Comparative Case Analysis of Crisis Decitions: Korea and Cuba." In Hermann (ed.) 41-55.

Parry, Clive
1968   "The Function of Law in the International Community." In Max Sorenson (ed.) MANUAL OF PUBLIC INTERNATIONAL LAWS. New York: St. Martin's Press.

Patcher, Martin
1965   "Decision Theory and National Action." JOURNAL OF CONFLICT RESOLUTION June, 164-76.

Pool, I. De Sola, and Kessler, A.
1965   "The Kaiser, the Tsar, and the Computer: Information Processing in a Crisis." THE AMERICAN BEHAVIORAL SCIENTIST 8/9, May, 31-38.

Possony, Stefan T.
1968   FOREIGN POLICY AND RATIONALITY. Orbis, Spring, #1, 132-60.

Postman, Leo and Bruner, J.
1948   "Perception Under Stress." PSYCHOLOGICAL REVIEW LV, 314-23.

Pruitt, D. G.
1969   "The 'Walter Mitty' Effect in Individual and Group Risk Taking." Proceeding of 77th Annual Convention of the American Psychological Assn. 4, 425-26.

Pruitt, D. G.
1971a "Choice Shifts in Group Discussion: An Introductory Review." JOURNAL OF PERSONALITY AND SOCIAL PSYCHOLOGY 20/3, December, 339-61.

Pruitt, D. G.
1971b "Conclusions: Toward an Understanding of Choice Shifts in Group Discussions." JOURNAL OF PERSONALITY AND SOCIAL PSYCHOLOGY 20:495-510.

Pruitt, D. G. and Teger, Allan I.
1967   "The Risky-Shift in Group Betting." JOURNAL OF EXPERIMENTAL SOCIAL PSYCHOLOGY 5:115-26.

Raack, R. C.
1970 "When Plans Fail: Small Group Behavior and Decision-Making in the Conspiracy of 1808 in Germany." JOURNAL OF CONFLICT RESOLUTION 14/1, March, 3-19.

Rabow, J., et al.
1966 "The Role of Social Norms and Leadership in Risk-Taking." SOCIOMETRY 29:16-27.

Raser, J.
1966 "Personal Characteristics of Political Decision-Makers: A Literature Review." Peace Research Society (International) Papers, 5, 161-81.

Raven, B.
1974 "The Nixon Group." JOURNAL OF SOCIAL ISSUES 30:297-320.

Rettig, S.
1966 "Group Discussion and Predicted Ethical Risk-Taking." JOURNAL OF PERSONALITY AND SOCIAL PSYCHOLOGY, LXIII, 83-88.

Rim, Y.
1964a "Social Attitudes and Risk-Taking." HUMAN RELATIONS 17:259-65.

Rim, Y.
1964b "Personality and Group Decision Involving Risk." PSYCHOLOGICAL RECORD 14:37-45.

Rim, Y.
1966 "Inter-Directedness Decisions Involving Risk." PSYCHOLOGICAL ABSTRACT 40:77-84.

Rimkus, Ray
1975 "Synthetic Organizations and Foreign Policy Crisis." Paper delivered at the Fifth Annual National Security Education Seminar, Denver, Colorado.

De Rivera, Joseph H.
1968 THE PSYCHOLOGICAL DIMENSION OF FOREIGN POLICY. Columbus: Charles Merrit.

Roberts, J. C. and Castore, C. H.
1972 "The Effects of Conformity, Information, and

Confidence upon Subject's Willingness to Take Risk Following a Group Discussion." ORGANIZATION BEHAVIOR AND HUMAN PERFORMANCE 8:384-94.

Robinson, James A.
1970 "Crisis Decision-Making: An Inventory and Appraisal of Concepts, Theories, Hypotheses and Techniques of Analysis." POLITICAL SCIENCE ANNUAL. Indianapolis: Bobbs-Merrill, 111-148.

Robinson, James A.
1972 "Crisis: An Appraisal of Concepts and Theories." In Hermann (ed.). 20-35.

Robinson, J. and Snyder, R.
1965 "Decision-Making In International Politics." In H. C. Kelman, ed. INTERNATIONAL BEHAVIOR: A SOCIAL PSYCHOLOGICAL ANALYSIS. New York: Holt, Rinehart, and Winston.

Robinson, J. A. and Majak, R. A.
1967 "A Theory of Decision-Making." In J. C. Charlesworth (ed.). CONTEMPORARY POLITICAL ANALYSIS. New York: Free Press, 175-88.

Robinson, John P., Rusk, J. and Head, K.
1968 MEASURES OF POLITICAL ATTITUDES. Ann Arbor: Institute for Social Research.

Robinson, M. J.
1975 "Understanding Television's Effects - Experimentalism and Survey Research: An Offer One Shouldn't Refuse." EXPERIMENTAL STUDY OF POLITICS 4:99-133.

Rogow, A.
1963 JAMES FORRESTAL: A STUDY OF PERSONALITY, POLITICS, AND POLICY. New York: McMillan.

Rogow, A.
1971 "Some Psychiatric Aspects of Political Science and Political Life." In G. Abcarian and J. Soule, SOCIAL PSYCHOLOGY AND POLITICAL BEHAVIOR. Columbus: Merrill.

Roig, C.
1973 "Some Theoretical Problems in Decision-Making Studies." In D. Siojanski (ed.). POLITICAL DECISION-MAKING PROCESSES. San Francisco: Josey-Bass, 19-54.

Rosenau, J.
1967a "The Premises and Promises of Decision-Making Analysis." In J. C. Charlesworth (ed.). CONTEMPORARY POLITICAL ANALYSIS. New York: Free Press.

Rosenau, J.
1967b DOMESTIC SOURCES OF FOREIGN POLICY. New York: Free Press.

Rosenau, J.
1969 INTERNATIONAL POLITICS AND FOREIGN POLICY. New York: Free Press.

Rosenau, James
1976 "Pre-Theories and Theories of Foreign Policy." In R. B. Farrell, ed. APPROACHES TO COMPARATIVE AND INTERNATIONAL POLITICS. Evanston: Northwestern University Press.

Rosenblast, P. C. and Miller, N.
1972 "Experimental Methods." In C. G. McClintock (ed). EXPERIMENTAL SOCIAL PSYCHOLOGY. New York: Holt, Rinehart and Winston.

Rule, B. and Evens, J.
1971 "Familiarization: The Presence of Others and Group Discussion Effects of Risk-Taking." REPRESENTATIVE RESEARCH IN SOCIAL PSYCHOLOGY 2:28-32.

Russett, Bruce
1967 INTERNATIONAL REGIONS AND THE INTERNATIONAL SYSTEM. Chicago: Rand McNally.

St. Jean, R. L.
1971 "Information and Interaction in Group Risk-Taking." DISSERTATION ABSTRACTS INTERNATIONAL 31 (7-A), 3641.

Sapin, B., and Snyder, R. C.
1954 THE ROLE OF THE MILITARY IN AMERICAN FOREIGN POLICY. Garden City, New York: Doubleday.

Scheff, T.
1963 "Decision Rules, Types of Error, and Their Consequences in Medical Diagnosis." BEHAVIORAL SCIENTIST 8:97-107.

Schlesinger, Arthur
1965 A THOUSAND DAYS. Boston: Houghton-Mifflin.

Schwartz, David C.
1967 "Decision Theories and Crisis Behavior: An Empirical Study of Nuclear Deterrence on International Political Crisis." ORBIS September #2, 459-90.

Schwartz, D. C. and Zill, N.
1971 "Psyphysiological Arousal as a Predictor of Political Participation." Presented at the Annual Meeting of the American Political Studies Association, September.

Schwartz, D. C.
1972 "Decision-Making in Historical and Simulated Crisis." In Hermann (ed). 167-84.

Schweitzer, Nicholas
1977 "Delphi as a Technique in Intelligence." Presented to the International Studies Association, St. Louis.

Sears, D. O.
1969 "Political Behavior." In G. Lindzey and E. Aronson. HANDBOOK OF SOCIAL PSYCHOLOGY v. 5. Reading, Mass.: Addision-Wesley.

Semmel, A.
1972 "Some Correlates of Foreign Policy Attitudes Among Foreign Service Officers." Ph.D. Dissertation, University of Michigan.

Semmel, Andrew K.
1976 "Group Dynamics and Foreign Policy Process: The Choice-Shift Phenomenon." Presented to Southern Political Science Association, Atlanta, November.

Semmel, Andrew K. and Minix, Dean A.
1978a "Foreign Policy Decision-Making in Small Experimental Groups: The Choice-Shift Phenomena." Washinton, D. C.: Military

Issues Research Memorandum, GPO.

Semmel, Andrew K. and Minix, Dean A.
1978b "Toward Caution or Risk: Who Should Make Foreign Policy?" Clifton Magazine, Winter 44-49.

Semmel, Andrew K. and Minix, Dean A.
1979 "Group Dynamics and Risk-Taking: An Experimental Examination." JOURNAL OF EXPERIMENTAL POLITICS, January.

Semmel, Andrew K. and Minix, Dean A.
1979a "Small Group Dynamics and Foreign Policy-Making: An Experimental Approach." In Lawrence S. Falkowski, ed. THE UTILITY OF PSYCHOLOGICAL MODELS FOR INTERNATIONAL POLITICS AND FOREIGN POLICY. Boulder: Westview Press.

Sewell, John W.
1977 THE UNITED STATES AND WORLD DEVELOPMENT: AGENDA. New York: Praeger.

Shackle, G. F. S.
1969 DECISION, ORDER AND TIME IN HUMAN AFFAIRS. Cambridge: Cambridge University Press.

Shapiro, M. J. and Bonham, G. M.
1973 "Cognitive Processes and Foreign Policy Decision-Making." INTERNATIONAL STUDIES QUARTERLY 17:147-74.

Sherif, M.
1936 THE PSYCHOLOGY OF SOCIAL NORMS. New York: Harper.

Shils, E. S. and Janowitz, M.
1948 "Cohesion and Disintegration in the Wehrmacht." PUBLIC OPINION QUARTERLY, v. 12"280-315.

Sidney, Hugh
1969 "White House Staff vs. the Cabinet." WASHINGTON MONTHLY. February, p. 106.

Siegel, S. and Zajonc, R. B.
1967 "Group Risk-Taking in Professional Decisions." SOCIOMETRY 30:339-49.

Sigal, Leon V.
1970   "The 'Rational Policy' Model and the Formosan
        Straits Crises." INTERNATIONAL STUDIES
        QUARTERLY. June, 121-56.

Silverthorne, C. P.
1971   "Information Input of the Group Shift
        Phenomena in Risk-Taking." JOURNAL OF
        PERSONALITY AND SOCIAL PSYCHOLOGY 20:451-61.

Simon, Herbert A.
1957   "A Behavioral Model of Rational Choice."
        MODEL OF MAN: SOCIAL AND RATIONAL. New York:
        John Wiley and Sons.

Simon, Herbert A.
1965   ADMINISTRATIVE BEHAVIOR. New York: Free Press
        Paperback.

Singer, J. David
1965   QUANTITATIVE INTERNATIONAL POLITICS. New
        York: Free Press.

Singer, J. David
1968   "Man and World Politics: The Psycho-Cultural
        Interface." JOURNAL OF SOCIAL ISSUES 24:
        127-56.

Singer, J. David
1969   "The Levels-of-Analysis Problem in Interna-
        tional Relations." In J. Rosenau, 20-29.

Singer, J. D. and Ray. P.
1966   "Decision-Making in Conflict: From Inter-
        personal to International Relations."
        Bulletin of the Menninger Clinic 30, January,
        300-312.

Singer, J. D. and Small, D.
1968   WAGES OF WAR. New York: Wiley.

Slovic, P.
1964   "Assessment of Risk-Taking Behavior."
        PSYCHOLOGICAL BULLETIN 51:220-233.

Smith, Barbara, Johnson, K. Paulsen, D. W. and
        Shocet, F.
1976   POLITICAL RESEARCH METHODS FOUNDATIONS AND

TECHNIQUES. Boston: Houghton Mifflin Co.

Smith, M. B.
1968 "A Map for the Analysis of Personality and Politics." JOURNAL OF SOCIAL ISSUES 24: 15-28.

Smith, M. B.
1972 "Is Experimental Social Psychology Advancing?" JOURNAL OF EXPERIMENTAL SOCIAL PSYCHOLOGY 8:86-96.

Snyder, Glenn H.
1972 "Crisis Bargaining." In Hermann (ed). 217-56.

Snyder, Richard C.
1962 DETERRENCE, WEAPONS SYSTEMS, AND DECISION-MAKING. China Lake, California: Project Michalson.

Snyder, R. C., Bruck, H. and Sapin, B.
1962 FOREIGN POLICY DECISION-MAKING. New York: Free Press.

Snyder, R. C. and Paige, Glenn D.
1958 "The United States' Decision to Resist Aggression in Korea: The Application of an Analytic Scheme." ADMINISTRATIVE SCIENCE QUARTERLY 3:34-78.

Snyder, R. C. and Robinson, J. A.
1960 NATIONAL AND INTERNATIONAL DECISION-MAKING. The Institute of International Order, Program of Research no. 40, New York.

Somit, A.
1972 "Biopolitics." BRITISH JOURNAL OF POLITICAL SCIENCE, April, 209-38.

Sorenson, Theodore C.
1963 DECISION-MAKING IN THE WHITE HOUSE. New York: Columbia University Press.

Sorenson, Ted
1966 KENNEDY. New York: Bantam.

Stagner, R.
1967   PSYCHOLOGICAL ASPECTS OF INTERNATIONAL
       CONFLICT. Belmont, California: Brooks/
       Cole.

Stauffer, R.
1969   "The Biopolitics of Underdevelopment."
       COMPARATIVE POLITICAL STUDIES 2 (Oct.)
       361-87.

Stauffer, R.
1971   "The Role of Drugs in Political Change."
       Monograph, New York: General Learning Press.

Steinbruner, John D.
1970   "Some Effects of Decision Procedures on
       Policy Outcomes." Center for International
       Studies, MIT.

Stenibruner, J.
1974   THE CYBERNETIC THEORY OF DECISION: NEW
       DIMENSIONS OF POLITICAL ANALYSIS. Princeton:
       Princeton Press.

Stephens, J.
1972   "An Appraisal of Some Systems Approaches in
       the Study of International Systems."
       INTERNATIONAL STUDIES QUARTERLY September
       321-49.

Stokes, J. R.
1971   "Effects of Familiarization and Knowledge of
       Others' Odds Choices on Shift to Risk and
       Caution." JOURNAL OF PERSONALITY AND
       SOCIAL PSYCHOLOGY 20:407-12.

Stoner, J. A.
1961   "A Comparison of Individual and Group
       Decisions Involving Risk." MA Thesis,
       Massachussetts Institute of Technology.

Stoner, J. A. F.
1968   "Risky and Cautious Shifts on Group Decisions."
       JOURNAL OF EXPERIMENTAL AND SOCIAL PSYCHOLOGY
       4:442-59.

Sullivan, M. P.
1976   INTERNATIONAL RELATIONS: THEORIES AND
       EVIDENCE. Englewood Cliffs, N. J.: Prentice
       Hall.

Swanson, G. E.
1951 "Some Problems of Laboratory Experiments with Small Populations." AMERICAN SOCIOLOGICAL REVIEW 16/3:349-58.

Teger, A. I. and Pruitt, D. G.
1967 "Components of Group Risk-Taking." JOURNAL OF EXPERIMENTAL SOCIAL PSYCHOLOGY 3:189-205.

Teger, A., Pruitt, D., St. Jean, R. L. and Haaland, G.
1970 "A Re-examination of the Familiarization Hypothesis in Group Risk Taking." JOURNAL OF EXPERIMENTAL SOCIAL PSYCHOLOGY 6:346-50.

Thibaut, J. W. and Kelley, H. H.
1959 THE SOCIAL PSYCHOLOGY OF GROUPS. New York: John Wiley.

Thomas, Edwin J. and Fink, Clinton
1965 "Effects of Group Size." In Hare, Borgatta, and Bales (eds). 525-36.

Thompson, J. C.
1968 "How Could Vietnam Happen? An Autopsy." ATLANTIC (Ap) 47-53.

Thorson, S. J.
"Axiomatic Theories of Preference-Based Choice-Behavior: An Overview." AMERICAN BEHAVIORAL SCIENTIST 20/1:95-110.

Thorson, T.
1970 BIOPOLITICS. New York: Holt, Rinehart, and Winston.

Tongberg, Sue
1970 RISK-TAKING JUDGMENTS IN ADULTHOOD. Ann Arbor: University Microfilms.

Torgerson, Warren G.
1958 SMALL GROUPS AND POLITICAL BEHAVIOR. Princeton: Princeton Press.

Torrance, E. P.
1954 "Some Consequences of Power Differences in Decision-Making in Permanent and Temporary Three-Man Groups." RESEARCH STUDIES, State College of Washington, Vol. 22, 130-40.

Triska, Jan., et al.
1964 "Pattern and Level of Risk in Soviet Foreign Policy-Making: 1945-1963." STUDIES OF THE COMMUNIST SYSTEM. Stanford.

Triska, J., et al.
1964 PATTERN AND LEVEL OF RISK IN SOVIET FOREIGN POLICY: 1945-1963. Stanford: Stanford University Press.

Ulmer, S.
1971 COURTS AS SMALL AND NOT SO SMALL GROUPS. New York: General Learning Press.

Van de Ven, A. H.
1974 GROUP DECISION-MAKING EFFECTIVENESS. Kent State University Center for Business and Economic Research Press.

Verba, S.
1961 "Assumptions of Rationality and Non-Rationality in Models of the International System." WORLD POLITICS 14:93-117.

Verba, S.
1961 SMALL GROUP AND POLITICAL BEHAVIOR. Princeton: Princeton Press.

Verba, S.
1964 "Simulations, Reality, and Theory in International Relations." WORLD POLITICS 16: 490-519.

Vidmar, A.
1970 "Group Compositions and the Risky Shift." JOURNAL OF EXPERIMENTAL SOCIAL PSYCHOLOGY 3:189-205

Vinokur, A.
1971 "Cognitive and Affective Process Influencing Risk Taking in Groups: An Expected Utility Approach." JOURNAL OF PERSONALITY AND SOCIAL PSYCHOLOGY 20:472-86.

Vinokur, A.
1971 "Review and Theoretical Analysis of the Effects of Group Processes upon Individual and Groups Decisions Involving Risk." PSYCHOLOGICAL BULLETIN 58:231-50.

Vocke, W. C.
1976   AMERICAN FOREIGN POLICY: AN ANALYTIC
        APPROACH. New York: Free Press.

Vogel, William, Raymond, Susan, and Lazarus, Richard S.
1959   "Intrinsic Motivation and Psychological
        Stress." JOURNAL OF ABNORMAL AND SOCIAL
        PSYCHOLOGY, LVIII 225-33.

Walker, T.
1976   "Microanalytic Approaches to Political
        Decision-Making: Methodological Issues and
        Research Strategies." AMERICAN BEHAVIORAL
        SCIENTIST 20/1:93-110.

Walter, T. G. and Main, E. C.
1973   "Choice Shifts in Political Decision-Making:
        Federal Judges and Civil Liberties Cases."
        JOURNAL OF APPLIED SOCIAL PSYCHOLOGY 2:39-48.

Wallach, Michael A. and Kogan, Nathan
1965   "The Roles of Information, Discussion and
        Consensus in Group Risk Taking." JOURNAL OF
        EXPERIMENTAL SOCIAL PSYCHOLOGY 1:1-19.

Wallach, M. A., Kogan, N. and Bem, D. J.
1962   "Group Influence on Individual Risk Taking."
        JOURNAL OF ABNORMAL AND SOCIAL PSYCHOLOGY
        65:75-86.

Wallach, M. A., Kogan, N. and Bem, D. J.
1964   "Diffusion of Responsibility and Level of Risk
        Taking in Groups." JOURNAL OF APPLIED
        SOCIAL PSYCHOLOGY 68:263-74.

Wallach, M. A., Kogan, N. and Burt, R. B.
1965   "Can Group Members Recognize the Effects of
        Group Discussion Upon Risk Taking." JOURNAL OF
        ABNORMAL AND SOCIAL PSYCHOLOGY 68:263-74.

Wallach, M. A., Kogan, N. and Burt, R.
1967   "Group Risk Taking and Field Dependence-
        Independence of Group Members." SOCIOMETRY
        30:323-38.

Wallach, M. A., Kogan, N. and Burt, R. B.
1968   "Are Risk-Takers More Persuasive than Con-
        servatives in Group Discussion?" JOURNAL OF
        EXPERIMENTAL SOCIAL PSYCHOLOGY 4:76-88.

Wallach, M. A. and Mabli, J.
1970 "Information Versus Conformity in the Effects of Group Discussion on Risk-Taking." JOURNAL OF PERSONALITY AND SOCIAL PSYCHOLOGY 9:101-106.

Weick, K. E.
1965 "Laboratory Experiments with Organization." In J. G. March (ed). HANDBOOK OF ORGANIZATIONS. Chicago: Rand McNally, 194-260.

Weil, Herman M.
1975 "Can Bureaucracies Be Rational Actors? Foreign Policy Decision-Making in North Vietnam." INTERNATIONAL STUDIES QUARTERLY 19/4: 432-468.

Weiner, Anthony J. and Kahn, Hermann
1962 CRISIS AND ARMS CONTROL. New York: Hudson Institution.

Whiting, Alan S.
1960 CHINA CROSSES THE YAHU: THE DECISION TO ENTER THE KOREAN WAR. New York: MacMillan.

Whyte, W. F.
1956 THE ORGANIZATION MAN. New York: Simon and Shuster.

Wiegele, Thomas C.
1973 "Decision-Making in an International Crisis: Some Biological Factors." INTERNATIONAL STUDIES QUARTERLY 17/3:295-335.

Wildavsky, A.
1964 THE POLITICS OF THE BUDGETARY PROCESS. Boston: Little-Brown.

Wilker, H. R. and Milbrath, L. W.
1970 "Political Belief Systems and Political Behavior." SOCIAL SCIENCE QUARTERLY 51: 477-93.

Wolfers, A.
1959 "The Actors in International Politics." In W. T. R. Fox, ed. THEORETICAL ASPECTS OF INTERNATIONAL RELATIONS. Notre Dame, Indiana.

Wolfinger, R. E.
1971 "Nondecisions and the Study of Local Politics."
AMERICAN POLITICAL SCIENCE REVIEW 65:
1063-80.

Young, Oran R.
1968 THE POLITICS OF FORCE. Princeton: Princeton Press.

Zajonc, R. B., Wolosin, R. J. and Wolosin, M. A.
1972 "Group Risk-Taking Under Various Group Decision Schemes." JOURNAL OF EXPERIMENTAL SOCIAL PSYCHOLOGY 8:16-30.

Zaleska, M. and Kogan, N.
1971 "Level of Risk Selected by Individuals and Groups When Deciding for Self and for Others." SOCIOMETRY 34:1980213.

Zinnes, Dina
1968 "The Expression and Perception of Hostility in Pre-War Crisis: 1914." In Singer (ed). QUANTITATIVE INTERNATIONAL POLITICS. New York: Free Press.

Zinnes, Dina A., Zinnes, Joseph, and McClure, Robert D.
1972 "Hostility in Diplomatic Communication: A Study of the 1914 Crisis." In Hermann (ed). 139-164.

INDEX

Acheson, Dean, 40, 131
Allison, Graham, 23, 64
alternative decisional structures, 162
ANOVA, 109, 143
anti-communist idea elements, 148
Arab-Israeli dispute, 1973, 24
Arab Nationalists, 93
Asch, Solomon, 64, 153
attenuated time perspective, 31
Bachrach, P., 72
Baddeley, A. D., 29
Bales, Robert, 41, 59
Ball, George, 171
bandwagon effects, 167
Barber, James David, 27
Bateson, N., 60
Bay of Pigs, 170-71
Bayesian Choice Models, 23
belief systems, 8
Berlin Blockade, 135
Berlin Crisis, 1962, 135
billiard ball model, 3
bolstering, 30, 32, 37, 146, 154
Bower, Joseph, 163
Bowles, Chester, 170
Brady, Linda, 25
Brecher, Michael, 20, 22
Broadbent, D.E., 29
Brown, Roger, 63, 66, 70, 138, 154, 160
Brzezinski, Z., 39
Bundy, McGeorge, 164
bureaucratic politics, effects on individuals, 7, 169
Burnstein, E., 72
Burton, J., 3
California Psychological Inventory (CPI), 95

Cambodia, 93, 112, 114, 116, 135-36
Campbell, Donald, 87, 88, 95
Cartwright, Dorwin, 58, 62
chief executive, 169
China, People's Republic of, 129, 131
Choice Dilemma Questionnaire (CDQ), 58, 59, 89-93, 174
choice-shift, 58, 176
choice theory, 23
Clark, R. D., 59, 71
"clotting point", 153
coalition formation, 3
cognitive processes, 3
cognitive rigidity, 29, 31
college students, 93, 97, 103, 111; inclination toward risk-taking, 105-21
commitment hypothesis, 66
communication, among group members, 59
concurrence-seeking behavior, 131, 169
conflict and conflict resolution, 3
conformity, 42
consolidation of decision-making, 40
contagion effect, 120
content analysis, 84
conventional national security machinery, 39
Coolidge, President Calvin, 30
Cooper, Chester, 43
crises, case studies, 83; concept of, 19-22; decision-maker's perception of, 75; decision-making models, 22-24; and international systemic change, 22
critical evaluator, 168

Cuban Missile Crisis, 1962, 22, 24, 26, 39, 40, 45, 135, 169
Dalkey, Norman, 165
decision-making analysis, 6, 124; by analogy, 29, 133-134, 171
decision options discussed, 130-35
decisional extremization, 37, 68ff, 104ff, 120, 123ff
decisional polarization, 37, 68ff, 104ff, 116, 123ff
decisional "quality" 9, 25, 37, 76, 172
"defective" decision-making, 137
Defense Department, 173
defensive avoidance, 37
degree of risk/risk-taking, 94
Delbecq, Andre, 164
Delphi technique, 165
devil's advocate, 171
diffusion of responsibility hypothesis, 60
Dion, K. L., 67
"discount rate" of decision-makers, 29
dissonance, cognitive, 167
"DMZ tree incident," 1976, 135
dominant percept of decision-makers, 29
East, Maurice, 5
economic decision-making theory, 23
efficiency prescriptions for deliberative quality, 167
elite perceptions/cognitions, 7-8

emergent-norm hypothesis, 62
Entebbe raid, 1974, 136-37
events data, 84
EXCOM, 1962, 137, 169
external validity, 175
familiarization hypothesis, 60, 69
final group decision, 38
foreign policy, comparative study of, 4
Foreign Service Officers (FSOx), 148, 155, 173
Fort Knox, Kentucky, 93
Fulbright, Sen. J. William, 170
game theory, 23
"Gary Powers incident," 135
George, Alexander, 27, 28, 30, 31, 43, 44, 49, 51, 75, 134, 163, 167, 171
global perspective, 2
Glover, Maraline, 86
Great Britain, 141
group, cohesion and solidarity, 32, 42ff, 95, 168; conformity, 146-47; extremization, 68, 96; leader, 124, 139, 169; membership variable, 147, 160; norms, 42, 75, 111, 146, 160; polarization, 68; pressure, 161; process hypotheses, 125ff; role structure, 38; size, 38, 39, 75; social-psychological benefit, 160ff; socialization influence, 160ff; structure, 42
Guetzkow, Harold, 175
Hague, The, 93, 112, 116
Haley, H. J.
Hare, A. P., 146
Helman, Olaf, 165
Hermann, Charles F., 5, 20, 22, 23, 25, 39, 41, 167
Higbee, K. L., 162

high-level crisis decision-making, 40, 41
historical analogy, as a decision-rule, 134ff; as a predictor of group extremization, 124
Holsti, Ole, 7, 8, 27, 30, 31, 75, 103
Huntington, Samuel, 144
hypervigilance, 37
ideal procedures, for decision-making, 37
identification, 160
images, of national leaders, 4
individual preliminary perceptual analysis (ranking), 42
individual pre-test scores, 159
Indo-China, 24
information and recall, 167
information search, processing, evaluation and execution by small group, 24, 168
informational exchange hypothesis, 72, 124
informational influence hypothesis, 69, 72
Interaction Process Analysis (IPA), 59
interdependence, 1
intergovernmental organizations, 2
international relations, 1
international systems level-of-analysis, 2
internationalism scale, 144
internationalists, 173
interpersonal communication, 160
interpersonal comparison hypothesis, 69, 70, 71, 149

interpersonal discussion, 169
interpersonal group dynamics, 23, 26
intra-psychic dynamics, 26
"Inverse U" curve of stress, 27
Iscoe, Ira, 20
isolationists, 173
Janis, I., 10, 24, 37, 42, 48, 49, 50, 137, 167-70
Jervis, Robert, 134
Johnson, Pres. Lyndon B., 171
Johnson, Norris, 62
Kahn, Herman, 19-20
Kelman, Herbert, 5, 8
Kennedy, Pres. John F., 170
Kennedy, Robert, 27, 137
Kirkpatrick, Samuel, 98
Kissinger, Secretary of State Henry, 1, 4
Kogan, N., 57, 71, 126
Kohl, Wilfred, 164
Korean War, 6, 24, 39, 128, 131, 135
Lamm, Helmut, 68, 69, 71, 126, 142, 149
Lazarus, R., 27
leadership, 93, 139, 154
Lenter, Howard, 40
levels-of-analysis, 1
Levinger, G., 64
Lewin, Kurt, 43
Lutzker, Daniel, 173
McCauley, C. R., 71
McClelland, Charles, 4, 20
McNamara, Secretary of Defense Robert, 170
MacArthur, General Douglas, 131
Mann, Leon, 37
majority rule, 69, 125
maladaptive coping mechanisms, 37
manipulated norm, 72, 161
May, Ernest, 134, 137

Mayaguez Capture, 1973, 135, 137
Mennis, Bernard, 8, 148, 173
Milburn, Thomas, 29, 31
Milgram, Stanley, 161
"military mind", 144
military socialization, 147
Miller, Kent, 20
mindguards, 170
Moscovici, Serge, 66, 67
multiple advocacy, 163
Munich, 1938, 135
Munich disaster, 1972 135
Murdoch, P., 126
Myers, David, 68, 69, 71 72, 142
nation-state level-of-analysis, 4
national security advisers, 94
Nixon, Pres. Richard M., 26
nominal group technique, 164ff
non-governmental organizations, 2
organizational response model, 25
Paige, Glenn, 6, 39
paired-comparison scaling technique, 94
Panamanian Navy, Panama Canal, 93, 111, 113
parallel groups, 169
participators (high and low), 42
Pearl Harbor, 1941, 135, 137
Persian Gulf - see Strait of Hormuz
personality effects, 167
persuasion/leadership hypothesis, 60, 65, 69, 139
pluralistic ignorance hypothesis, 64
policy-making process (social factors), 38
Political Belief Scale (PBS), 94, 145
political beliefs, 94
Political Involvement Scale (PIS), 95
post-decisional regret, 37
post-test (group responses), 90, 94, 96, 105, 111, 147
power politics paradigm, 3
premature closure, 31, 153
pre-test (individual means), 90, 94, 95, 96, 105, 111, 147
productivity, 167
Pruitt, Dean, 63, 65, 66, 68
psychological flexibility, 94, 144
Rabow, J., 62, 161
Rand Corporation, 166
Raser, J., 86-87
rational calculation, 31
rational capacities, 73
rational choice models, 23
reduced attention span due to stress, 31
reduced crisis decision-making set, 38
reduced cue awareness due to stress, 31
reduction of in-group conflicts, 43
Reedy, George, 171
release/contagion hypothesis, 65
relevant arguments hypothesis, 66, 70, 72, 154
rhetoric-of-risk (caution) 61, 130
risk-as-value hypothesis, 138
"risky-shift", 57ff
De Rivera, Joseph, 131

Robinson, James, 6, 8, 23, 39
Rosenau, James, 4, 6, 8
ROTC Cadets, Army and Airforce, 93, 97, 103, 111; inclination toward risk/caution, 105ff
Rule, B. G., 59
Rusk, Dean, 170
Russian Revolution, 141
SALT I, 93, 112, 114, 140
St. Jean, R., 66
scale-of-risk, 91
Schneider, D. J., 64
Schreiber, E. G., 72
scientific generalization, 87ff
second-chance meeting, 172
self, presumed others, and ideal scores, 70-71
sex, as a predictor of risk-taking, 59
"shift" scores, 94-97, 110ff
Singer, J. David, 2, 3
size of decisional unit, 21
small groups, 9; and crisis decision-making, 24ff, 159ff
Snyder, Richard, 6. 8
social-comparison hypothesis, 63
social norms, 115-120
social-psychological level-of-analysis, 5-11, 174ff
social support, 161
South Africa, 174
South Korea. 93, 114, 131
Soviet Union, 92, 129, 131
Stanley, James, 87, 88
State Department, 173
status-ranking, 42

Stoner, James, 68, 154
Strait of Hormuz, 92, 114, 129, 133, 136
Stress, effects on analysis and evaluation, 50; effects on decision-makers, 21-33, 133; effects on spatial and temporal focus, 30; as a stimulant, 26
sub-samples, 146
Swanson, Guy, 85
systems level-of-analysis, 2-3
Teger, Alan, 59, 68, 72
threat, stress related, 27
transnational actors, 2
Truman, Pres. Harry S., 131
United Nations Security Council, 91, 131, 140
United States Army Officers, 93, 103, 111, 130, 131; inclination toward risk/caution, 105ff
USS Pueblo incident, 1962, 129, 135, 137
value-complexity, 30, 32
value hypothesis, 62, 63
Verba, Sidney, 24, 25, 175
Vietnam, 24, 93, 171, 172
vigilant information processing, 37
Vinokur, A., 58, 61, 72
Wallach, M. A., 57, 126
"Walter Mitty" effect, 65, 139, 153, 155, 160
Wiener, A., 20
Yule's Q statistic, 118-119
Zavalloni, M., 66, 67

ABOUT THE AUTHOR

Dean A. Minix is presently an Assistant Professor of Government in the Division of Social Science at Campbell University in Buie's Creek, North Carolina. Prior to his position at Campbell, Dr. Minix was a doctoral student in the Department of Political at the University of Cincinnati where he was awarded the Ph. D. degree in 1979. The author graduated from Georgetown College in Kentucky with a B. A. degree in 1973. His research and teaching interests are in the areas of foreign policy (U.S. and comparative), International Relations theory and methodology, as well as a geographical interest in the politics of the Middle East. Dr. Minix has published several articles (some co-authored) on the formation of foreign policy. In 1981, he was a participant in the Middle East Seminar of the Scholar-Diplomat program of the U.S. Department of State.